The Sociology of Welfare

ASPECTS OF SOCIAL POLICY
General Editor: J. P. Martin
Professor of Sociology and Social Administration University of Southampton

Penal Policy in a Modern Welfare State
A. E. BOTTOMS

The Social Context of Health Care
P. BREARLEY, A. MILES, E. TOPLISS, G. WOODS, J. GIBBONS

Reorganising the National Health Service
R. G. S. BROWN

Social Policy: A Survey of Recent Developments
edited by MICHAEL H. COOPER

Images of Welfare: The Mass Media, Public Attitudes and the Welfare State
PETER GOLDING and SUSAN MIDDLETON

The Poverty Business
JOAN M. HIGGINS

Understanding Social Policy
MICHAEL HILL

The Family, the State and the Labour Market
HILARY LAND

Capitalism and Social Welfare
ROGER LAWSON

The Child's Generation
JEAN PACKMAN

The Organization of Soviet Medical Care
MICHAEL RYAN

Provision for the Disabled
EDA TOPLISS

Alternative Strategies for Coping with Crime
edited by NORMAN TUTT

Efficiency in the Social Services
ALAN WILLIAMS and ROBERT ANDERSON

GRAHAM ROOM

The Sociology of Welfare

Social Policy, Stratification and Political Order

BASIL BLACKWELL · Oxford
MARTIN ROBERTSON · Oxford

First published in 1979 by Basil Blackwell & Mott Ltd, Oxford and Martin Robertson & Co. Ltd, 108 Cowley Road, Oxford OX4 1JF.

ISBN 0 631 10471 2 (case edition)
ISBN 0 631 10481 X (paperback edition)

Filmset by Vantage Photosetting Co. Ltd., Southampton and London. Printed and bound by Richard Clay Ltd. at the Chaucer Press, Bungay, Suffolk.

Contents

CONCLUSION

Preface

It is all of eight years since I began working on the ideas developed in this book. In that period I have incurred debts to very many colleagues and friends and can mention only a few of them here.

During the time I was preparing the work as a doctoral thesis I was most fortunate in my two supervisors. A. H. Halsey has been a continuing source of encouragement and inspiration and has crowned that support by kindly writing a Foreword to this published version. John Goldthorpe offered detailed and painstaking criticism that helped me to clarify and justify my argument. Such rigour as this book may now possess owes much to him.

All chapters were read in draft form by Peter Fairbrother and Robert Holman, who both made invaluable suggestions for change. Adrian Webb was my principal counsellor when I converted the thesis into a publishable version.

My thanks are also due to a wide range of other colleagues at Oxford and Bath: for guidance when I was losing my way, for criticism when I was losing clarity and for encouragement when I was losing heart.

Graham Room
School of Humanities, University of Bath

For Susan

Foreword

Economic growth has been the characteristic feature of the so-called capitalist or 'first world' countries over the past two centuries. We understood it, or thought we did, until recently when work appeared by such writers as Fred Hirsch (Hirsch, 1977; Hirsch and Goldthorpe, 1978), but what are less well understood, and certainly less well analysed by social scientists, are the causes and consequences of the more general phenomenon of 'modernisation' of which economic growth has been part. This book is, I think, a major contribution to that analysis. In it Dr Room has argued for a particular view of the social face of modernisation that includes the development of new forms of the division of labour and of elaborated relations between government and the governed. He has written an account of the development of social policy in Britain that is, in my view, essential reading for those who would understand contemporary social developments and one that interprets the social as well as the economic division of labour and the social as well as the political relations between the state and the individual.

Necessarily this is an ambitious enterprise. It is made the more timely by recent economic events—international inflation, the oil crisis, faltering economic growth and high rates of unemployment—which together have generated current debate, conventionally phrased in terms of the relation between economic and social policy under conditions of possibly permanent zero growth. This debate, if it is to be fruitful, must escape from the false simplicity of separating the economic from the social, and particularly of seeking economic explanations and prescriptions from which social phenomena are excluded as somehow residual. The level at which Dr Room conducts his analysis avoids this kind of mistake, while at the same time also avoiding vacuous generalisation.

Capitalism bequeathed us three distinct interpretations of social

ix

policy. The first was essentially an apologia: liberalism, with its central doctrine that the social services are a mechanism evolved by advanced industrial societies to respond to certain social needs, such as the need to tame the violence of the market and to protect workers from those social dislocations that are occasioned by industrialisation. The second was a critique: Marxism, with its central doctrine that the social services are a means of damping down radical protest or revolutionary movements. The third was not so much a doctrine as a social movement: Social Democracy, with its faith and affirmation that through the extension of social services new rights of citizenship could and would be established and a fundamentally new social order born.

All three traditions have evolved and diversified. Marxism especially has spawned separated and hostile sectarian movements. Nevertheless, these are the three traditions that contend for dominance and, while appreciating the diversity of their doctrines, Dr Room has presented an illuminating evaluation of them in precisely the way we expect of a skilled social scientist. He has formulated their theories powerfully, and he has tested their strength empirically. All three fail in crucial respects when inferences drawn from them are compared with the actual history of, for example, social security and pension schemes, the reorganisation of the National Health Service, the unification of the personal social services, or the introduction of educational priority areas.

However, it is the Social Democratic tradition of thought to which Dr Room gives most support in the course of his clarifying analysis of the nature of class, market and state in the society in which we live. Avoiding many of the errors of both Marxism and liberalism, modern Social Democratic theory owes much to perhaps the most distinguished British sociologist of the twentieth century—T. H. Marshall. It is a theory that recognises the importance of class and of status in determining the distributive, redistributive and 'welfare' activities of the state, while refusing to follow Marxists into an exclusively class explanation or liberals into, so to say, an exclusively classless explanation. Citizenship, with its underlying principle, as Durkheim might have put it, of the sacredness of the individual, has been an evolving force in British social history sometimes allied with, but more often inimical to, class interest, sometimes inegalitarian, but more often egalitarian in its effects, sometimes supporting but more often supplanting the traditional status order. But above all, citizenship is the social organisation of the right of the individual to dignity and freedom *vis à vis* the massive social forces of the economy and the state. Social policy and its evolution have to be understood in these terms, and Dr Room's book advances theories that enable us to do this more clearly and with more sophisticated appreciation of the struggles and tendencies that we see around us in politics, in industry, in communities and even within the family itself. He thus poses the challenges and obstacles that face Social Democracy as an intellectual and political force in the late twentieth century.

Social science itself is likely to be advanced only by those who know how to stand on the shoulders of their predecessors, and in this form of athletics Dr Room, in his first book, shows an adroitness born of deep learning and a vivid sociological imagination.

A. H. Halsey
16 November 1978   *Nuffield College, Oxford*

CHAPTER 1

Introduction

> *Our society must restore the consciousness of its organic unity.... No doubt these ideas will become truly efficacious only if they spread out into the depths of society, but for that it is first necessary that we elaborate them scientifically in the university. To contribute to this end to the extent of my powers will be my principal concern, and I shall have no greater happiness than if I succeed in it a little.* [*Emile Durkheim, Inaugural Lecture at Bordeaux, quoted in LaCapra* Emile Durkheim: Sociologist and Philosopher *p. 37*]

I CAPITALISM AND SOCIAL POLICY

In 1848, the year of revolutions, there appeared two influential analyses and prognoses of the 'Manchester System' of laissez-faire capitalism, whose home was England and which, with the repeal of the Corn Laws in 1846, was in its heyday. Marx and Engels published their *Communist Manifesto*, which became the *locus classicus* for subsequent Marxist writing on capitalism and its prospects. John Stuart Mill, whose intellectual apprenticeship had been in classical liberalism, published the first edition of his *Principles of Political Economy*.

For Marx and Engels, the adequate analysis of bourgeois capitalism provided at the same time a prognosis of its downfall. 'The chief requisite for the existence and rule of the bourgeoisie is ... the formation and increase of capital. The chief requisite for capital is wage labour.' Yet the development of large-scale industry destroys the isolation of workers and hence also that competition among them upon which the system of wage labour depends. It thereby 'cuts from under the feet of the bourgeoisie the ground upon which

1

capitalism controls production and appropriates the products of labour. Before all, therefore, the bourgeoisie produces its own grave-diggers. Its downfall and the victory of the proletariat are equally inevitable.' Palliatives are ultimately useless, for 'the life of the bourgeoisie has become incompatible with the life of society' (quoted in Mills, 1963, p. 58).

For Mill, in contrast, a system of private property is and must remain the basis of civilised and prosperous societies. 'A continual increase of the security of person and property' will have as 'one of [its] most unfailing effects . . . a great increase both of production and of accumulation.' Various reforms in the distribution of property may well be necessary, for example by placing restrictions on inheritance. This would however suffice, given also 'a conscientious or prudential restraint on population', to ensure that 'society would exhibit these leading features: a well paid and affluent body of labourers; no enormous fortunes, except what were earned and accumulated during a single lifetime; but a much larger body of persons than at present, not only exempt from the coarser toils, but with sufficient leisure, both physical and mental, from mechanical details, to cultivate freely the graces of life.' (Mill, 1848, Vol. 2, pp. 245–6, 307, 310.)

Here, then, are two radically opposed evaluations of capitalist market society. Moreover, classical liberalism and Marxism have indeed provided the principal perspectives for the analysis of this society over the last 150 years (Giddens, 1972, pp. 32–3). These classical analyses, like the sociological tradition proper as it emerged in the later part of the nineteenth century, were centrally concerned with 'the nature of the transformation which destroyed "traditional" society and created a new "modern" order' (Giddens, 1973, p. 17). However, in so far as classical liberalism and Marxism derived philosophically from the natural law and Hegelian traditions respectively, their proponents generally had particularly strong value-commitments *vis à vis* the market society—in contrast to the pleadings for value neutrality common among later sociologists. Liberal writers were thus especially critical of social developments that appeared to subvert the 'natural' social order of the market place; while the Marxist commitment to historicist prognoses—whether stated in weak or strong form—produced hostility to developments appearing to impede the abolition of capitalist society and radical social transformation. Among these developments has been the rise of social policy, in various forms, in all the major advanced Western societies.

In this book, our interest is in the role and significance of social policy in such societies. They have historically been organised in capitalist market terms and it is within the context of a system founded on private property rights that this social policy has developed. Accordingly, we must start by delineating the outlines of this capitalist market order, drawing on the classical liberal and Marxist characterisations. As we shall see, however, social policy developments in Britain over the last 150 years seem to pose major problems for continued advocacy of either of these traditions. Indeed, it was partly in response to these that a third intellectual tradition and political ideology came to the fore in the later part of the nineteenth century—that of Social Democracy. The exploration of this intellectual context will be our concern in chapter 2. In the following chapter, we go on to outline the arguments advanced by contemporary neo-Marxist, liberal and Social Democratic analysts of social policy.

Of course, although we have spoken of liberalism, Marxism and Social Democracy as traditions, any attempt to define such 'traditions' or schools and to identify their exponents runs the danger of naïve oversimplification. Such definitions serve merely as ideal types, to which actual writers may in varying degrees approximate. As with all ideal types, it is their usefulness in permitting explanation that must constitute the criterion for their construction and selection (Weber, 1949, p. 92).

The contrasting and conflicting sets of arguments by contemporary writers, which we set out in chapter 3, provide the issues for empirical investigation in Part II. There we seek to evaluate these opposing approaches by reference to post-war developments in British social policy: none is found to be wholly satisfactory. In these empirical investigations we are necessarily selective—not only in terms of the questions we pose, but also, for reasons of space, in terms of the substantive areas we explore. Nevertheless, we make explicit the criteria on which this selection is made and the limitations upon generalising from the conclusions reached. We make complementary use of case studies of particular policy developments and target groups and macro-studies at a national level. Again, the questions we are raising properly invite a far greater wealth of both types of study than can be marshalled here, but we indicate as we proceed the peculiarities of the material used and the limitations on the conclusions reached.

II THE WIDER LITERATURE

Such is our task. However, in recent years several other studies have appeared that may seem to have a similar intent—notably those by George and Wilding (1976), Mishra (1977) and Hall, Land, Parker and Webb (1975). All of them review divergent political philosophies and social theories and seek to evaluate them by examination of empirical developments in social policy. What, then, is distinctive about the present work?

George and Wilding come closest to the classification of contemporary 'schools' used here. However, they fail to show how the current lines of debate have emerged from long-standing classical traditions and thereby to root thinking about social policy within a firmly historical treatment of intellectual change. Second, in expounding these various schools, we will seek to identify the principal dimensions of theoretical conflict in such a way as to permit more rigorous and systematic empirical evaluation than they achieve. Third, George and Wilding limit their empirical investigation to a single chapter; ours will be much more extensive. The cost, however, is a much less detailed textual exegesis of theorists than the one they offer.

Mishra's classification of thinkers is rather different. He largely ignores the market liberalism of such writers as Friedman, despite its continuing intellectual and political vitality in the 1970s. He also fails to recognise the similarity of the perspectives of such writers as T. H. Marshall and Titmuss—whom we take as the clearest recent British exponents of Social Democracy. Nevertheless, the merits of these various taxonomies can properly be judged only in terms of their fruitfulness as tools for the empirical investigation that follows. In his own empirical discussion, Mishra's study has the merit of attending as much to socialist as to capitalist societies—a comparative perspective that we have had to sacrifice in favour of a more detailed and extensive investigation of British developments.

Finally, Hall and her colleagues take as their theories to be evaluated various processual models of policy-making derived principally from political science. The *main* focus is on the semi-private or invisible processes of policy formulation within government. In contrast, the theoretical debates under consideration in the present work are macro-sociological. While this involves an interest in policy formulation, this is principally in terms of policies' implications, once implemented, for social stratification, political order, etc. In short, Hall's concerns are complementary and adjacent to our own, rather than overlapping with them. She is able to attend as little to our macro-sociological debates as we do to her political science controversies.

Pinker has argued that 'the discipline of social administration lacks that body of theoretical material which might give it a greater intellectual unity and perspective' (1971, p. 5). These various studies may all be seen as responses to this deficiency, attempts to relate the study of social policy to broader debates in the social sciences. The present book seeks to continue and strengthen, therefore, an existing but comparatively new debate in academic social policy writing.

III THE WIDER CONTEXT

The legacy of Marxism and liberalism as competing views of—and prescriptions for—society is not, of course, peculiarly British or even Occidental. So too, while the contemporary writers on whom we draw in chapter 3 are principally Anglo-Saxon, their debates are not proceeding in isolation. Nevertheless, the non-British reader will inevitably detect that the intellectual map offered in Part I displays emphases distinctively British. This is probably most true of the Social Democratic tradition expounded there, which, as Halsey (1978) has recently argued, includes a set of intellectual traditions, insights and aspirations centring in the political ideal of fraternity, although also, as we shall see, strongly infused with paternalism.

The British focus is still more marked in the empirical discussions of Part II. This was, for some writers of an earlier era, entirely appropriate, given their interests and the status of Britain as the first industrial nation. Weber, concerned with the 'spirit of capitalism' engendered by the Protestant work ethic, focused on the English divines (1930). Marx likewise used England as the chief illustration of the capitalist mode of production and declared to less advanced nations, *'De te fabula narratur!'* (1970b, Preface to first German edition). Today such a selection is much more problematic. Bell, while explicitly disavowing Marx's attempt to set out a 'deterministic trajectory' in which England's fate adumbrates that of other societies, nevertheless takes the United States as his 'singular unit of illustration' of the coming of post-industrial society, 'because the processes of change are more advanced and visible here' (1974, p. x). This assumption about the United States has been common in post-war academic sociology.

Nevertheless, if one recognises a variety of futures available to present-day advanced Western societies, then an investigation devoted to any one of them can be of value to students and citizens elsewhere, enquiring into the range of alternatives available. More strongly, it can be argued that, despite its relative industrial and economic decline, Britain's experience of seeking out a new basis of democratic social integration, appropriate to a mature industrial society in which traditional authority and economic power no longer suffice to ensure political order, holds out lessons likely to be of pressing relevance to her Western neighbours over the next half-century. Or, as Halsey again writes, it is possible to present Britain as 'a country with a deep and lively tradition of democracy and one which is leading the world rather than trailing behind it in pursuing the application of democratic principles beyond the polling booth in the factory and workplace, the home and the school' (1978, p. 123). Bell, discussing similarly the theme of change in British society in the present century, counters that 'to assume that developments in Britain have been shaped, as some new ideologues would have it, by the forces of "social democracy" . . . is to betray a shocking ignorance of history and of the structural contexts . . . that have transformed *all* of Western society' (1978, p. 62). Which view is more valid—and hence in what respects the non-British reader may learn from the British experience—is in part the subject of this book.

PART I

The Idea of Social Policy

CHAPTER 2

The Capitalist Market Society

If these systems remain valuable to posterity, that is not in spite of their strictly historical character but because of it. To us, the ideas expressed in them are ideas belonging to the past; but it is not a dead past; by understanding it historically we incorporate it into our present thought, and enable ourselves by developing and criticising it to use that heritage for our own advancement. [R. G. Collingwood The Idea of History *p. 230]*

I INTRODUCTION

In recent decades, discussion of social policy has been dominated, in the Anglo-Saxon world at least, by three main 'schools' of thought. First, neo-Marxist writers have predicated their contributions to the debate on the assumption that Marx's categories of socio-economic analysis retain their relevance for the investigation of Western advanced societies. Second, there have been two varieties of liberal writer: 'market liberals' such as Milton Friedman and 'political liberals' such as Kerr and Galbraith. Third, writers such as Titmuss and T. H. Marshall have articulated a Social Democratic approach, often as an explicit critique of liberal and neo-Marxist analyses.

Notwithstanding their differences, these various approaches agree in recognising the importance of the capitalist market context within which social policy, as we know it today, has developed. They likewise agree in recognising the early and mid-nineteenth century as the heyday of laissez-faire capitalism, in England at least, and in seeing the social policy measures of that period—most notably the Poor Law Amendment Act of 1834—as supportive of this capitalist system. Their different attitudes to this system have then informed their differing evaluations of those early social policy measures;

9

while their views on the extent to which it has changed over the last 150 years inform their analysis of concomitant changes in the significance and role of social policy.

In the present chapter, we spell out the principal features of the nineteenth-century capitalist market order. Their definition and significance are not, of course, unproblematic. Indeed, it was largely as divergent assessments of these features that Marxism and the various strands of liberalism received at this period their classical statements. Accordingly, we proceed by delineating three fundamental aspects of capitalist market society over which these intellectual disagreements seem to have been greatest: the division of labour, social change and social integration. We assume, therefore, that by setting out this threefold divergence in classical liberal and Marxist analyses we adequately span the intellectual matrix within which debates about laissez-faire capitalist society have been conducted. Only then can we understand the role of social policy in the heyday of capitalism and evaluate subsequent changes in its significance.

However, in addition to distinguishing between these classical definitions of capitalism, we point to changes in our society that seem to undermine their common assumptions, hinder the empirical articulation of their analytical categories and contradict their predictions. Limitations on space prevent more than a general survey of such changes in the society at large. Moreover, the material and authorities cited have, in the main, to be presented uncritically. Our conclusion, however, will be that a demonstration that contemporary social policy has a significance and role essentially the same as that of social policy in the heyday of laissez-faire capitalism is a precondition for maintaining the relevance of those classical analyses. This conclusion will then lead on logically to a consideration in chapter 3 of competing views of contemporary social policy, including views put forward by those claiming to bear the mantle of these classical writers.

II THE DIVISION OF LABOUR AND CLASS INTERESTS

The classical Marxist and liberal traditions agreed in recognising an advanced division of labour in a market society as one of the central distinguishing features of capitalism. Competition in the market place promoted specialisation and cooperation in the workplace, in the production of goods for sale, i.e. commodities. However, it was not only goods that were distributed on market principles; in addition, the various 'factors of production'—land, labour and capital—were allocated among productive enterprises by markets. The competitive market thus complemented the division of labour in two respects. First, each individual was engaged in specialised production and could gain access to the products of other specialised activities only by exchange. Second, each productive enterprise would typically require the collaboration of various skills and of the different factors of production, which were differentially distributed among the individuals in the society, but whose cooperative activity could be organised on the basis of factor markets. Members of civil society were related through the 'cash nexus': social bonds and social evaluations were defined by the market. The conclusion drawn was that such a market organisation of an advanced division of labour permitted an unprecedented productivity and efficiency.

Both traditions agreed that the 1834 Poor Law reinforced this social order. The cash nexus reigned for all who were unwilling to submit to the loss of esteem and of civil and political rights that receipt of relief entailed. Indeed, this loss of citizenship rights served as a powerful deterrent to those tempted to abandon the struggle in the market place. Hence 'the Poor Law was an aid, not a menace, to capitalism, because it relieved industry of all social responsibility outside the contract of employment, while sharpening the edge of competition in the labour market' (Marshall, 1965, p. 97).

For the liberal, this market organisation of society was not merely a possible basis for social harmony. It was, rather, a *sine qua non* for prosperity, equity and freedom in advanced society. For the Marxist, in contrast, the cash nexus involved the denial to the mass of the population, except on condition of their alienation to the capitalist of both product and productive activity, of access to the means of production and hence to the means of life. It was, therefore, both the consequence and the basis of inequality in advanced capitalist societies and its abolition was the *sine qua non* of social harmony and individual freedom.

These differences may be understood as arising from contrasting analyses of the way in which the rights of private property, in a society organised in terms of the cash nexus, define individuals' interests. The liberal denied that private ownership of the means of production need compromise an identity of interests among owners of different factors of production. The right of each individual to dispose of his property and labour power in the market place, free from interference and in accordance with his own judgement, permitted the unhindered pursuit of self-interest by each and every citizen. Such inequalities as might result would reflect diverse initial endowments of goods and skills, together with differences in the effort and wisdom devoted to production and exchange. They could not, however, be construed as resulting to any extent from inequitable exchanges, for each individual had been free to enter into such transactions only as promoted his own self-interest. Moreover, a market organisation of society, far from setting individuals' interests in conflict with one another, rather served to identify them. Liberals influenced by the natural law tradition thought of this identity as being 'natural': Adam Smith, for example, saw the market as an 'Invisible Hand'. Those more in the utilitarian tradition preferred to look to an artificial identification of interests, under suitable legislative action by the state; yet in the early nineteenth century that action was generally seen in terms of a policy of laissez-faire, under which the remaining impediments to a free market economy would be removed. (Hence, for example, we find Ricardo advocating free trade in corn, in order to remove, through appropriate legislative action, the conflict of interest between protected landowners and other social classes—Halevy, 1972, especially pp. 273ff and 338ff.)

For Marx, however, this formal equality in the market place must not be allowed to mask the difference in the situations and interests of those in whose hands were concentrated the means of production and those whose sole property was their own labour power. Indeed, it was a peculiarity of capitalism that labour power was treated as a commodity, that this commodity was, for the mass of the population, the only property they possessed, and that, in consequence, it was only by the sale of labour power that access to the means of life was gained. It followed that the wage bargain could not be seen as equally freely entered into by both parties: the bargain was a precondition of access to the means of life for the labourer only. Moreover, Marx's labour theory of value implied that it was the peculiarity of the commodity labour power that its use value (to the capitalist) was the production of surplus value, i.e. of an exchange value greater than its own. Consequently, the liberal's own principle of the individual's natural right to the produce of his labour was violated and this violation was the *sine qua non* for the continued existence of capitalism. The legal and political arrangements that upheld private property rights in the means of production and that protected the concentration of property in a few hands therefore involved an opposition of the interests of the wage labourer to those of the capitalist. They perpetuated an essentially unequal exchange as the basis of the capitalist mode of production. Moreover, as we shall see in the next section, this opposition increased as capitalism developed.

Such, in outline, were the contrasting approaches taken by the classical liberal and Marxist traditions to inequality and class interests in a society permitting unlimited private accumulation of property in the means of production and organised in terms of the cash nexus.

However, we may argue that certain empirical developments in the British socio-economic order over the last 150 years render of declining applicability the notion of a cash nexus as the predominant form of social relationship. To this extent, the liberal–Marxist debate over the implications of the cash nexus for the definition and reconciliation of class interests within a complex division of labour is of declining relevance.

We may distinguish three elements to the cash nexus in which the wage earner in a capitalist society, as depicted by both of the classical traditions discussed above, is typically involved:

(i) his access to the means of life or to life chances is wholly dependent on his disposable income;

(ii) his disposable income is determined by the wage he receives in return for the sale of his labour power;

(iii) this wage is struck at a level dictated by a competitive labour market—the individual worker enjoys a formal freedom, in the sense that he enjoys the civil right to dispose of his labour power through an individual contract involving a wage bargain.[1] (It was, of course, a common observation among the classical economists that, if supplies of labour were unlimited, the wage would settle at a level merely sufficient to supply the basic subsistence needs of the labourer.)

Consider the empirical relevance of these three elements in reverse order.

(i) There has been growing social regulation of the wage bargain and of access to sub-sectors of the labour market. In these two ways, the typical worker approximates decreasingly to the classical notion of the individual worker freely offering his services to any employer and competing with other workers in the search for a satisfactory wage bargain. Such regulation has been undertaken by both the state and various occupational associations. Organisations of employees have developed to protect their members' interests and these have in the long run tended to reflect the changing map of diverse skills in the labour force. Protective measures have affected both rewards and employment opportunities. Thus, for example, the development of collective bargaining machinery in this century has involved the specification of 'a recognised union rate for ... jobs embodied in a formal collective agreement' (Wootton, 1962, p. 71), and has occurred not only among manual workers but also, particularly in recent decades, among clerical and professional workers (Lockwood, 1958). Control over recruitment and training facilities and systems of professional licensing have likewise been means whereby such organisations regulate access to the labour market. State intervention in negotiation of the wage contract, through wage councils, arbitration procedures, incomes policies, etc., has similarly grown in importance in this century (Wootton, 1962, Ch. 3).

(ii) The direct identification of wage and disposable income is likewise to a decreasing extent an adequate description of the British labour force. *Prima facie* there has taken place a progressive divorce of wage and disposable income, in at least three ways. First, the nineteenth century saw an increasing range of private attempts to mitigate the consequences for the individual worker of the vagaries of the market and the insecurity of families whose livelihood depended critically upon the health and employment of its head. Friendly Societies offered such benefits as sick pay, old age pensions and funeral benefits and by 1905 their members numbered six million (Bruce, 1961, p. 96). The trade unions, whose right to engage in collective bargaining was recognised by an Act of 1875, offered similar benefits. Their membership was concentrated among skilled workers prior to the 1890s but thereafter moves were made to organise unskilled and badly paid trades, fostering a rapid growth of unionisation. Second, there has grown up an extensive social security system organised by the state. Under the Poor Law of 1834, relief was to be granted to paupers in workhouses, such that the pauper would be less well off than the poorest independent worker. This constituted, therefore, a divorce of labour market rewards and livelihood for the pauper, whereas (in principle) for the free worker in the labour market the identification of wage and disposable income operated fully. The social reforms of the period 1905–14 involved the public recognition of the break-up of the Poor Law and built upon the experience of private insurance schemes, organising them into a more coherent whole. This system of social security received its present shape, in the main, from the Beveridge Plan of 1942 (Beveridge, 1942). This plan, which pre-supposed the maintenance of full employment by state action, sought to provide a certain minimum disposable income for all, according to their social needs. Third, there has been the development of the income taxation system (incorporating various forms of allowance and relief).

It is, of course, true that these three mechanisms whereby the direct identification of disposable income and labour market rewards is dissolved may nevertheless permit the continuation of a marked degree of indirect identification. Thus Atkinson, for example, uses the definition of poverty implied by the Supplementary Benefits scale to examine the causes of poverty. His results map out the degree of identification of wage and disposable income for low-income groups and indicate those categories or groups of individuals among the poor for whom that identification largely persists (1969, Part I). Titmuss, in his study *Income Distribution and Social Change* (1962), examines for higher-income groups the extent to which the taxation system divorces market rewards from disposable income. He investigates opportunities for such groups to substitute for some of their disposable income, as defined for income tax purposes, various fiscal and occupational welfare benefits, including the conversion of income into capital and redistribution of income among their kinship groupings; he demonstrates that an *indirect* identification of market rewards and disposable income largely persists. However, it is precisely the indirect character of this identification that leads Titmuss in his conclusion to call for more detailed investigation of the new social mechanisms for rearranging, transforming and spreading income and for a new and more adequate approach to the collection and presentation of income data. Our conclusion holds, therefore, that in respect of the direct identification of market rewards and disposable income, the classical ideal types have grown increasingly inadequate.

(iii) In various ways access to life chances would seem to be decreasingly dependent upon disposable income. In particular, there has been the development of state agencies distributing services and benefits in kind for which the recipient is not required to pay the full cost (Halsey, 1972b, especially Chs 6 – 7, 10 – 12). Among such measures are public and social services.[2] Rather less obviously, the cost—and hence the accessibility—of commodities is affected by the state's imposition of indirect taxes, or, indeed, by its provision of subsidies on, for example, food.

Thus, this dissolution of the cash nexus has been effected most clearly in and through the changing role of the state. By intervention in the wage-bargaining process, by divorcing disposable incomes from wages and by distributing services in kind without imposing full charges on the consumer, the state would seem to have rendered access to life chances decreasingly dependent on the individual's disposal of property and labour power in the market place and increasingly dependent on publicly defined and guaranteed social rights. The latter, indeed, constitute 'the new property' (cf. Reich, 1964). *Prima facie*, then, such measures of social policy have a significance very different from the 1834 Poor Law.

III Capital Accumulation and Social Change

A second area of debate and disagreement between the classical liberal and Marxist traditions concerns the dynamics of change in capitalist market society. They have generally agreed in recognising the continuing search for private profit, via the accumulation of capital, as the central determing factor in such change. Moreover, both recognised the cumulative and dynamic implications of capitalist development and the centrality to capitalism not of *trade*, whereby given resources are reallocated among trading partners within an essentially static context, but rather of *industry*, involving 'the engagement and the application of man's ingenuity to make and shape the products he wants'. As Pasinetti has further noted, industry, unlike trade, 'requires [cumulative] changes in the organisational structure of society' (1965, pp. 573–4); hence both liberals and Marxists have concerned themselves with the wider social implications of this continuing capital accumulation. For example, both classical traditions examined its consequences for the changing pattern of life chance distribution among members of the population. They also acknowledged that the seemingly inexorable advance of the power of capital, coupled with its apparently supreme embodiment of rationality and efficiency, imposed on the society a particular system of values and progressively overturned those of earlier epochs.

In the classical liberal view, a policy of laissez-faire on the part of the state would permit progressive realisation of the beneficial potential of a market-dominated civilisation; social progress had as its necessary and sufficient condition the untrammelled pursuit of capital accumulation. Marxists, however, have generally argued that such laissez-faire accumulation must have two consequences wholly at variance with the expectations of the liberals. First, unimpeded capital accumulation, far from proceeding smoothly and without limit, must rather encounter recurrent crises of increasing gravity, which would not only interrupt its progress but also undermine claims as to its rationality and conformity to some supposedly 'natural' economic order. Second, the benefits of increasing productivity would be distributed among social classes in such a way as to foster growing inequality: the proletariat would suffer relative, if not absolute, immiseration.

More specifically, both traditions assumed that it was the rate of economic surplus, determined essentially by the surplus of production over consumption, that determined the rate of investment and of capital accumulation (Kaldor, 1955–6), which in turn determined the rate of economic growth, as measured by the increase in aggregate output of commodity values. This focus on commodity values, permitting quantification as a means of formulating relatively precise economic laws on the model of the physical sciences, enabled classical political economy to become the principal liberal contribution to an understanding of the process of, and prospects for, capital accumulation. Likewise Marx, while differing sharply from many proponents of the liberal tradition as to the ontological status of these 'laws', employed the instruments forged by classical political economy for his own prognoses, at the same time as he submitted the uses hitherto made of them to ideological critique. He adopted and adapted certain of their principal doctrines: notably the belief in a declining rate of profit, the emphasis on increasing returns to scale and the belief that poverty for much of the labour force is the *sine qua non* of capital accumulation.[3]

For some of the classical political economists, the secular tendency of the rate of profit to decline meant that eventually capital accumulation and hence economic growth must cease; a 'stationary state' would arrive. Such a prospect was viewed with varying degrees of gloom. For Marx in contrast, the decline of the rate of profit was an expression not of a natural law but rather of the fetters placed upon further development of the forces of production by capitalist property relations; for such decline would arise principally out of the periodic and increasingly violent crises to which capitalism would become subject (1970b, Chs 25 and 32). For Marx, therefore, the prognoses advanced by proponents of the 'dismal science' were well founded. Their diagnosis, however, was mystifying in attributing to invariant natural laws the ailments afflicting the historically specific mode of production with which they were concerned; their prescription of resigned submission to such laws involved a similar reification of a particular economic system as eternally valid. The doctrines of such other liberals as Spencer would presumably have appeared to Marx as offering even less insight into the prospects for capitalism, being centred less upon the immanent development of a system of commodity production than upon the exaggerated application of a biological metaphor in an optimistic social evolutionism. In Spencer there occurred the same reification of the laws of societal evolution as Marx criticised in the case of 'economic laws'.

There are then further disagreements between classical liberalism and Marxism as to the pattern of distribution of life chances consequent upon continuing unimpeded accumulation. Early contributors to the liberal tradition such as Locke were more concerned to justify the right of unlimited accumulation and appropriation by those with property than with the likely empirical consequences for the distribution of life chances. As Macpherson has argued (1962, Ch. 5), Locke attempted to justify, on the basis of private property rights and the right of the property owner to purchase labour as a commodity in the market place, his natural right also to the surplus produced by that labour, and to the unlimited accumulation of capital that such a surplus permitted. The classical political econo-mists, in contrast, were more concerned to investigate the supposed economic laws governing distributive outcomes. Indeed, for Ricar-do an investigation of these laws constituted 'the principal problem of Political Economy' (Sraffa, 1951–5, Vol. 1, p. 5). For such classical economists, Malthus' theory of population provided the foundation for a widely accepted 'iron law of wages', according to which wages could not long rise above subsistence level because of the increased procreativity of the labouring classes consequent upon any such rise. Ricardo, among others, interpreted this as meaning that labour, like other commodities, has 'its natural price ... i.e. that price which is necessary to enable the labourers, one with another, to subsist and perpetuate their race, without either increase or diminution' (Sraffa, 1951–5, Vol. 1, p. 93). His prog-nosis of the coming stationary state therefore involved the persis-tence of contemporary inequalities.

The Marxist tradition represents a radical critique of the classical liberal views of distribution. Already in the previous section we have seen how Marx understood the sale of labour power and the expropriation of the surplus in very different terms from such liberals. His investigation of the 'general law of capitalist accumula-tion' led him to conclude that through the preservation and progres-sive expansion of the industrial reserve army of unemployed labourers the wage rate was kept close to subsistence level. 'It follows therefore that in proportion as capital accumulates, the lot of the labourer, be his payment high or low, must grow worse.... Accumulation of wealth at one pole is, therefore, at the same time accumulation of misery ... at the opposite pole' (1970b, Vol. 1, p. 645). Such a distribution could not be deemed 'natural'; rather, it was the necessary fruit of the legal and political framework uphold-ing private property rights in the means of production.

To conclude this introduction, both liberals and Marxists recog-nised that the 'Manchester system' of laissez-faire capitalism en-joyed increasing sway not only in its home, England, but also over an increasing area of the world as a whole, and that the values it embodied were being imposed over a continuously growing area of social life. However, we have also seen the very different ontologi-cal status attributed by classical liberalism and Marxism to these values and to the laws that enforced them. For some liberals they were 'natural' but would not be realised except through active promotion of a policy of laissez-faire; for others, such as Spencer, their realisation was guaranteed through an ineluctable evolutionary process (Peel, 1971, Chs 6 and 8). For Marx, however, the implication of his critique of liberalism was that the values of the market system could claim no privileged status, and that the supposedly natural laws of capitalist development would produce growing crises whose resolution would be possible only through the transcending of the capitalist mode of production and distribution itself. As, therefore, with other aspects of his critique of liberalism, Marx here accepted its definition of a key element in capitalist market society, but then submitted it to criticism to reach very different conclusions.

However, over the last 150 or so years, changes have taken place in the British socio-economic order that put in question the prognoses of both sides in this debate and suggest the declining applicability of their concepts.

First, we may argue that the rate of capital accumulation is no longer determined by the rate of surplus. Kaldor, as a leading representative of the Cambridge school of economics, presents this case in a particularly clear form.[4] He argues that Britain's economy has been the first of the advanced economies to reach a situation of 'labour scarcity', in the sense that it is labour, rather than capital or land, that is relatively the most scarce factor of production and is hence the effective constraint upon economic growth. Reserves of disguised unemployment in agriculture have been exhausted and, contrary to Marx's expectations, the industrial reserve army has not been extended but largely eliminated. Such a transition to a state of labour scarcity, from that of the capital scarcity depicted by Marx or even of the land scarcity upon which Ricardo focused his anxieties, renders inoperative the classical reaction mechanism under which the size of the available surplus determines the rate of capital investment. Rather, in Kaldor's view the rate of long-run capital investment, like the rate of overall economic growth, is now principally dependent upon the rate of growth of the labour force—or, more strictly, of the labour force in manufacturing industry. Consequently, among the possible policy implications flowing from Kaldor's analysis are attempts to reallocate labour from tertiary to secondary activities (1966).[5]

However, one may surely argue that Kaldor should properly

concern himself also with possible changes in the *quality*, as well as the quantity, of such scarce labour. Moreover, since formal institutions that deal with such changes lie in the tertiary sector, attempts to reallocate labour towards the manufacturing sector, which Kaldor believes to be the sector whose growth largely governs the overall rate of economic growth, might in principle be counterproductive. Rather, if one accepts his conception of our economy as labour scarce, tertiary activities effecting qualitative change in the available labour force become a crucial area for empirical investigation. Indeed, in his more theoretical writings Kaldor has acknowledged the importance of such changes. He has examined the processes of learning-by-doing, which he sees as the inextricable concomitant of capital accumulation. At a given rate of capital investment, the rate of growth of productivity will be the greater 'the more "dynamic" are the people in control of production, the keener they are in search of improvements', etc. (1961, p. 207). The main implication for economic policy designed to foster growth is then the stimulation of the 'technical dynamism' of the economy (Kaldor and Mirrlees, 1962, p. 190).

This leads us into a more general consideration of the second element in the classical mechanism of economic change, namely the dependence of the rate of economic growth upon the rate of capital investment and accumulation. This element also would appear no longer to hold so strictly for our advanced economic order. We have just seen that in some of his theoretical writings Kaldor emphasises the dependence of the rate of economic growth upon not only the rate of capital investment but also the degree of 'technical dynamism' in the economy. Much more generally, however, and in various ways, economists of widely differing viewpoints appear to agree that, over the last 150 years, the skills and expertise of the labour force have become increasingly crucial in determing the growth potential of an advanced economy. In his historical studies of the Industrial Revolution in this country, Hobsbawm has distinguished two phases. The former, lasting from about 1780 to 1840, was dominated by cotton manufacture, the technology of which was fairly simple, requiring little scientific knowledge on the part of the entrepreneur and the workers. Consequently, many skills in demand in the early decades of this phase were progressively destroyed by mechanisation and often women and children came to be employed in the increasingly unskilled jobs. In contrast, the second phase, 1840–95, saw the need for new skills in the capital goods industries. In addition, the further the second phase proceeded, the more did science play an important role in technology; the electrical and chemical industries, two important growth industries of the later decades of the nineteenth century, were based wholly on scientific knowledge. Thus 'by the end of the nineteenth century it was already clear, especially from the experience of the German chemical industry which led the world, that the output of technological progress was a function of the input of scientifically qualified manpower, equipment and money into systematic research projects' (Hobsbawm, 1969, pp. 90–3, 117, 174). What economists have termed 'human investment' was thus the essential obverse of the new technology.

During the present century, such human investment would seem to have continued its growth in importance. As Galbraith writes, 'investment in human beings is, *prima facie*, as important as investment in material capital. The one, in its modern complexity, depends on the other' (1962, p. 221). Studies such as those of Denison (1967) on the contribution of education and other forms of human investment to economic growth may be subjected to severe criticism on both conceptual and methodological grounds (Balogh and Streeten, 1963); nevertheless, there seems to be general agreement among economists that an educated, healthy labour force enjoying reasonable living conditions is a necessary precondition for the effective operation of a modern economy and that 'improvements in the quality of the labour force can have dramatic effects on economic growth' (Blaug, 1968), particularly when there are limits on the availability of labour.[6]

The conclusion of this discussion, therefore, is that both elements in the basic mechanism of economic change postulated by classical liberalism and Marxism alike have been substantially undermined and rendered inapplicable to the contemporary British socio-economic order. Moreover, we have argued that it is those processes of human investment affecting the 'technical dynamism' of the labour force that have been of fundamental importance in these changes. Central among these processes are, surely, the contemporary state's social policies: for, with the greatly expanded role of the post-war state, access to life chances has, as argued in the previous section, become increasingly mediated by state agencies.[7]

It may of course be objected that, in the 1970s, rising unemployment demonstrates the impermanence of Kaldor's labour scarcity. The state's role in affecting and promoting the technical dynamism of the labour force lacks the significance we have accorded it. However, if we regard the current international recession as short run and as signifying no necessary fundamental change in the pattern of Western economic development, Kaldor's account of the long-run maturation of advanced capitalist economies may still stand. In any case, Kaldor does not assert that this maturation necessarily involves continuing full employment. On the contrary, for an economy like Britain, where maturation has taken place early and at relatively low levels of productivity, international competition from less mature rivals with ample labour supplies is likely to threaten employment, as domestic manufacturing industry loses profitable markets at home and abroad. Kaldor's emphasis on labour scarcity in manufacturing industry as a developing constraint on economic growth will remain valid, however, for the advanced capitalist world as a whole and for each individual economy as yet immature—as also will our inferences in regard to social policy. For Britain, admittedly, it may be less clear that social policy initiatives over the quality and redeployment of the labour force will retain the central economic role we have ascribed to them. Nevertheless, some of the Cambridge school have argued, in part because of Britain's 'premature maturation', the need for still more broad-ranging state intervention, which might well include the vigorous use of social policy instruments, in pursuit of a 'social contract' aimed equally against unemployment and inflation (see, for example, Kahn and Posner, 1977).

Early in this section it was seen that classical liberalism and Marxism also included empirical predictions as to the pattern of life chance outcomes, expressed in terms of wages and profits, that would result from continuing capital accumulation. We may, therefore, add an assessment of the adequacy of such predictions, by reviewing briefly the empirical evidence on income distribution. Hobsbawm, as we have seen, distinguishes two phases of the Industrial Revolution in this country. In addition to the difference in dominant form of technology between the two phases, they would appear to have been characterised by rather different patterns of income distribution, at least at the macroeconomic level.

The generation prior to 1795 had seen a rising real income for the upper reaches of the wage-earning classes and also for the middle and upper classes. In the new industrial areas of the north and Midlands, this prosperity was even more general (Perkin, 1969, pp. 134–49). However, there is a long-standing debate among present-day writers as to what changes took place in the living standards of wage earners during the first phase of industrialisation. Meliorists such as Hartwell argue for a continuing rise in real wages over this period (1971, Chs 5, 13, 14), while deteriorationists such as Hobsbawm consider that there was certainly no significant general improvement (1969, pp. 92–3). Opinions are much influenced by the terminal dates considered. However, it seems certain that improvements in real wages were slower than the growth of per capita real national income. 'Thus [even] on the most "optimistic" view of the question, there occurred a decisive shift in the distribution of income away from wages' (Perkin, 1969, p. 138). Furthermore, since it is known that certain favoured groups of workers were enjoying a rapidly increasing standard of living, it follows that the mass of the working class were suffering, to a serious extent, relative (if not absolute) immiseration. The conclusion must be that the more 'optimistic' of classical liberal expectations as to the pattern of distributive outcomes cannot be said to have held true for this period. They cannot, therefore, claim to represent an adequate general theory of income distribution under capitalism—at least at a macroeconomic level. Rather, this discussion gives support to the more pessimistic of the classical economists in their presentation of political economy as the 'dismal science', and also, of course, to Marx's theory of the relative immiseration of the wage-earning section of the population.

However, there took place a general rise in real wages from the mid-1840s. The so-called Great Depression was, for the working class, a period of significant growth in real incomes, for this was a period of falling prices, of especial benefit to lower-income groups (Saul, 1969, especially pp. 30–4). Hobsbawm considers that 'the most rapid general improvement in the conditions of life of the nineteenth-century worker took place in the years 1880–95' (1969, p. 162). The question arises, therefore, as to the changing shares of wages and profits in national income during the second phase of the Industrial Revolution and beyond. Kaldor refers to 'the relative stability of these shares in the advanced capitalist economies over the last 100 years or so, despite the phenomenal changes in the techniques of production, in the accumulation of capital relative to labour and in real income per head' (1955–6, p. 350). In contrast, Glyn and Sutcliffe cite recent studies indicating a long-run increase in the share accruing to labour; however, they point out that, in assessing such trends, the inclusion or non-inclusion of salaries as part of the rewards of labour is crucial, because of the progressive expansion of salaried occupations (1972, pp. 43–4; cf. Deane and Cole, 1962, p. 246). On either view, however, the Marxist expectation of a continuing relative immiseration of the labour force—which we interpret here as meaning a declining share of wages in national income—is contradicted. We are bound, therefore, to conclude that neither the empirical propositions advanced by classical liberalism as to the developing pattern of income distribution under capitalism, nor those of Marxism, can claim general validity for British society over the last 200 years.

Finally, the foregoing puts in question the assessment by liberals and Marxists alike of the historical significance to be given to the values of capitalist market society. As we have seen, it was classical political economy that made the major contribution to a liberal understanding of the processes whereby those values appeared inexorably to be imposed over ever-widening areas of social life: for the presentation and examination of those values in terms of the quantifiable exchange values of commodities facilitated the elucidation of well-defined economic 'laws' of development. Similarly, it was against these political economists that Marx developed his immanent critique of liberal prognoses. However, our discussion suggests that 'human investment', including measures of social policy by the state, has undermined the operation of these laws. Such contemporary social policies then appear to have a significantly different role from those of 1834. Investigation of their implications for the modes of action and values dominant in society and for the directions and dynamics of social change will need to draw on the tools not of political economy but rather of political sociology.

IV SOCIAL INTEGRATION AND SOCIAL TRANSFORMATION

The classical liberal and Marxist traditions were both, in important respects, offspring of the eighteenth-century Enlightenment. It is, therefore, appropriate that the third respect in which we should compare and contrast their analyses of capitalist market society centres on their views as to the rationality of its organisation. Both traditions proposed an image of a rationally organised society, the virtue of whose organisation would readily be perceived by its members, who would freely and willingly concur in its ethos and contribute to its functioning. Social integration, however, would be no less real for being predicated upon this free acquiescence, while individualism would be no less valued for being expressed within such a rational order. However, consistently with the differences seen in previous sections, these classical traditions differed radically as to the character of such a social order. These differences may best be highlighted by considering in turn their respective views of the relationship to social integration of (i) a system of market disciplines, (ii) forms of group membership and group allegiance, and (iii) the free and spontaneous concurrence of individuals in social functioning.

(i) First of all, both schools acknowledged that capitalist market society imposed on its members a system of constraints or disciplines. For those liberals inspired principally by the natural law tradition, the demand for laissez-faire was an attack on regulations interfering with the individual's natural right to dispose of his goods and person as he wished. The edifice of disciplines and constraints harking back to medieval guild privileges and feudal ties was to be dismantled; the new disciplines of the market would take their place. Liberals inspired more by the utilitarian tradition searched for a system of social disciplines that would identify the pursuit of self-interest with the promotion of the common utility. As seen above, in the earlier part of the nineteenth century this system was taken to be the free market, at least so far as economic interests were concerned (Halevy, 1972, pp. 498–9). (Only in the mid-nineteenth century did such a search lead, instead, to advocacy of greater state intervention in the market system and greater regulation of the rights of private property—Brebner, 1948.) Their advocacy of laissez-faire was therefore no less emphatic than that of their fellow liberals.

Such a prescription cannot be fully appreciated without brief consideration of the moral philosophy that in general accompanied it. Dominant in the ethos of the society experiencing the Industrial

Revolution, particularly among members of the middle class, was a work ethic whose origins may be traced back to the Protestant work ethic of the seventeenth century (Weber, 1930; Tawney, 1938). In the words of one nineteenth-century writer, 'Habitual exertion is the greatest of all invigorators' (quoted in Burn, 1964, p. 106); moral self-discipline and development could best be achieved through diligent application to one's vocation. Complementing the work ethic was an acceptance, in the mid-nineteenth century, of the existing social order as essentially just and eternally valid, although marginal reforms might be made. A nominalist view of society was prevalent by mid-century; early social reformers, deeply concerned with 'the social evils of the time, . . . explained them largely in moral terms and sought to remove them by reforming the individual' (Roberts, 1960, p. 173). In short, as laissez-faire capitalism entered its heyday, 'it was fundamental to the mid-Victorian outlook that material and moral progress were to be regarded as complementary' (Burn, 1964, p. 106). Accordingly, the 1834 Poor Law appeared not only as an essential step in extending the domain of market principles, through which individuals might have their natural rights respected and their self-interested activity rendered a means of promoting the common good, but also as a form of moral discipline and an incentive to self-development through work. Its stigmatisation of the pauper and its 'less eligibility' principles were 'intended to force into the labour market those who were hesitating on the edge of it: their labour would be for the good of the country at large; it would also be the means of restoring to them the self-respect and the capacity for social usefulness which years of semi-mendicancy had deprived them of' (Burn, 1964, pp. 106–7).

The Marxist perspective on this system of disciplines is very different. As seen earlier, it was only on condition of alienation of his labour power to the capitalist that the proletarian was able to gain the means of life. The institution of private property rights in the means of production, together with the right of unlimited accumulation, rendered proletarian an increasing proportion of the population, with interests essentially opposed to those of the ruling capitalist class and, indeed, to class society as such. The market could not, therefore, be seen as permitting harmonious social integration. The disciplines it involved or that accompanied it—the legal and political protection of private property rights, the removal of communal responsibility for individual welfare, the stigmatisation of pauperism—must be seen as essentially coercive. Such an order, far from promoting the moral development of the individual worker, rather increased his alienation and debilitation.

(ii) Both classical liberalism and Marxism saw the continuing development of such a laissez-faire capitalist market system as undermining traditional forms of association and grouping. Marx, in particular, appears somewhat ambivalent towards these developments. For while he recognised that capitalism had brought many out of the 'rural idiocy' of traditional village life, he also bemoaned the destruction of 'all feudal, patriarchal and idyllic relationships', for which only 'crude self-interest and unfeeling "cash payment"' had been substituted (*Communist Manifesto*, quoted in Mills, 1963, pp. 48–9). Liberals in general accepted less reservedly such social consequences of laissez-faire. They especially decried 'the spirit of corporation', i.e. the existence of 'a particular society formed within the general society, whose interests clash with those of the general society'. Such corporations served merely to 'prolong the prejudices of the past' (Halevy, 1972, p. 117); their demise, through the fuller operation of the free market, would permit the substitution of loyalties and allegiances to the market civilisation as a whole, arising out of recognition of the harmony among individual interests that such a market organisation entails.

Again in contrast, Marx saw the development of the capitalist system as forging new allegiances very different from these liberal expectations. Central to these was the emergence of the proletariat as a class-for-itself, conscious of its common interest in the abolition of class society. As seen in our opening pages, Marx explored the various immanent changes that were likely in the capitalist mode of production, producing the instruments, the agent and the conditions of its own abolition. Concentration of workers as the scale of production develops makes visible to them their common interests; immiseration worsens their situation and makes clear the incompatibility between their interests and those of private property; recurrent and growing crises dispel the pretensions of capitalist organisation to rationality and efficiency and demonstrate that these private property rights are a fetter on further development of the forces of production. Appeals to a supposed common interest among classes lose all credibility; the ideological power of the ruling class no longer serves to mystify social antagonisms; 'at long last, people are compelled to gaze open-eyed at their positions in life and their social relations' (*Communist Manifesto*, quoted in Mills, 1963, p. 49).

(iii) Out of these developing contexts of social discipline and group allegiance, liberals and Marxists saw the emergence of a social order that would conform to the true nature of man. It will be convenient to begin by outlining the very different philosophical anthropologies typical of classical liberalism and Marxism. Liberals generally conceptualised man in pre-social, abstract terms: individuals have desires, instincts, interests, etc., which are given prior to their historical social situations. Under this general view of the individual, as Lukes writes, 'social and political rules and institutions are . . . regarded collectively as . . . a means of fulfilling independently given individual objectives' (1973b, p. 73). Those liberals influenced by the natural law tradition tended to view socio-political arrangements as 'a means which men decide to form in order to defend . . . the person and goods of each individual member' (Colletti, 1972, p. 150), thus securing each individual's natural rights. Each thereby enjoyed a freedom: freedom 'from' society and from undue interference by others. Liberals influenced more by Benthamite utilitarianism preferred to criticise and justify social arrangements not in terms of natural rights, but rather as a means to the maximisation of the common good; nevertheless, their conception of the individual was generally no less abstract (but see below, p. 33).

In contrast to this abstract individualism, Marx and his sympathisers were among those denying that the individual can be thought of in such pre-social and ahistorical terms. Rather, human needs, desires and interests are historically created in the continuing 'metabolism of man and nature', whereby man creates and transforms his world, together with his consciousness of it and of himself. Social arrangements could not, therefore, be seen merely as a means to fulfilling certain pre-social individual objectives. Likewise, individual freedom could not be enjoyed simply by the exclusion of others; rather, a real freedom for the individual required the liberation of the total society.

These differences in philosophical anthropology then inform divergent evaluations of the social order that would permit man's self-realisation. Liberals and Marxists agreed that the competitive market system makes self-interest the norm; each individual seeks to make others means in his life projects. For those liberals drawing principally upon the natural law tradition, such a market society was the only context conforming to the true nature of man, as an abstract individual, for whom social arrangements were properly merely a means. Indeed, it was by virtue of its 'natural' character also a rational social order, and could but be perceived as such by its members, each of whom had as his prime concern the pursuit of his private self-interest. For liberals more in the utilitarian tradition, the rationality of such a market order consisted more in its identification of individual interests. For both strands of liberalism, therefore, at least in the earlier part of the nineteenth century, opposition to such a social order was deemed irrational; an enlightened citizenry could not but freely concur in such a market civilisation.

Marx, in contrast, denied that the egoism of civil society was the 'natural' behaviour of abstractly conceived individuals. Rather, it was an aspect of the alienation entailed by the cash nexus. Nor did it permit an identity of interests, but rather exacerbated their opposition as between proletarian and capitalist. The capitalist market society could not, therefore, be seen as permitting man's free expression of his species-being; and this was but one sense in which it must be deemed irrational. In its orientation to the production not of use values but of exchange values, the capitalist mode of production, far from promoting man's historical autogenesis, rather created a world of objects that progressively impoverished its producers (see the chapter on 'Alienated Labour' in Marx, 1970a). Even in terms of productive efficiency, the private property relations of capitalism, as must become increasingly evident, would contradict and in time come to act as a fetter upon the essentially social and cooperative productive forces. The proletariat, in acting as a 'class-for-itself' concerned to abolish the capitalist order that both depended upon and increased its own alienation and exploitation, would establish through its practical critique of capitalism a social order in which the individual would be not a means but an end and where there would be a real and visible community of interest (Avineri, 1968, Ch. 5).

Such, then, are the divergent liberal and Marxist views on social integration. However, as in previous sections, it may be argued that certain changes in the British socio-economic order over the last 150 years have put in question the relevance of these analyses and the validity of their predictions. Let us proceed by taking in turn the three themes discussed above.

(i) As we have seen, the system of disciplines imposed by the laissez-faire capitalist market society included two principal elements. First, there was the impersonal competitive market, under which the price mechanism enforced a strict *quid pro quo* in exchange; unilateral transfers of goods, services or cash were absent. The 'laws' of the market place enforced the discipline of the cash nexus. As we have also seen, it was such an order that classical liberalism sought to promote in British society and that the Marxist tradition took as the object of its critique. Second, to those who, for whatever reason, withdrew from such a regime, unilateral transfers were made, as the sole means of ensuring their continued livelihood, given the decay of traditional local networks of support. Yet such provision was granted only on condition of humiliation, stigmatisation and moral supervision, the paradigm being the 1834 Poor Law.

However, in Section (II) we presented a *prima facie* case for believing that, over the past 150 years, there has occurred a progressive and by now substantial dissolution of the cash nexus. At the same time, there has been the substantial 'break-up' of the 1834 Poor Law. For the 'independent workman' portrayed by classical liberalism, therefore, the disciplines of the cash nexus have been reduced in their effects; while for the recipient of social policy benefits the price is no longer the loss of civil and political rights and liberties. Moreover, the boundary once drawn between the independent workman and the recipient of such benefits seems to have been progressively dissolved through the creation of universal social services distributing benefits on criteria independent of labour market status or income. Overall, then, the disciplines of capitalist market society as classically conceived appear to have been of waning significance, notably on account of the changes in social policy over this period.

(ii) Next, we considered the patterns of group allegiance expected progressively to emerge as capitalist society developed. Liberals, we saw, envisaged that as traditional 'corporations' were dismantled new allegiances to the emerging market civilisation would follow necessarily from the identification of individual interests through the market. However, Macpherson, in his critique of classical liberalism, argues that such an allegiance is contingent upon 'the apparent inevitability of everyone's subordination to the laws of the market'. Such a condition, however, was not enforced by capitalist society as it developed in the nineteenth century. Rather, this 'inevitability became increasingly challenged as an industrial working class developed some class consciousness and became politically articulate.... The development of the market system ... [produced] a class which could envisage alternatives to the system' (Macpherson, 1962, pp. 272–3).

Not, however, that such class consciousness resulted in the action anticipated by Marxists, who, as we have seen, envisaged the progressive homogenisation, concentration and immiseration of workers as producing a revolutionary class-conscious proletariat. That even relative immiseration has actually occurred is doubtful, as argued in the previous section. Similarly, writers such as Lockwood have followed Weber's discussion of differentiated, rather than homogeneous, class situations and have emphasised the persistence of status considerations in workers' life projects (Lockwood, 1958, especially Introduction; also Weber, 'Class, Status and Party', p. 182, in Gerth and Mills, 1948). Whether or not, therefore, it is claimed that the proletariat still suffers a '*total loss* of humanity and ... can therefore redeem itself only through the *total redemption of humanity*' (Marx, 1975, p. 256), the conditions for such a redemptive act appear in large measure not to have materialised. The problems posed for Marxist writers by the failure of the proletariat in most advanced Western nations to achieve revolutionary class consciousness have often been rehearsed (Goldthorpe *et al.*, 1969, Ch. 3).

We may, however, add that in these accounts the observation is often made that Social Democratic parties have in general had to come to terms with the rather ambiguous implications for their practice of Marxist and socialist theory. Central to this problem has been the possibility of changing society by piecemeal and democratic means. The belief that such possibilities existed was fostered in particular by the extension of the franchise, i.e. of political rights of citizenship, and by the development of social policies, granting social rights and security against the vicissitudes of the market society. Bismarck's *Sozialpolitik*, introduced initially as a means of dissipating support for socialism, nevertheless appeared to present means for the peaceful transformation of capitalist society into a form of socialism, given a sufficient degree of electoral support and Parliamentary democracy (Giddens, 1970).

(iii) Finally, then, such Social Democracy came to appear to many as a political movement and programme for the humanisation of society, not by revolutionary class action but by persuasion and reform. The empirical development that may be said to have put in question the expectations of classical Marxism is the much greater electoral success of Social Democratic candidates than of orthodox Marxist parties, at least in Britain, the home of laissez-faire capitalism.

For the utilitarian strand in liberalism, which became of increasing importance relative to the natural law tradition in the course of the nineteenth century, the belief that a sufficient condition for social integration and harmony was the organisation of society in such a way as to identify the pursuit of self-interest and the furtherance of the common good was predicated upon the assumption that individuals were aware of, as well as desiring to pursue, their own self-interest. In the early nineteenth century, such utilitarians tended, as we have seen, to laissez-faire views; here an individual's self-interest could be considered to receive immediate and clear definition by the market. By mid-century, however, the utilitarianism of writers such as J. S. Mill and of practitioners such as Chadwick no longer advocated laissez-faire. Of especial relevance here, appreciation developed of the need for education of the populace, if they were to be capable of intelligent and responsible exercise of the duties of citizenship—including the new political rights—in an advanced capitalist society. Such education, however, if it was to be compulsory must also be free and provided by the state (Halevy, 1972, pp. 506–8). Within the liberal tradition itself, therefore, we find a move towards a more insociate and developmental conception of the individual and a continuing dilemma as to the proper limits of such state intervention. J. S. Mill and Alfred Marshall are but two examples of liberals perplexed by the attempt to reconcile the free acquiescence of an enlightened and rational citizenry in a market civilisation with the measures of state intervention outside the market place—including the growing range of social policies—without which such enlightenment could not exist (see Marshall's essay 'The Future of the Working Classes' in Pigou, 1925). It was from among such liberals that the rising tide of Social

Democracy, emphasising the role of the state in promoting the positive freedom of the citizen, drew many of its recruits.

V CONCLUSION

The classical liberal and Marxist analyses of capitalist market society, as developed in the early and mid-nineteenth century, have provided the principal components of the intellectual matrix within which debates about advanced industrial societies have been conducted. In this chapter, we have considered three key elements of market society, which, while receiving central attention by both classical traditions, have been interpreted and analysed in sharply contrasting ways. Yet we have also argued that fundamental changes have taken place over the last 150 years in the British socio-economic order that appear to contradict such predictions as are advanced by each tradition and that render increasingly irrelevant the assumptions and concepts employed in their debates. Furthermore, as Giddens points out, these classical traditions 'are in accord in minimising the influence of the "state". The political is seen as secondary and derived' (1972, pp. 32–3). Yet central among the developments we have traced are the extension and apparently changed role of the state's social policies.

The later part of the nineteenth century saw the rise of Social Democracy as a political movement and of academic sociology as an intellectual enterprise. Each must be seen as in part a response to the apparent declining relevance of classical Marxism and liberalism as tools of social analysis and guides to political action; each involves a reappraisal of the positive role of the state. We have already briefly referred to Social Democracy as a political movement. In concluding this chapter let us, therefore, note some of its main features as an intellectual current drawing on the new sociology.[8]

Weber and Durkheim are generally recognised as the principal figures in the sociological tradition as it was defined on the Continent in the decades immediately preceding the First World War. Their biographical and intellectual relationships to Social Democracy in Germany and France are not unambiguous—although this ambiguity is itself partly symptomatic of the turbulence, both political and intellectual, in which this alternative to Marxism and classical liberalism arose. Thus, for example, the German Social Democratic Party was avowedly Marxist until the turn of the century; only towards the end of his life, with the increasingly revisionist Social Democrats now integrated into the parliamentary system, did Weber see himself as being, if not its intellectual mentor, then at least its sympathetic goad (see Rimlinger, 1971, pp. 122–30; Giddens, 1970; Beetham, 1974).

Weber in particular was concerned to emphasise the positive role of the state: as an agent of life chance distribution, as an instigator of societal change and as a promoter of social integration. He saw social policies as central to this role, as his leading place in the *Verein für Sozialpolitik* suggests. For him, it was the relationship between political leadership and bureaucratic administration that must form the starting point for sociological analysis of contemporary society, rather than the relationship between wage labour and capital on which the classical liberal–Marxist debate had focused (Beetham, 1974, Ch. 3; Giddens, 1972, especially Ch. 3). Only in so far as Social Democratic thought acknowledged this had it, in his view, attained maturity.

First, such a mature perspective would need to recognise that the state's activities generated patterns of interests distinct from those of the market place. Among the mass of the population, entitlement to the new social welfare provisions meant that wage labourers had less and less of a common interest in the wholesale abolition of the existing order. (Indeed, Weber pointed pessimistically to signs that all sectors of the population were coming to embrace the security that such welfare provisions afford, no matter what the cost in terms of individual independence.) Social Democratic thought would need equally to recognise that political leaders—of any hue —typically become professionalised, developing interests within the existing order that divert them from pursuing radical change. They come to live *off*, not *for* politics (Beetham, 1974, pp. 228–30).

Second, Weber bemoaned the German Social Democrats' continuing reliance upon mechanistic laws of capitalist development to undermine the prevailing order, to make visible to the working class its interest in a radically different society and thus to ensure transition to a fully humanised one. He argued, rather, that the process of societal change was centrally dependent upon political activity, which enjoyed an autonomy *vis-à-vis* the dynamics of capital accumulation; that it was only via political leadership that patterns of common or conflicting interest within and between collectivities became apparent; and that there was a plurality of societal futures available, incorporating a variety of values, none of which was historically privileged but one of which must be politically chosen. In short, he called for political leaders who would live by the 'ethic of responsibility' (Beetham, 1974, p. 174), choosing and imperiously defining social values for their followers, having full regard to the probable consequences, rather than surrendering fateful societal decisions to the putative dictates of historical inevitability. Equally, however, he sought to expose the dangers to such an ethic and to 'substantive rationality' in policy-making (i.e. the conscious political choice of policy goals) posed by the increasing powers of the bureaucratic administrators, and to awaken political leaders—including the Social Democrats—to the need to mobilise democratic control of such powers.

Third, Weber challenged the prognoses that the liberal and Marxist traditions offered of a rationally organised society whose virtues would be immediately and sufficiently evident to evoke the freely willed acquiescence of its members. This acquiescence, he argued, could not be purely self-interested. It must, rather, involve the acceptance and discharge of social duties and obligations as morally binding. In no society, moreover, would this acceptance arise spontaneously. Rather, to engender and mobilise such obligations—and hence to secure the legitimacy of the prevailing order (Weber, 1964, pp. 124–5)—was a central task of political leadership. It was the failure of Social Democratic leaders responsibly to accept this necessity that Weber deplored. Indeed, the centralised bureaucratic administration that they appeared to be proposing as the heart of their socialist society would tend, in Weber's view, to undermine this task of engendering wider civic obligations, by holding forth 'formal rationality', i.e. the procedural correctness of individual action, as a sufficient criterion of social organisation (Beetham, 1974, especially Chs 3 and 6 and pp. 144–7, 222ff.).

Durkheim, similarly, was a sympathetic critic of Social Democracy and shared its intellectual inheritance. He saw the rise of the state—intervening in life chance distribution, promoting the division of labour and societal advance and pursuing social integration—as the 'normal' concomitant to advancing industrialisation. However, his critique of existing society and his prescription for the state's activity were rooted in his fundamental assertion that 'society is *par excellence* a *moral* entity'. In the previous section we traced the classical debate over the disciplines of market society, the emerging patterns of group allegiance and the conditions for spontaneous individual concurrence in societal functioning. For Durkheim, these were the elements of moral life, yet his analysis departed from both of the classical traditions (see Durkheim, 1961, Part I; cf. Lukes, 1973a, pp. 110–19). The disciplines and allegiances of a market civilisation were chimerical, for the pursuit of untrammelled self-interest, which liberalism enjoined, corroded all stable social groupings. Equally, however, the Marxist hopes for an emerging allegiance to the proletariat as a class-for-itself embodying a moral life antithetical to that of the market place were as utopian as they were particularistic, in looking not to the rational action of the state but to the revolutionary action of the disaffected for the moral reconstruction of society.

Current conflict was, then, an expression of moral malaise and the task of the state was to promote the moral reconstitution of society. 'The task of the most advanced societies', proclaimed Durkheim, 'is a work of justice' (1933, p. 387); of *justice* because only a just social order would engage the moral commitment of its members and a *task* because without this commitment, social disorder was endemic. This justice, moreover, centred in respect for the rights of the individual citizen; in a highly complex society, where men have only their humanity in common, 'the individual ... has become tinged with religious value; man has become a god for men' (1951, pp. 333–4). Complementing this promotion of the 'sacredness of the individual' at a societal level, Durkheim prescribed reconstruction of more local loyalties to secondary groups—in particular, to professional associations (1951, pp. 378–84). It was to a recognition of, and commitment to, this moral task that he then summoned the Social Democrats of contemporary France (Lukes, 1973a, Chs 12 and 17, pp. 268–74).

Nevertheless, it was on Britain that classical liberalism and Marxism had focused and with Britain that our empirical investigation in Part II will be concerned. What, then, were the principal components of Social Democratic thought as it emerged to prominence in England during this period? As in France and Germany, British Social Democracy attained maturity and coherence as a unified but distinct intellectual force in the first two decades of the present century—overshadowed as they were by the anticipation and experience of war. It was the Webbs and Tawney who were most influential in attempting to harness the British strands of social philosophy and analysis to a political strategy for Social Democracy. It is on them, therefore, that we concentrate. (Winter, 1974).[9]

Tawney's intellectual position has certain parallels with that of Durkheim. For both of them, contemporary class conflict was an expression of the moral anarchy that a market society breeds. For neither, therefore, could such conflict be removed by economic or bureaucratic reorganisation alone. The positive role each of them prescribed for the state consisted, then, in its promotion of a principled moral order that was 'planned ... to emphasise and strengthen ... the common humanity which unites' men and that, indeed, had a sacred character (Tawney, 1964, p. 49). This alone could engage the freely willed moral commitment and obligation of the mass of the population.

For Tawney, it was in face of the war-time exigencies that the significance of this positive role was particularly and publicly evident. Full mobilisation on the military and industrial fronts required a mobilisation on the social front also—in the sense of an equality of sacrifice and a collective commitment to a more egalitarian society. This alone, in Tawney's view, could secure popular acquiescence during the war and its aftermath: an acquiescence that would go beyond either sullen or deferential compliance and would rather involve citizens as a collective force for social transformation. Out of the international conflict engendered by unprincipled capitalism would come the re-ordering of society as morally just and hence socially cohesive. For Tawney, then, Social Democracy involved 'a dialectic between legislation from above *and* active citizenship from below' (Terrill, 1974, p. 261; cf. Tawney, 1964, p. 219). This insistence on the necessarily democratic character of any effective programmes of social reform, with moral solidarity or fraternity both their seed and their fruit, was perhaps Tawney's principal intellectual legacy to the Social Democracy that came to political dominance only in the aftermath of another war. At the same time, however, his failure to confront the implications for such fraternity of the value plurality affirmed by Weber led him also to neglect the ethic of responsibility by which the political leader must properly live: the leader's fateful and imperious enunciation of political values tended, in Tawney, to be neglected because fraternity was treated as morally unambivalent (cf. Winter, 1974, pp. 92–3 and Terrill, 1974, pp. 223–9).

Nevertheless, it was the Webbs whose ideas had the greater

influence on British Social Democratic thought.[10] For them, Social
Democracy as a pathway and as a goal centred in social administration and reform from above. Their confidence in the political
efficacy of rational argument and their optimism as to the harmony
of interests that these reforms would promote attest their indebted-
ness to the liberal tradition and to utilitarianism in particular.
However, these hopes, which among the Webbs' heirs flowered into
euphoria in the 1940s, the heyday of Social Democracy, held
dangers of intellectual myopia, as we shall see. In brief, these were
at least threefold. First, the Webbs' social theories and political
strategy encouraged a reliance on Labour governments at least to
pursue policies that aimed at radical social transformation and that
would heed the findings of the rational social investigator. Yet, as
Weber had pointed out, constellations of interest typically develop
that link political leaders to advantaged groups in the wider society,
in the face of which early vision may fade and the findings of social
enquiry be ineffectual. Second, the welfare professional and administrator tended to appear as benignly countering the depradations of urban–industrial change. As one Social Democrat wrote in
mid-century: 'It is [the professions'] business . . . to construct a scale
of human values . . . it rests with them . . . to find for the sick and
suffering democracies a peaceful solution of their problems' (Marshall, 1965, p. 179). Only more recently have Social Democratic
writers developed a critique of such professionalism, not unlike that
which Weber offered of the state official. Third, these Social
Democratic apologists, while recognising the social legislation of
the 1940s as both an expression and a catalyst of widespread
commitment to shared social purposes, tended to neglect the difficulties inherent in the political task of mobilising such commitments in the face of self-interested action. Again, it was to the
problems of such mobilisation that Weber had pointed. To these
various weaknesses we shall in due course return.

Finally, then, and to repeat, the rise of Social Democracy as an
intellectual current and a political movement in the later part of the
nineteenth century was in part a response to the perceived failings
of classical liberalism and Marxism. Those, therefore, who would
maintain the continuing validity of either of these two traditions
when applied to contemporary society must demonstrate that the
empirical changes we have discussed, notably those in the field of
social policy, are only superficial and apparent. That is, social policy
today has a role and significance not essentially and necessarily

different from the social policies of the early nineteenth century; the Social Democratic alternative forged in the later part of that century was fundamentally misleading as an intellectual current and as a political movement. In the next chapter, therefore, we investigate the analyses of contemporary social policy advanced by the heirs of these three traditions, before going on, in Part II, to an empirical evaluation of their competing claims.

NOTES

1. See Marshall's discussion of the historical development of this civil right (1965); and Weber's analysis of the 'formally free' labour force of Occidental capitalism (1968, Vol. 1, Ch. 2).
2. For discussions of the distinctions between these, see Titmuss (1974) Ch. 9, and Pinker (1971) Ch. 4.
3. See P. Colquhoun *A Treatise on Indigence* (1806) pp. 7–8: 'Without a large proportion of poverty there could be no riches, since riches are the offspring of labour, while labour can result only from a state of poverty' (quoted in Marshall, 1965, p. 94).
4. For a general survey of growth theories, see Hahn and Matthews (1965).
5. See too Cripps and Tarling (1973). This is part of Kaldor's notion of the 'maturation' of an advanced economy. In other writings he explores other con-stituents of this process—see, for example, 1968, pp. 385–91. For a critique (by a neo-Marxist) see Rowthorn (1975). Kaldor's reply (1975) includes modification of his views on maturation.
6. See Shonfield's discussion of Sweden's 'active manpower policy', whose focus 'is on the use of the labour force—how to increase its size, how to improve its quality, how to achieve its more rapid deployment in response to changing needs' (1969, p. 201).
7. Patterns of international migration will also, of course, affect the seriousness of the labour scarcity of which Kaldor writes. Here is a further major sense in which the state's social policies may affect the size, quality and deployment of the labour force and hence, in a labour-scarce economy, the rate of economic growth. For a comparative study of such policies, see Castles and Kosack (1973).
8. It is, of course, important not to exaggerate the links between the two. In addition, the intellectual content of any political theory is likely to be vulgarised—and even emasculated—when it becomes the agenda of a popular movement. (For discus-sion of this in relation to Marxism, see Avineri, 1968, pp. 250–1.)
9. Winter takes G. D. H. Cole as representing a third strand—but goes on to argue that Cole eventually shifted into 'the Webbian centre of socialist thought' (1974, p. 283).
10. But on whether these ideas were an authentic and essential part of the socialist and labour traditions, see Hobsbawm (1964) Ch. 14.

CHAPTER 3

Alternative Interpretations of Social Policy

Sociology and history teach that achievement is inevitably meas-
ured with out-dated tools and the concepts and preoccupations of
previous generations. [*P. Townsend and N. Bosanquet* Labour
and Inequality *p. 9*]

I INTRODUCTION

The conclusion of the previous chapter was that certain fundamental changes in the British socio-economic order over the last 150
years present serious problems for the principal varieties of social
analysis developed in the early and mid-nineteenth century. We
argued, additionally, that it has been the rise of state intervention,
including in particular the development of a wide-ranging social
policy, that has been central among these problems. It follows that
any contemporary attempt at a general understanding of our socio-
economic order must give central attention to the investigation of
such social policy.

We now set out the conflicting interpretations of social policy
advanced by contemporary neo-Marxists, liberals and Social
Democrats, as a prelude to their subsequent empirical investigation. Each group of writers is strongly influenced by the traditions
discussed in the previous chapter, although we shall make little
attempt to assess how faithful they are to their respective predecessors. At the same time, they have to a considerable extent developed their principal arguments about contemporary social policy

in industrial society through continuing mutual criticism. We focus selectively on their responses to the empirical developments discussed in the previous chapter.

II Neo-Marxist Interpretations of Social Policy

The term neo-Marxist may be taken as referring to those contemporary writers who assert the continuing relevance of Marx's categories of social and economic analysis, albeit with modification of concrete detail. As observed in chapter 1, the degree to which any particular writer conforms to this typification will not always be unproblematic. Nevertheless, the writers to be considered in this section are obvious contributors to the contemporary articulation of orthodox Marxist analysis. In seeking to uphold the principal tenets of the Marxist tradition, they have, to varying extents, confronted the empirical changes discussed in chapter 2. In their comments on the historical development and contemporary functioning of social policy, they argue that no fundamental change has been wrought in Marx's delineation of (i) conflicting class interests, (ii) the significance of capital accumulation, and (iii) the revolutionary role of the proletariat.

(i) It is denied that for the mass of the population the cash nexus has been transcended, either through the divorce of disposable income from wages or through the freeing of access to life chances from full dependence on disposable income. The class interests of the owners of property and those who have only their labour power to sell are no less well-defined and no less opposed than in Marx's day. The social security system, which appears at first sight to divorce market rewards and disposable incomes, in the main merely redistributes earnings over the individual's life cycle and within the working class. Fiscal and occupational welfare provisions, being regressive, undermine any egalitarian effect of the social services and ensure the perpetuation of a strong link between the earnings of a household and its disposable income (Kincaid, 1973; Westergaard and Resler, 1976, Part 2, Ch. 4).

Moreover, while access to the life chances distributed by the other social services may formally be partly independent of disposable incomes, the class gradients in outcomes have not been significantly altered by the establishment of the post-war welfare state (Blackburn, 'The Unequal Society' in Blackburn and Cockburn, 1967). In sum, then, it is the individual's sale of his labour power that determines, for the mass of the population, access to life chances; the rise of social policy does not reduce the relevance of the Marxist analysis of class interests. 'Property, profit and market . . . remain the prime determinants of inequality' (Westergaard and Resler, 1976, p. 17).[1]

(ii) It is also denied that Marx's analysis of capital accumulation and social change needs any major modification in order to be relevant to contemporary Western societies. Neo-Marxist economists would, in the first place, oppose Kaldor's view that, in Britain at least, there has taken place a transition from a situation of capital scarcity to one of labour scarcity. Such studies as Baran and Sweezy's *Monopoly Capital* (1968), attempting to compute the size of the surplus in the American economy, are therefore not at all misplaced for any of the Western economies, including the British. So too, many neo-Marxists have been quick to deny that the rise of 'human investment' puts in question Marx's analysis. The labour force may, in contrast to that depicted by Marx, appear to display increasing heterogeneity; yet, in the face of growing bureaucratic regulation of all but the most privileged groups of employee, both manual and non-manual grades occupy situations similar in their powerlessness and in the alienation they involve (Gough, 1975b, p. 67). Relative immiseration of the mass of the population—albeit construed no longer principally in economic terms—remains the consequence of progressive accumulation.

Nevertheless, there seems to be an increasing recognition among some neo-Marxists of the need to analyse the role of the modern state apparatus in social policy formulation and implementation. Such analyses are directed towards a demonstration that the dominant mode of social action remains the pursuit of private profit and the expansion of exchange values. This permits the neo-Marxist to designate the contemporary state a *capitalist* state, to lay bare the expression of capitalist contradictions within this state's social policies and to give contemporary detail and relevance to orthodox Marxist prognoses on the resolution of such growing 'structural' contradictions.

O'Connor's analysis *The Fiscal Crisis of the State* (1973) has proved a significant recent contribution to the neo-Marxist position. He accepts that human investment has indeed become a precondition for the expansion of exchange values, as argued in chapter 2. Yet the pursuit of such investment through the state's social policies testifies to the political power of private capital; these social policies involve no societal objective challenging the pursuit of private profit. O'Connor goes on to expose the 'contradiction' between collective expenditure on social policies and the private appropriation of their economic fruits—a contradiction likely to be increasingly evidenced by the inadequacy of the state's tax base for non-inflationary financing of the expenditures properly required for an expansion of the forces of production. (For more extended expositions, see Gough, 1975a, b.)

Difficulties arise in regard to the coherence and consistency of O'Connor's argument, vitiating his treatment of certain key issues. They are not, however, peculiar to O'Connor. To start with, it is by no means clear precisely how the interests of the capitalist class come to mould the state's social policies. Does O'Connor intend an account in terms of certain supposed 'systemic' demands and constraints; or are capitalists seen as constituting a self-conscious and politically dominant group capable of orienting social policies to their own well-defined ends? The former would tend to be predicated upon an ahistorical, functionalist perspective, in which the state has no real autonomy; the latter is consistent with a historically oriented concern with continuing class struggle over policy.

This leads us, therefore, into a brief consideration of contemporary neo-Marxist debates over the 'relative autonomy' of the capitalist state, centring upon the question of how that state can simultaneously be deemed to enjoy some autonomy and yet be a *capitalist* state. Drawing in part on the recent Poulantzas—Miliband debate (including 'The Problem of the Capitalist State' in Blackburn, 1972), Gough argues that 'it is the incapacity of the capitalist classes to organise itself [*sic*] as a political force which requires the State . . . to act as a class-conscious political directorate' (1975b, p. 64). Cleavages of immediate interest among sub-sections of the economically dominant class would otherwise inhibit the implementation of their 'common, longer-term political interests' (Gough, 1975b, p. 65; cf. O'Connor, 1973, pp. 65ff; see too Westergaard and Resler, 1976, Part 3, Ch. 6). Here, then, is not only a recognition of the inadequacy of quasi-functionalist appeals to systemic demands as an explanation of the supposed subservience of social policies to the developing needs of the capitalist system, but also an acknowledgement of the problematic character of the processes whereby the capitalist class becomes conscious of, and secures policy formulation in accordance with, its long-term common class interest. However, it remains unclear, first, by what means the state becomes aware of this interest. As Offe argues, the neo-Marxist must demonstrate that 'the State apparatus . . . display[s] a selectivity aimed at distilling . . . out of narrow, short-term, conflicting, incompletely formulated interests . . . only those which coincide with the "collective interest of capital", which indeed help the latter to be articulated in the first place'. Second, what prevents the agencies of the state apparatus developing and pursuing their own interests and goals, and 'which *internal structures* within the political system guarantee the implementability of initiatives and interests arising from the process of accumulation'? (Offe, 1974, pp. 35–7).

This exposition of the 'relative autonomy' of the capitalist state is sometimes also taken as permitting simultaneous recognition of the role of working-class struggle in the development of post-war social policies, which 'undoubtedly . . . sometimes went further than the dominant class would have wished'; although, in general, 'social policies originally the product of class struggle will, in the absence of further struggle, be absorbed and adapted to benefit the interests of the dominant classes' (Gough, 1975b, pp. 69, 76; cf. Westergaard and Resler, 1976, pp. 177–8). Without this latter qualification, it is perhaps rather unclear how the modern welfare state can properly be designated 'capitalist'. For, as Offe argues, the neo-Marxist must demonstrate how the state tends selectively to 'protect . . . capital against anti-capitalist interests and conflicts' (1974, p. 38). Also unclear is the compatibility of such neo-Marxist emphases on class struggle as a factor in the development of social policy with their arguments, to be considered below, that political debates over social policy have served as an opiate for the working class. Finally, there is surely a need for explication of the relationship between the interests of different classes and the alternative principles of social policy around which debates and struggles have actually centred.

(iii) Their commitment to the Marxist tradition has meant that the central sociological paradox with which they have been confronted has been the failure of the working class to develop a revolutionary class consciousness, becoming a class-for-itself. As against the arguments of the previous chapter, they deny that attempts at non-revolutionary reform are other than misconceived or that the social policies developed over the past century introduce fundamental changes in the dominant mode of social integration. On the contrary, welfare state institutions have served as relatively successful agencies for the perpetuation of a 'false consciousness' among members of the working class. Through its social policies, the state is able to mitigate the most glaring deprivations wrought by the capitalist system and to pretend to a concern with social welfare. The irrationality of capitalism and the real conflicts of interest between different classes are thereby masked and any radical criticism of the status quo is deflected.

In recent decades, these arguments have been elaborated within several variants of neo-Marxism. In the Frankfurt tradition, Marcuse sees false consciousness as almost universal in contemporary neo-capitalism. The technology of such societies satisfies a seemingly unending series of new human needs—needs that, however, 'have a societal content and function which are determined by external powers over which the individual has no control'. This technology thereby 'serves to institute new, more effective and more pleasant forms of social control and social cohesion' (Marcuse, 1968, pp. 22, 13). Among these new techniques for the sublimation of class conflict are social policies. Anderson draws on Gramsci's analysis of the 'hegemony' of the ruling class. This hegemony 'not merely sets external limits to the actions and aims of the subordinated bloc, it structures its intimate vision of itself and the world, imposing contingent historical facts as the necessary coordinates of social life itself' (Anderson, 'Origins of the Present Crisis' in Anderson and Blackburn, 1965, p. 30). Not dissimilarly, Westergaard argues that 'conflict is regulated through a series of compromises which define, not only the means and procedures of conflict, but also the area of conflict . . . only a small band of the full range of alternative policies is effectively ventilated and disputed' ('The Myth of Classlessness' in Blackburn, 1972, p. 140). Conflicts over social policies are typically predicated upon—and reinforce—uncritical acceptance of the legitimacy of the more fundamental patterns of property ownership and control (Habermas, 1976, p. 70). Parkin summarises these views: the social services 'damp down radical or revolutionary movements', so that 'the relatively low costs incurred by the dominant class in the provision of welfare [will be] more than offset by the prevention of a more drastic kind of redistribution' (1971, pp. 124–5). Those Social Democratic politicians who make extension of the social services a prime objective are then seen as naïve or treacherous (Gough, 1975b, p. 66).

For Marx himself, the continuing development of the capitalist mode of production, as elucidated by the study of political economy, would realise the objective preconditions for revolutionary class consciousness and class action on the part of the proletariat. In contrast, the prognoses offered by contemporary neo-Marxists are vague and only loosely articulated with the study of change in such objective conditions. Indeed, as Goldthorpe has observed, there has been a 'decomposition of the relatively integrated approach of Marxist orthodoxy', so that 'the more sociologically informed and sophisticated treatments . . . tend also to be the ones that lack any articulation with economic analysis', while neo-Marxist economists attempting new departures tend to be sociologically naïve (1972, pp. 364–5).

For some of the writers we have discussed, analysis of change must focus on the possible contemporary agents of opposition to the cultural and ideological hegemony of the ruling class. For Marcuse, this agent is 'the substratum of the outcasts and outsiders, the exploited and persecuted . . . , the unemployed and the unemployable', whose opposition alone 'hits the system from without and is therefore not deflected' by the 'totalitarian tendencies of the one-dimensional society' (1968, p. 200). Others look to a 'hegemonic' socialist party which can be 'the bearer of *universal values,* which are recognised and experienced as such by a majority of all those whose humanity is denied and dislocated by the social order' (Anderson, 'Problems of Socialist Strategy' in Anderson and Blackburn, 1965, pp. 241–2). Little account is offered, however, of what developments in objective conditions may be expected to encourage and prosper such cultural opposition. Anderson declares that British society is suffering 'a slow, sickening entropy . . . The "law" of uneven development has produced its customary dialectical reversal' (Anderson and Blackburn, 1965, p. 47). Miliband speaks of 'profoundly destabilising forces at work in capitalist society'—including a conflict between the 'spirit of sociality and cooperation' that these societies require from their members and the 'dominant impulse' of private appropriation (1969, pp. 264, 268). Neither offers more specific analysis.

Other writers consider how the contradictions espied by Marx in the developing capitalist mode of production have been 'displaced' into the state sector and attempt a prognosis of these new contradictions. O'Connor, for example, argues that there is a contradiction of growing intensity within the dual role of social policy—in facilitating private capital accumulation and in legitimising the capitalist order. For the legitimising function is directed chiefly at disguising the immiserising consequences of the accumulation (1973, pp. 158–68; cf. Bowles and Gintis, 1976, pp. 231–5). He fails, however, to make clear how this contradiction engenders not only a 'fiscal crisis' but also a demystification of subordinate classes' perception of societal arrangements.[2] Offe argues that through its social policies the state promotes an image of itself suggesting that 'use values like education, . . . health, welfare . . . are the final purpose of its measures'. Yet 'the more and more visible conflict between promise and experience' undermines acceptance of the state's legitimacy and promotes growing frustration of citizens' expectations' ('Legitimacy versus Efficiency' in Lindberg *et al.*, 1975, p. 256). Schroyer (1973) draws on O'Connor and Offe in seeking a 'unified critical theory' uniting 'cultural criticism to a critique of political economy'. He recognises that this requires, *inter alia*, analysis of the ways in which societal changes are creating 'propitious circumstances' for emancipation. He finds it necessary, however, to set aside orthodox Marxist notions of class consciousness and conflict, with their associated emphasis on the milieux of industrial production, and instead to focus upon institutions dealing with 'health, education, welfare, environmental conditions . . . [as] a social space for emancipatory movements' (pp. 239, 248–51). That is, he finds an adequate prognosis must be predicated upon recognition of the central role of social policy that we spelled out in the previous chapter.

III Liberal Interpretations of Social Policy

The term 'liberal' is currently applied to two broad groups of social analyst: 'market liberals' such as Milton Friedman and the Institute of Economic Affairs, who extol the virtues of a laissez-faire market society, and 'political liberals' such as Kerr and Galbraith. By examining their respective views of social policy, some of the similarities and differences between these two variants of liberalism will become clear.

Market liberals

It is the market liberals who more obviously share the view of market society held by the classical liberalism depicted in the previous chapter. The competitive market grants freedom in the disposition of each individual's skills and property; the cash nexus identifies self-interest and the common interest. Private ownership of the means of production promotes capital accumulation and its fruit, prosperity for all who share responsibly in productive activity. Indeed, such a market-organised system of private appropriation is the epitome of rational social organisation and its unimpeded operation cannot but evoke the free and whole-hearted acquiescence of all rational citizens.

Such market liberals, then, see themselves as taking the 'freedom of the individual, or perhaps the family, as [their] ultimate goal in judging social arrangements'. More specifically, this freedom is the individual's 'freedom to make the most of his capacities and opportunities according to his own lights'; it therefore entails an equality of opportunity. It does not, however, necessarily entail a 'material equality or equality of outcome' (Friedman, 1962, pp. 12, 195), even though a trend to such may indeed be the outcome of unimpeded capitalist development.

It follows that these writers adopt a twofold approach to social policy. First, they deduce from their conception of market society the role that social policy may play without threatening market principles of social organisation, or, stated more positively, the ways in which social policy may be organised to support and reinforce the operation of the market system. Second, they assess the extent to which actual social policies conform to such a role, and seek to explain deviations. In this second aspect of their analysis they have had to take up the argument of the previous chapter that, in certain key respects, the classical liberal conception of the character and future of capitalist market society is of dubious contemporary relevance.

It is a general argument of market liberals that, to the extent that our society departs from a capitalist market organisation, the freedom of the individual, as celebrated in the classical liberal tradition, is put seriously at risk. Among these departures is the growth of state social policies. Hayek, for example, interprets the growing range of state activity as steps along a 'road to serfdom'; for 'only within . . . a competitive system based on free disposal over private property . . . is democracy possible' (1944, p. 52). For Friedman, similarly, the only alternative to the 'voluntary cooperation of individuals—the technique of the marketplace" is totalitarianism and coercion (1962, p. 13). These are essentially normative arguments, predicated upon the classical liberal conception of individual liberty (see above, p. 29). For Friedman and Hayek, such liberty can be enjoyed only in a market-organised society: it is then sufficient for them to point to invasion of the market by social policy institutions, *inter alia*, in order to make their point.

Such market liberals judge that many of the benefits realised through a market civilisation are necessarily less likely under alternative forms of social organisation. Along with invasions of individual liberty, therefore, are likely to come social discord, inequitable distribution of rewards (Friedman, 1962, Ch. 10) and reduced growth in prosperity. For example, it is argued that social policies that divorce access to life chances from labour market rewards tend to reduce work incentives and hence prosperity. Moreover, they reduce the bread-winner's individual responsibility for his family's well-being, and for the pursuit of independence they substitute permanent mutual dependence as the much more fragile basis of mutual respect (Bremner, 1968, pp. 52–3). In sum, such social policies undermine the 'two "natural" . . . channels through which an individual's needs are properly met: the private market and the family' (Titmuss, 1974, p. 30), and thereby threaten the very foundations of social integration. Extensive social policies also entail high levels of taxation, which not only discourage work effort but may also render more difficult the fiscal control of the economy, and hence act as a burden on stable and sustained growth. This burden is, moreover, exacerbated by the invariable tendency of the state's monopolistic welfare bureaucracies to become cost-inefficient (Friedman, 1962, Ch. 12; Hicks, 1966; Niskanen, 1973).

These market liberals then outline blueprints for social policies that would reinforce and uphold the capitalist market system and that would therefore not hinder but multiply the benefits of a market civilisation. Their proposals, then, are for a system of social services that will not represent a distributive system at odds with the cash nexus, that will be a means of 'human investment' organised in the interests of economic productivity and growth alone, and that will reinforce the social disciplines and mode of social integration of the market society. Two elements, given varying weights by different writers, are generally present (cf. the two elements in the classical liberal view of social disciplines, pp. 26–7 above).

First, there is the idea that state-organised social policies should, on grounds of compassion and in the interests of political stability, provide a minimum for all, a safety-net below which no citizen should be allowed to fall. This may be achieved by the provision of a minimum income, education vouchers, etc., which may be used in the market place for the purchase of basic life chances, in combination with individuals' own resources. In this way, inequalities in such resources do not prevent all from having a basic minimum purchasing power. Friedman is a particularly strong advocate of such a system. State intervention, he argues, must be focused on individuals rather than on institutions, for 'the subsidisation of institutions rather than of people has led to an indiscriminate subsidisation of all activities appropriate for such institutions, rather than of the activities appropriate for the state to subsidise' (1962, p. 100). Alternatively, such a common minimum might be achieved, it is argued, through state distributive agencies—such as a state education system—for those who cannot do better for themselves privately. In this way, a universal enjoyment of at least the most basic life chances can be assured.

The second element involves what Titmuss has termed the 'Industrial Achievement–Performance Model' of social policy. According to this, 'social needs should be met on the basis of merit, work performance and productivity' (1974, p. 31). Market liberals see this element as being realised through private market distribution of life chances such as housing, education and health care; for they assume that individuals' incomes adequately reflect their merit, work performance and productivity. Under this second element, therefore, the social services represent no challenge to the cash nexus; they involve a programme of human investment in individuals on the basis of their past individual contributions to the economy, as the only guide available to their potential future contributions to productivity and growth; and they rigidly enforce the work ethic. Moreover, many liberals adopt what Titmuss terms an 'optimistic automated model' of industrial development (1968, p. 157), according to which economic growth can and will, without the aid of redistributive social policies, eliminate poverty. The corollary is a declining importance of the first, 'safety-net', element of the liberal proposals, in favour of the second. The liberals conclude that such proposals do not significantly contravene the principles of the cash nexus, they are not in essential conflict with a distribution according to need and they serve, like the 1834 Poor Law, 'to support industrialism and the attempt ... to establish a completely competitive, self-regulating market economy founded on the motive of individual gain' (Titmuss, 1968, p. 189).

Finally, these liberals would point out that, in many respects, actual social policies have approximated to these blueprints. For example, the Beveridge conception of the British post-war Welfare State was close to that just described; and innovations in social policy have often been justified by reference to the supposed requirements for economic productivity and growth. In so far as the modern Western state's social policies have deviated from this liberal model, the explanation is either the pressure of self-seeking sectional interests, or else misguided attempts to create a more egalitarian society that disregard, by intent or otherwise, the consequent loss of individual liberty.

Political liberals

Turning to the political liberals, three broad arguments sufficiently characterise their view of contemporary social policy; although, as in the case of the neo-Marxists and, to a lesser extent, the market liberals, social policy generally receives their attention only in the course of more general studies. (For a succinct statement of what follows, see Lipset, 1964.)

(i) While acknowledging that working-class movements arose in the nineteenth century in part because of a perceived conflict between the interests of that class and the prevailing mode of social organisation (see above, Ch. 2, section IV), they argue that class conflict is a feature peculiar to a society where industrialism is replacing agriculture as the dominant mode of social existence. 'Unrest peaks early':

it is the social dislocation caused by early industrialisation that accounts for social discord, immiseration of the labour force and such social problems as inadequate urban sanitation and mass illiteracy. However, with the solution to these problems, in part through various measures of state intervention, 'civic reintegration of the labour force' is achieved. 'The industrialising societies universally come to contain, to control, and to redirect the response of industrial workers to the transformation of society. . . . The potential benefits to the individual worker nearly everywhere appear to transcend the negative consequences of industrialisation' (Kerr, 1964, pp. 187, 185). Consequently, it may be expected that calls for fundamental social reorganisation and action to back those calls will continue to decline in intensity. There may be continuing conflict, but its resolution is by widely agreed procedures. This argument concludes, then, by deducing that categories of sociological analysis that focus on class conflict and exploitation may safely be discarded.

It follows that the developments in social policy discussed in section IV of the previous chapter cause no embarrassment for these political liberals. Rather, such social policies are among the most significant factors making for this civic reintegration of the labour force. They help to promote an identity of interest among all social groups and have rendered irrational as well as anachronistic any life project that looks to collective revolutionary action on the part of the working class for the achievement of its goals. Instead, the atomised individualistic pursuit of occupational 'status' and of income has become the norm. (Such life projects are, for example, assumed in the methodology employed by Blau and Duncan, 1967.) Equality of opportunity in a meritocratic system, accompanied and supported by an equality of citizenship rights, cannot but evoke consensus among all major social groups.

(ii) The political liberals generally argue for the existence of a 'logic of industrialism'—whether this appears as the convergence theories of Kerr and Galbraith or as the neo-evolutionism of Parsons and the structural-functionalists. The former see the development of industrial society, including changes in the system of social stratification, as being largely determined by technological changes. Moreover, in so far as the technological systems of industrial societies are becoming increasingly similar, so too are their systems of social stratification and their ideologies. This hypothesis on the 'logic' of industrialism is generally presented as an optimistic prognosis: the logic is leading to a more meritocratic and harmonious social structure, enjoying no great concentrations of power but rather a 'pluralism' of competing interests.

  Sociologists of the structural-functional school have attempted to delineate the 'functional prerequisites' of an advanced industrial society. These include the social services, viewed as a mechanism evolved by society in response to certain objective social needs, such as the need to tame the violence of the market, the need to protect the labour force from the social dislocation consequent upon industrialisation and the need to discourage unrest among the working class. These sociologists have sought to incorporate notions of social change into their functionalist theory by employing an evolutionary scheme, by analogy with the evolution of biological species. This is especially evident in Parsons' later work, where he postulates certain 'evolutionary universals', with reference to the achievement of which societies may be compared for evolutionary advance (1964; 1966). Among these are a money economy, a market system of life chance allocation and a bureaucratic system of administration. (For a critical exposition, see Gouldner, 1971, pp. 362ff.) In turn, this leads such sociologists to see the ultimate goals of such evolution as given in terms of material prosperity and the maintenance of social order. The requirement for the former is continuing technological advance, while that for the latter is an adjustment or adaptation of the existing social system 'as the requirements and consequences of this advance unfold, and sufficiently to contain social dissensus and conflict to a manageable level' (Goldthorpe, 1971, p. 275).

  Belief in such a 'logic of industrialism' or social evolution leaves little or no role for purposive political action by the state, which cannot therefore make genuine choices among various possible future developments of the society. Rather, actions by the state have an essentially instrumental character and 'the crucial questions are defined as ones which require special expertise for their proper comprehension' (Goldthorpe, 1971, p. 275). In consequence, Kerr argues, 'Parliamentary life may appear increasingly less significant and political parties merely additional bureaucracies: the great political causes of old may become little more than technical issues' (1964, p. 228). No essentially political element is therefore involved in such matters as the determination of the distribution of life chances—including distribution effected through social policies. Rather, questions of distributive justice are surrendered to immanent laws of socio-economic development.

Such political liberals, confronted with the changes in British society discussed in section III of the previous chapter, would presumably subscribe to the increasing significance of 'human investment'. Social policies undertaken by the state create and sustain the technically competent labour force that is a functional prerequisite of an advanced society. Their continuing extension must and will be informed by the logic of industrialism. Our supposition that the formulation of social policy and decisions by the state that affect the distribution of life chances are irreducibly political matters will be judged misplaced. For at the same time as the state's activity has been extended over an ever wider area of the society, its concerns have become increasingly technical and instrumental in character.

(iii) While the market liberal assumes that equitable transactions and a natural harmony of interests must obtain and can only obtain in a free market system, to which there is free access, political liberals commonly focus their attention on free access to the political 'market place' by a plurality of competing interest groups. It is assumed that such free access will ensure distributive justice among the various interest groups involved and that, since such an arrangement cannot but commend itself to the parties concerned, social harmony is also assured. Through his multiple group affliations, the individual then obtains just treatment (Wolff, 1968, p. 133). Consequently, while the political liberal is likely to emphasise the continuing importance of the market and of the cash nexus in advanced societies, this advocacy is likely to be much more qualified than in the case of the market liberal. Faced with the discussion in section II of the previous chapter, where we traced the apparent challenge to the cash nexus posed by the growing range of state intervention in general and of social policy in particular, he is unlikely to be over-critical (Bell, 1976, Ch. 6), provided that free access to the political processes through which social policy is formulated can be guaranteed. Such free access is deemed likely to foster meritocracy: by it, all legitimate interest groups are able to demand formal equality of treatment, in the sense of a common set of rules being applied to all. In Parsons' terms, there is a shift from particularism and ascription to universalism and achievement as the basis of life chance allocation. Meritocracy, then, appears here as the fruit of free access to the political market place; just as earlier it was seen to be a requirement of the logic of industrialism and a means of effecting the civic reintegration of the labour force.

As indicated above, those political liberals who also expound a supposed 'logic of industrialism' imply that, to an increasing extent, the concerns of this pluralist system must become increasingly technical. Hence

> participation in the democratic process must, for the mass of the population, necessarily be of a decidedly restricted and indirect kind. It becomes in effect limited to joining in organised groups which can seek, via their own officials and experts, to influence key decision-makers; and to periodic voting on alternative sets of national political 'leaders', who will tend increasingly to bid for electoral support on the grounds of their superior technical or 'managerial' competence.

Such competence, indeed, 'must become an important new basis of social power' (Goldthorpe, 1971, pp. 276, 284; but cf. Bell, 1974, pp. 376–7, 481–2). Thus, Kerr writes, 'the benevolent political bureaucracy and the benevolent economic oligarch are matched with the more tolerant mass' (1964, p. 228).

IV THE SOCIAL DEMOCRATIC INTERPRETATION OF SOCIAL POLICY

From among those writings on contemporary social policy that differ significantly from both the liberal and neo-Marxist approaches, we may select the defining elements of a Social Democratic standpoint. Titmuss and T. H. Marshall are two major figures who stand firmly within the Social Democratic tradition developed around the turn of the century. They have articulated—or at least sketched—a macro-sociological account of social policy that may be set alongside the contemporary neo-Marxist and liberal accounts we have already considered, and they attempt to unite this account with detailed empirical study of individual social policies. Marshall, as Lockwood has recently noted (1974), provides in his essay 'Citizenship and Social Class' an analysis of the development and significance of social policy that is the direct heir to—but also advances beyond—the classical accounts of change in social stratification and political order offered by Durkheim and Weber. Titmuss, while eschewing the jargon of the macro-sociologist, is also continually concerned with the mutual implications of social policy and social stratification, social change and social integration. While there are some differences in their theoretical emphases, empirical concerns and intellectual battle-grounds, they may be treated, for our present purposes, as defining a Social Democratic school. (At the same time, moreover, they dispel the somewhat anaemic connotations with which the term 'Social Democratic' has in recent years tended to be surrounded.)

Had the main concern of this book been to provide a detailed intellectual map of contemporary thinking about social policy, it would of course have been necessary to look also at Townsend, Donnison, Abel-Smith and others within this school. Yet they seem generally much less clear than Titmuss and Marshall in spelling out systematically a macro-sociological view of social policy in industrial society, however important their contributions to studies in social administration. The reader must judge whether the selection of writers used here in characterising the Social Democratic approach—and, indeed, its competitors—involves serious distortion and omission.

Even in the case of Titmuss and Marshall, however, some explica tion will be needed of what they leave in part only implicit—a task already begun by such commentators as Lockwood (1974) and Reisman (1977). We expound their approach by taking the same three dimensions of comparison as those used in chapter 2 and in the preceding sections of this chapter: (i) interests, inequalities and the cash nexus; (ii) the dynamics of social change and of social policy development; and (iii) the interrelationship of social policies and patterns of social integration.

(i) We argued in chapter 2 that the rise of social policy appeared to have undermined the cash nexus characterising capitalist society. For contemporary Social Democrats—as for those reviewed in the previous chapter—the progressive dissolution of the cash nexus through social policy is indicative of a contrast between two very different distributive systems. Through a historical study of the developing meaning of the notion of a national citizenship in this country, T. H. Marshall has presented this contrast in terms of the distinction between civil and social rights. Capitalism, realised most completely in the early nineteenth century, involves the extension to all of the civil right to dispose freely of one's property and labour power in the market place. This right is the basis of the formal equality, but substantive inequality, of the members of a capitalist society ('Citizenship and Social Class' in Marshall, 1965, pp. 95–7). Under such a distributive system, access to life chances is wholly dependent upon the intelligent exercise of these civil rights and upon one's initial individual endowment of skills and property. The latter, in turn, depends mainly upon inheritance, the right of inheriting property being itself one expression of these civil rights of the market society. Civil rights, then, are essentially permissive, granting to the individual a guarantee of non-interference. The use that is made of them and the fruits of their exercise are of no necessary and direct interest to the state; it is for the individual to bring to the attention of the courts any infringements of those rights.

Titmuss frequently argues the inadequacies of civil rights as a guarantee of equitable treatment. Protection against the infringement of such rights is the province of the courts and requires that the agent of infringement be identifiable, in order that compensation may be extracted. Yet in our advanced urban–industrial civilisation, the generation of diswelfares results from processes that it is increasingly difficult to identify clearly. Reliance on civil rights therefore involves the danger that increasingly 'social costs and diswelfares of the economic system [will be allowed] to lie where they fall' (Titmuss, 1968, p. 133; cf. 1974, Ch. 5). (This argument forms part of Titmuss' general critique of the 'optimistic automated model' of industrialisation employed by market liberals.)

In contrast, social rights are publicly defined and guaranteed claims to certain life chance outcomes: notably those distributed through the contemporary social services. Rather than being essentially permissive as in the case of civil rights, their exercise and fruits are of immediate concern to the state; for it is in terms of the guarantee of a publicly recognised *outcome*, rather than merely of an opportunity for private activity, that they are defined. Moreover, while the guarantee and protection of civil rights is a matter for the courts, it would be inappropriate to say that social rights are *legally* guaranteed. Their substantive content is, rather, a continuing political decision. For, as T. H. Marshall writes,

Benefits in the form of a service have . . . [the] characteristic that the rights of the citizen cannot be precisely defined. The qualitative element is too great. A modicum of legally enforceable rights may be granted, but what matters to the citizen is the superstructure of legitimate expectations. . . . And so we find that legislation, instead of being the decisive step that puts policy into immediate effect, acquires more and more the character of a declaration of policy that it is hoped to put into effect some day. . . . The rate of progress depends on the magnitude of the national resources and their distribution between competing claims [1965, pp. 114–15, 103].

Civil rights, therefore, involve a guarantee that others will be excluded from interfering with the individual's exploitation of market opportunities and his free disposition in the market place of initial endowments received by private inheritance. Social rights, in contrast, involve a guarantee of the individual's free access, through social policies, to an endowment from a common patrimony.

Titmuss and T. H. Marshall argue that the post-war British welfare state approximates in important and significant respects to such a distributive system, altogether different in principle from the capitalist market. Its social policies group and treat individuals not according to their economic power but rather according to their needs; the substantial dissolution of the cash nexus has proceeded *pari passu* with the increasing realisation of a 'needs nexus'. It follows that individual interests can no longer be adequately conceptualised and explored within the parameters of the classical liberal–Marxist debate. More particularly, while the neo-Marxist claim that class gradients in life chances are as great as ever may have some justification, such a pattern of empirical outcomes of the various forms of distributive principle present in our contemporary society does not necessarily result from a continuing dominance of the cash nexus. Rather, an investigation is necessary of, for example, possible new social mechanisms whereby the equality of treatment implied by new social rights has been impeded or subverted. The market liberals, in turn, identify valid needs with effective market demands and argue that, in so far as social policy subverts the market system and the cash nexus, it thereby impedes the satisfaction of such valid needs. In contrast, this Social Democratic approach argues that the realisation of the 'needs nexus', and the radically different principles governing social policy and the market as (ideal-typical) distributive systems, together expose the value-judgements implicit in the liberal definition of 'need'. This is a major theme of Titmuss' writings in particular. As against the political liberals, who view contemporary social policy and the cash nexus of the market as complementary foundations of a meritocratic order, the Social Democratic approach sees social rights in terms not of merit but of need, and thereby raises for the sociologist the question of the conceptual and empirical relationship between these two notions. In conclusion, then, advocates of this interpretation of social policy argue that it incorporates principles of life chance distribution fundamentally at variance with the capitalist market, and that neither those principles nor their empirical embodiment in the post-war British Welfare State can be adequately understood within the neo-Marxist definition of the cash nexus, the market liberals' conception of need, or the political liberals' delineation of meritocratic distributive justice.

(ii) We also suggested in chapter 2 that the rise of social policy has undermined classical analyses of the role of capital accumulation in social change and the associated prognoses. In the present chapter, however, we have seen that both neo-Marxists and liberals deny the need for any radical rethinking of those analyses. These schools represent two forms of historicism, deriving philosophically from the Hegelian and natural law traditions respectively (although historicist tendencies are rather weak among most market liberals). The laws of capitalist development, although accorded different ontological status by the two traditions, enforce a particular set of values as the organising principle of society. For the market liberal, these are the values of the market. For the political liberal they are expressed in terms such as Parsons' 'evolutionary universals'. For the neo-Marxist, the continuing enforcement of market values involves the progressive devaluation and dehumanisation of the proletariat and thereby guarantees the revolutionary substitution of an alternative, humanised social organisation.

In contrast, it is a central theme of the Social Democratic approach to social policy that its formulation involves real value choices: the future is 'open' and contemporary political decisions have fundamental implications for the future of Western industrial society. In Weber's terms—and avoiding the strictures he levelled against the Social Democrats of his own day—they demand an ethic of responsibility in policy-making (see above, p. 35). For example,

Titmuss opposes those 'who argue from theories of political and economic convergence that we are today approaching the end of the ideological debate'. As a corollary, he holds that, far from the individual actor being the prisoner of inexorable historical processes, 'instruments and institutions of [social] policy have a potential role to play in sustaining and extending personal freedoms' (1973, pp. 18, 272; cf. his Introduction to Tawney, 1964). Proponents of this approach would therefore agree with Goldthorpe when he argues more generally that the sociologist, in his prognoses, should properly focus not so much on 'degrees of probability' as on 'ranges of possibility'. He continues:

> To the extent that alternative futures really are spelled out . . . , to that extent . . . there is revealed the true range of socio-political choice, the degree of existing social conflict and the possibilities for future action. It may further be added that the approach in question entails no presumption in favour of piecemeal social policies. The viability of designs for the future based on piecemeal methods is to be as critically considered as that of designs of a more sweeping character [1971, p. 287].

With the new focal importance of social policy in our contemporary socio-economic order, it is in this arena that the fundamental value choices are being made. These are real and irreducibly political; they concern the very meaning to be given to individual freedom and social harmony, for example. Or in Halsey's words: 'Liberty, Equality and Fraternity . . . are . . . courts of appeal before which policy and practice appear as plaintiffs or defendants in an evolving trial of promise and performance' (1978, p. 10). With the development of the political rights of citizenship, moreover, which Marshall traces over the nineteenth and early twentieth centuries and which he sees as the harbinger and spur to those social rights we have already discussed (1965, pp. 84–6), it is the mass of the population that comes to participate in that trial. The powers they enjoy by virtue of their established political and social rights make their critical evaluation of policy a crucial influence on its development.

In addition and more particularly, however, the Social Democratic writers seem to affirm—although this is generally left implicit—two further arguments in regard to the dynamics of social policy development. In both they echo a major theme of their British forebears, particularly Tawney (see above, pp. 37–8). First, social policies are chosen and pursued in part in response to—and in search of—support among the population at large. Thus Titmuss argues on the one hand that the post-war social legislation was a response to 'the demand for one society; for non-discriminatory services for all without distinction of class, income or race; for services and relations which would deepen and enlarge self-respect; for services which would manifestly encourage social integration' (1968, p. 191). Equally, however, he sees those reforms of the 1940s as having been a precondition for popular cooperation and acceptance of the austerities of war and reconstruction, as we shall see shortly. Once introduced, they could not be dismantled after those austerities were past, in a return to the *status quo ante*: their enjoyment had established expectations that could be disappointed only at the cost of reduced political legitimacy. Second, it is only in the course of seeking to implement social rights that the obstacles to their realisation are exposed and rendered a matter for political concern. Such obstacles may, indeed, include the unanticipated consequences of social policies themselves. The pursuit of social policies permits, then, an immanent learning and critique, in which the social scientist has a central role. Summarising these two points, therefore, the development of social policies is, in part, governed by the search for and the maintenance of popular support for political objectives; and yet it tends perennially to promote an extension of social criticism.

(iii) In the previous chapter we also argued that the rise of social policy appeared to have modified the conditions for establishing a harmonious and rational social order. Contemporary Social Democratic writers echo their forebears' argument that the modern state is able, through its social policies, to promote forms of social integration fundamentally different from those obtaining in classical capitalist market society. Let us consider in turn, then, their views on (a) social integration and the possibilities of social harmony; (b) the role of social policy in such integration; and (c) the implications of social policy for individual action and group formation.

(a) For the liberal, social integration proceeds from the manifest rationality of a society organised in market or meritocratic terms: each citizen perceives that such a form of organisation identifies his own self-interested endeavours with the common good. In contrast,

Titmuss and T. H. Marshall believe that an advanced urban–industrial society cannot, even in principle, be organised in such a way that the pursuit of self-interest is a sufficient basis for social integration and social harmony. A subordination of self-interest to the common interest must be evoked. The neo-Marxist sees social integration under capitalism as effected through coercion and ideological manipulation. Appeals to the common interest run counter to the true interests of the proletariat, whose position in, but not of, civil society means that these interests cannot but be wholly in conflict with those of other classes and, indeed, with the maintenance of class society as such. Against this view the Social Democrats argue, first, that whatever the merits of Marx's analysis of the society of his own day, there exists in contemporary society some potential community of interest among members of different classes. Social integration need not, therefore, be wholly coercive but may, in part at least, be rooted in interests common to all. Second, they would deny that in our advanced Western societies coercion and ideological manipulation are sufficient to secure political stability. Rather, it requires some degree of freely willed acquiescence in—and commitment to—the socio-political order, and popular legitimation of the collective purpose it embraces (cf. Terrill, 1974, pp. 150–1). At the risk of over-simplification, therefore, we might summarise by saying that against the neo-Marxist view that the social integration of contemporary Western society cannot but be coercive and the liberal view that it is basically self-interested or calculative, these Social Democratic writers echo Durkheim's thesis that social integration must be seen as essentially a *moral* phenomenon (see above, p. 36). They grant, of course, that any *actual* society will involve a mixture of self-interest, coercion and moral obligation. Their contention, however, is that attempts to extend the domain of self-interest or of authoritarian coercion will typically tend to promote not spontaneous social cohesion but sullen compliance or overt conflict.

(b) Social policy is then seen in terms of its potential for evoking such moral commitment to the common welfare. It realises, to this extent, a novel system of social disciplines, which contrast both with the work ethic and market incentives applauded by classic liberalism and with the monopolisation of access to the means of life that, in classical Marxism, is deemed the basis of the coercive power of the capitalist. Titmuss emphasises this theme most notably, perhaps, in his first and last major works. In *Problems of Social Policy* and elsewhere he examines the war-time crucible in which the post-war Welfare State was forged. Universalist social policies aimed at meeting the primary needs of all citizens became an instrument for fostering moral commitment to the national war effort and sustaining public morale, notwithstanding the additional obligations and social disciplines that this enlargement of social policy entailed (1950, especially Chs 2 and 17). Titmuss summarises his argument thus:

> The waging of modern war presupposes and imposes a great increase in social discipline: moreover this discipline is only tolerable if—and only if—social inequalities are not intolerable.... It follows that the acceptance of these social disciplines—of obligations as well as rights—made necessary by war, by preparations for war and by the long-run consequences of war, must influence the aims and content of social policies not only during the war itself but in peace-time as well.... The aims and content of social policy, both in peace and in war, are thus determined—at least to a substantial extent—by how far the cooperation of the masses is essential to the successful prosecution of war ['War and Social Policy' in Titmuss, 1963, pp. 85–6].

Here again, Titmuss' debt to Tawney is especially evident. In *The Gift Relationship* (1973) he is likewise concerned with the consequences of different social policies for the readiness of citizens freely to place collective needs before their own individual interests, and is thereby concerned with the uses of social policy as an instrument of *moral* discipline.

(c) To round off this discussion of social integration, consider the implications of social policy for group formation and individual action. We have, by implication, just considered Titmuss' view of the way in which universalist social policies define as a group all those enjoying the social rights of citizenship. His study *The Gift Relationship* examines citizens' subjective perception of that group membership and their readiness to act in the interests of this group, whereby they acknowledge their membership of a moral community. For T. H. Marshall, the extension of the social rights of citizenship involves the granting of a common status—in this case, to all those of British nationality. (Marshall's analysis therefore represents one example or application of Weber's more general critique of Marxist views of stratification, emphasising the potential significance of interests and modes of group formation other than those oriented to class situation.) Such shared honour, moreover, will be subjectively perceived by the citizens concerned and will be manifested in a willingness to discharge the duties, as well as enjoying the rights, of this new status. It involves a 'direct sense of community membership based on loyalty to a civilisation which is a common possession'. Marshall is not, however, altogether confident that this loyalty will emerge strongly. Certain duties of citizenship are, of course, compulsory, so that 'no act of will is involved'. Others, however, are vague—'the community is so large that . . . obligation appears remote and unreal'. A possible 'solution . . . lies in the development of more limited loyalties, to the local community and . . . the working group' (1965, pp. 101, 129, 131). (Here Marshall echoes Durkheim's concern to balance civic duties towards the society at large with ones more localised—see above, p. 37.)

Not, however, that the social integration thus evoked is akin to the civic reintegration hailed by the political liberals, which involves consensus and acquiescence in the stable functioning of the open—indeed, the good—society. For the Social Democrats, however, the experience of the moral community that social rights realise tends to engender new expectations and popular demands for further social transformation—in the occupational division of labour, for example. Here are possible lines of increased conflict rather than its abatement. Hence the pursuit of social integration cannot, *contra* the political liberals, be portrayed in static systemic terms. It is, rather, essentially historical and tends, moreover, to promote an extension rather than a reduction in the range of societal life subjected to popular political scrutiny (Lockwood, 1974).

Such, then, is the Social Democratic response to contemporary liberal and neo-Marxist arguments. Our exposition will have made clear what we shall be taking as the principal differences and lines of conflict between the Social Democratic approach and those of its intellectual rivals, when we proceed to empirical evaluation in Part II. Nevertheless, this should not lead us to regard the thought of these writers as ossified. The account we have presented is perhaps best seen as hailing from the immediate post-war era, when Social Democracy was in its heyday as an intellectual current and political programme. Over subsequent decades, they have modified their arguments, albeit without fundamentally changing them, at least as much as their liberal and neo-Marxist critics. Thus their optimism wanes over the sufficiency of universalist services alone to secure social rights and to change fundamentally the pattern of inequalities and interests; although their response is, for instance, to place new hopes in additional measures of positive (or 'affirmative') discrimination towards the underprivileged (Titmuss, 1968, pp. 134–6; for a recent American view, see Glazer, 1975). Likewise, their confidence declines over the capacity of citizens, by virtue of their political and social rights alone, to exercise and retain control over the dynamics of social policy development. Instead, and explicitly recalling Weber's fears (see above, p. 36), Titmuss points for example to new and largely invisible concentrations of power —including public and private welfare bureaucracies—that mould social policy decisions 'without any proper awareness or public discussion of what is involved in terms of the common good, and what consequences may flow from the choices made' (1963, p. 239). Finally, they voice their fears that in face of the acquisitive individualism enjoined by the market place and the ostensibly meritocratic educational system, the efficacy of social policies in moral reconstruction and social reintegration is limited and may, indeed, be progressively undermined (Titmuss, 1973, Ch. 14); although the need for such moral reconstruction is simultaneously increased—as, for example, Hirsch's study has recently argued (1977). Nevertheless, these modifications in their position if anything emphasise their distinctiveness from the liberal writers, without, however, drawing them fundamentally closer to the neo-Marxist emphasis upon private property, profit and the market as the continuing bases of social organisation and development.

V PROBLEMS OF METHODOLOGY

In Part II we shall attempt an empirical evaluation of these rival perspectives. Nevertheless, it is worth pausing briefly to consider some of the methodological weaknesses that they variously exhibit, although, of course, such criticism raises fundamental issues in the methodology and subject matter of the social sciences upon which we can here only touch.

(i) Some of the historical accounts that these writers offer on the development of social policy exhibit logical deficiencies. For example, Goldthorpe has discussed the strengths and weaknesses of functionalist accounts and his comments are broadly relevant to the various forms of *political liberal* we have considered. Functionalist writers attempt to explain the growth of social policy 'in terms of the objective "demands" of certain social situations, which are seen as virtually imposing particular courses of action'. The value of these attempts lies in the attention paid to 'the description and analysis of actual social conditions and the social problems which arose out of these'. They thereby serve as a counterbalance to certain earlier approaches, such as Dicey's emphasis on 'the new ideas conceived and propounded by great men' and market liberals' explanations in terms of powerful and selfish sectional interests (Goldthorpe, 1964, pp. 50–1, 45).

Goldthorpe goes on to apply two familiar criticisms of functionalist attempts at explanation. First, explanation in terms of 'functional prerequisites' begs the question as to the way in which particular social necessities are defined as such. The historian of social policy must show 'not only . . . the existence of a social problem, but, also, how this was made known to contemporaries and how the gravity of its consequences was brought home to those in positions of influence and authority'. He must also study 'what kind of case had reformers to be able to make out in order to prevail against vested interests opposed to reform, or even simply inertia? What, in fact, were the ends to which social policy had convincingly to be related before its "necessity" was accepted?' Second, functionalist explanations neglect the actual historical processes by which the social institutions in question came into existence. If the historian is to explain the particular form taken by social policy measures, he will need 'to think . . . in terms of the purposive actions of individuals and groups in pursuit of their ends—. . . with the emphasis on the diversity of these'. Goldthorpe's criticisms are, then, predicated upon acceptance of 'an "action" frame of reference; that is, analysis in terms of the ends of individuals and groups rather than in terms of the "needs" of society considered as a whole' (1964, pp. 54–6).

However, adherence to these historiographical precepts also suggests criticisms of the *market liberals* and *neo-Marxists*. The former emphasise, as an explanation of the growing range of state social policies, the hostility of powerful interest groups 'to a system of economic liberalism that would allow them no more than their due share in the growing prosperity of their society' (Goldthorpe, 1964, p. 47). In general, however, they have failed to investigate the public justifications of policy modifications provided by reformers. That rational justifications could be presented and broadly accepted for progressively greater intervention by the state in the market economy is, for them, a contradiction in terms.

For the neo-Marxists, measures of social policy have typically been instigated and administered in accordance with the interests of the capitalist ruling class, such as the maximisation of the economic surplus and the maintenance of political stability. However, while such arguments may be of value in *suggesting* explanations, they can hardly count as explanations as they stand. Rather, among the questions that must surely be raised are the extent to which social policies have indeed been instituted overtly in furtherance of the interests of the capitalist class; the processes whereby social policies, whatever the reason for their instigation, have been subverted to serve the interests of that class; and, not least, the processes whereby the capitalist class has been made aware of its collective interest in particular forms of social policy (see above, pp. 44–5).

Turning to the *Social Democratic* writers, Sinfield has recently shown how Titmuss tends sometimes to embrace a technological determinism in his accounts of urban–industrial change and its associated costs, rather than 'examining the power, political and economic, of the different classes in society and the many ways in which its distribution influences the form and outcome of state intervention or inaction' (Sinfield, 1978, p. 146). Marshall, however, in his historical studies such as *Social Policy* (1975), does seek to identify the actions of the various groups involved, as they pursue diverse ends in regard to the formulation of social policy. In addition, the unanticipated consequences of social policies are given due attention, as are their implications for the redefinition of individual interests and for group formation.

(ii) A related ground for criticising some of these schools is their failure to give central importance in their analyses to the actor's perception of and commentaries upon his situation. It is the *Social Democratic* writers who seem most ready to acknowledge this importance. For example, in investigating whether or not actors' experience of universalist social policies leads them to sense membership in a moral community of citizens, Titmuss and Marshall make such commentaries the test of their own analyses as sociologists.

In contrast, the *neo-Marxists*, as we have seen, give considerable attention to the cultural hegemony exercised by the capitalist ruling class, which perpetuates a false consciousness among the mass of the population. The individual labourer fails to perceive his exploited situation and the identity of his interests with those of his fellow labourers. His definition of his situation is of little value, therefore, to the neo-Marxist sociologist in indicating the true character of contemporary society. Moreover, while the definition of the situation indeed informs the individual's goals and life projects, a proper explanation of his life chances and life experience must focus on the cultural processes whereby conformist attitudes are inculcated, and on the objective features of class situation that determine the actual, as distinct from the subjectively intended, fate of the individual. As seen earlier, neo-Marxists vary in their 'pessimism' as to the likely permanance of this pervasive false consciousness. Few, if any, provide a coherent prognosis of changes in the objective situation of the mass of the population likely to demystify the consciousness of the typical wage labourer.

Marx's own position is subtly, yet fundamentally, different. He agrees in attributing a false consciousness to the mass of the working class in his own day, which he accounts for in terms of the 'commodity fetishism' induced by the dominance of the cash nexus (1970b, Ch. 1, section 4), together with the ideological power of the ruling class. The worker's perception of his situation is superficial and distorted; only at the dusk of the capitalist epoch will the proletariat attain full and true consciousness of its situation and interests. However, it is precisely because immanent development of the capitalist mode of production creates the conditions for demystification that Marx is prepared to speak of the proletariat as a class. It is by its revolutionary action as a class, oriented to the abolition of its proletarian condition and therefore necessarily to the abolition of private property, that the proletariat then vindicates Marx's analysis. In and through such revolutionary *praxis* the proletariat, in consciously and deliberately transforming the social order, appropriates and expresses man's species being as *homo faber* in unalienated form (Avineri, 1968, Chs 2, 5, 6).

To the extent, therefore, that the neo-Marxists assert a persisting and impenetrable false consciousness, they not only diverge from the broadly Weberian precept that the initial datum of the sociologist must include actors' definitions of the situation, but also depart from Marx's own philosophical anthropology. They may then be charged with a failure not only to advance hypotheses regarding actors' perceptions and actions that are empirically testable in terms acceptable to 'bourgeois' sociologists, but also to demonstrate the necessary development of conditions for their own vindication *à la* Marx.

More briefly, the liberal writers we have examined likewise depart from the canons of *Verstehendesoziologie*. The *political liberals*, whether presenting their case as a neo-evolutionist adaptation of structural-functionalism or in terms of the logic of industrialism, see the individual as learning, through forms of socialisation evolved so as to facilitate change without conflict, to adapt and conform to the changing imperatives of his society. The sociologist may, therefore, safely neglect individuals' perceptions of their society and concentrate on these imperatives, save when deviant cases of maladjustment are his concern.

The *market liberals* also ignore, but in a rather different sense, the actors in the society on which they are commenting. As we have seen, their arguments are in considerable measure normative, being predicated upon a particular notion of individual freedom, which is taken as being of supreme value. Connected to this is a particular conception of the rational individual as concerned with meeting his needs, defined in pre-social terms, through the instrumental use of social arrangements. It is on the basis of these assumptions that a blueprint for the social services is drawn up and existing social policies criticised. Concern with the perceptions held by actual individuals has little place in such a scheme.[3]

(iii) We may criticise the conceptualisation of a social system that some of these writers adopt. Dawe (1970) has contrasted 'two sociologies: a sociology of social system and a sociology of social action. They are grounded in the diametrically opposed concerns with two central problems, those of order and control'. For the former, 'the notion of a social system [is] ontologically and methodologically prior to its participants'. For the sociology of social action, in contrast, 'society is the creation of its members; the product of their construction of meaning, and of the action and relationships through which they attempt to impose that meaning on their historical situations'. Dawe goes on to draw out certain corollaries of these differences. For the systems approach, 'subjective meanings are ... ultimately derived from the central value system' and do not, therefore, 'have to be treated as a significant variable'. Moreover, this central value system structures roles and sub-systems so that 'when survival is threatened, ... the system adjusts in such a way as to restore equilibrium'. In contrast, for social actionism integration pertains not to the central values of the social system but rather to the biography of the individual in terms of an overall life-meaning, as he attempts to control his ongoing situation in accordance with some integrated life project. Social actionism, then, gives an essentially historical perspective, in which 'social systems are conceptualised as the *outcome* of a continuous process of interaction' and in which 'equilibrium' has little meaning.

As Dawe points out, structural-functionalism is the most obvious example of the social systems approach. Parsons' later work on such systems contrasts with his earlier focus on individual social action. The attempt to dynamise this basically static approach through the postulation of evolutionary universals, however, hardly involves any properly historical perspective (Peel, 1971, pp. 254–8). Likewise, those *political liberals* espousing a logic of industrialism see this as deriving from the changing technological constraints of industrial society, rather than as the outcome of social interactions among actors in pursuit of their life projects. The absence of real political choices among alternative possible futures is then one expression of the unproblematic nature of the value assumptions of the status quo.

In the case of the *market liberals*, it might appear at first sight that the perspectives of social actionism receive clear illustration, for the value espoused is the freedom of the individual actor to pursue his own self-interest. However, we have also seen that the market liberal treats as unproblematic the ends and values that rational individuals will choose for their life projects; for these are defined in pre-social, ahistorical terms. The form of social organisation within which these ends may harmoniously be pursued, namely the market, is likewise defined in ahistorical terms; it is not conceived as the outcome of continuous interaction, which rather takes place only *within* it. Equilibrium and harmony are guaranteed by the identification of individual interests through the market. For such liberals, therefore, the unproblematic definition of individual interests as pre-social and as finding their natural expression in a market organisation of society provides the basis for a quasi-sociology closer to the social systems approach than to social actionism.

Marx, particularly in his earlier humanistic writings, emphasises man's autogenesis through social labour and his objectification of his 'species-being' in an objective world. Society then appears as the creation of cooperative human activity. For Marx, this does not conflict with the idea that it is men's social being that determines their consciousness. For neither 'society' nor 'man' may be properly considered ontologically and methodologically prior; rather, they exist in a dialectical relationship. Notwithstanding, therefore, the 'natural' appearance of the laws governing capitalist development, the capitalist mode of production represents one stage in man's creation of himself and in the progress towards a 'humanised' social order, wherein man, far from being subject to such laws, will instead exhibit the free creativity that is distinctively human.[4]

However, it is arguable that many of the *neo-Marxists* we have considered tend to adopt a more static, social systems approach. 'Capitalism' is construed as a well-integrated, basically unchanging 'system'. Hobsbawm, for example, describes contemporary Marxism as a form of structural-functionalism, which engages in 'the analysis of the structure and functioning of [social] systems as entities maintaining themselves in their relations both with the outside environment—non-human and human—and in their internal relationships' ('Karl Marx's Contribution to Historiography' in Blackburn, 1972, p. 273). He goes on to argue that Marxism is distinguished by its inclusion of disruptive elements within the system; but he retains the ontological priority of the latter. Likewise Poulantzas attacks social actionism as hindering 'the study of the objective co-ordinates that determine the distribution of agents into social classes and contradictions between these classes' ('The Problem of the Capitalist State' in Blackburn, 1972, p. 242). These neo-Marxists might therefore be accused of hypostatising 'capitalism' as an enduring historical reality, rather than treating it as an ideal type of socio-economic organisation, to be used as a category of historical explanation (cf. Avineri's discussion of the inapplicability of this criticism to Marx himself, 1968, p. 157–60).

More specifically, we saw earlier that it is in considerable measure their assumption of the persistence and integration of the capitalist system that leads many neo-Marxists to interpret contemporary social policy as an integral element of advanced capitalism. The false consciousness of the proletariat is effected by appropriate socialisation and mystification, in part through measures of social policy. Man's species-being as world-creator is sublimated in the pursuit of false needs by the happy robot. As Goldthorpe notes, such analysis is in many respects 'Parsons through the Looking Glass' (1972, p. 25). Moreover, whereas social actionism and Marx's humanistic notion of man as a world-creator are essentially historical and dynamic perspectives, some of these neo-Marxists seem to conceive of the capitalist system in terms hardly less static than the basic structural-functionalist approach. As seen earlier, they fail to spell out the character of immanent change in the system and resort to vague prognoses of 'contradiction' and 'crisis'.

The *Social Democratic* writers, in contrast, seem generally to avoid a static, social systems approach. Indeed, as Titmuss writes, 'the concept of policy is only meaningful if we ... believe we can effect change' (1974, pp. 23–4). This approach conceives of social policy not as the mere adjunct to a well-integrated and essentially static social system ontologically prior to the actors who inhabit it, but rather as a positive instrument of social transformation by the actors themselves, in the course of which value choices as to the appropriate pattern of citizenship rights and social integration are unavoidable and perennial.

The methodological canons used here in criticising these competing perspectives are predicated on a broadly Weberian view of social science (1949)· a view that will continue to inform our discussion. Nevertheless, this procedure may admittedly involve implicit prior commitment to a methodology vitiating a proper appreciation of, for example, neo-Marxist arguments on the role of the capitalist state's social policy. Such has been a major theme of the Poulantzas–Miliband debate, concerned with epistemological as much as with substantive issues (see Laclau, 1975). It is, in this case, the position represented by Poulantzas that is then the less acceptable in terms of the arguments of this section, and that we shall accordingly tend to exclude from our own 'epistemological terrain'. Yet such dangers seem unavoidable.

VI Conclusion

Here, then, are the macro-theoretical perspectives that we shall be seeking to evaluate empirically in Part II. Of course, the issues around which they join battle change somewhat from one decade to the next. In the late 1970s it is the significance of social policies for unemployment, inflation and social discord that attracts popular concern and academic debate; in this debate one welcome development is growing recognition of the necessity for a multi-disciplinary analysis. Nevertheless, the broad theoretical and ideological divides mapped out here go back more than a century, as we have seen; and as Halsey argues, they continue to dominate our collective attempt 'to know ourselves' (1978, Ch. 1).

NOTES

1. The neo-Marxists also, of course, argue the continuing relevance of Marx's analysis of the interests of property owners—see Blackburn, 'The New Capitalism' in Blackburn (1972). We confine our discussion here to their general analysis of social policy; but will need to investigate these interests of the propertied in Part II.

2. Hence his analysis need offer little threat to a liberal writer such as Janowitz, who is equally alert to the delegitimising impact of the 'fiscal crisis' (1976, esp. Chs 1 and 4), but who looks to incremental 'institution building in social welfare'—including, for example, increased citizen participation—as both a viable and a sufficient remedy (Chs 8–9).

3. The Institute of Economic Affairs has admittedly undertaken surveys of popular attitudes to alternative social provisions—for example, Harris and Seldon (1971). Yet the covert aim seems to have been political propaganda—not necessarily an unworthy pursuit—rather than academically rigorous investigation: see Donnison (1971).

4. Not that such an interpretation of Marx is uncontentious; but it follows that of such writers as Avineri (1968).

PART II

The Investigation of Social Policy

CHAPTER 4

The Development of Social Policy

If princes are superior to populaces in drawing up laws, codes of civil life, statutes and new institutions, the populace is so superior in sustaining what has been instituted, that it indubitably adds to the glory of those who have instituted them. [*N. Machiavelli* The Discourses *I.58*]

I INTRODUCTION

We now embark on an empirical evaluation of these contrasting approaches to social policy. We focus on the three lines of discussion developed in Part I, albeit in a rather different order. The relationship of social policy to the cash nexus is the concern of chapter 5, where we consider what Titmuss has termed the social division of welfare. In chapter 6 the implications of social policies for social integration and conflict are examined. First, however, we investigate the dynamics of change in social policies, looking at their instigation and their development once established.

It is Weber who has bequeathed the most influential perspective on the dynamics of social action and policy-making in state bureaucracies. He provides us with an ideal type of such a bureaucracy, in which policy-making displays both formal rationality—the procedural correctness of individual action by officials—and substantive rationality, i.e. the conscious and public political choice and pursuit of policy goals. However, this ideal type was developed by Weber less in celebration of the virtues of existing bureaucracies than as a tool for analysing their departures from such rational policy-making and for exposing it as empirically problematic (Gerth and Mills, 1948, Ch. 8; Beetham, 1974, Ch. 6).

Consider, therefore, what is involved in the substantive rationality of policy development. First, there is typically the recalling—necessarily selective—of those publicly declared objectives, for whose promotion the existing measures were originally established. These objectives are either reaffirmed as remaining broadly appropriate, even in a somewhat different situation, or else they serve as a focus of criticism, leading to the articulation of alternatives. Second, these objectives are taken as a criterion for assessing existing measures. There is a retrospective—and, again, necessarily selective—evaluation of their effectiveness, and an analysis and explanation of what are seen as having been their principal deficiencies. Policy innovations are then justified in terms of the restatement of objectives and this particular 'reading' of previous measures. Third, this policy-making process is *public*: it is through democratic scrutiny that the government is held accountable for its previous measures and through democratic debate that policy innovations are agreed. Special significance is thereby accorded to those public declarations of social objectives that are embodied in legislation, for these become the criteria against which the state's performance is subsequently judged.

However, in any empirical situation, none of these elements is unproblematic. First, the question is raised of the wider ends and values in terms of which alternative social policy objectives and measures are judged and justified. It is, moreover, necessary to relate these ends and values to the goals of the various contending individuals and groups involved in policy formulation, and to see the measures actually chosen as the outcomes of continuing power struggles. Second, the sense in which the 'deficiencies', retrospectively identified, are such is not unproblematic. To start with, the particular 'reading' of past experience that is used as the basis of policy formulation will, presumably, be as much a matter of contention among the various interest groups involved as is the choice of social policy goals. Our attention is again, therefore, directed to the power of these different groups to secure acceptance of their desired 'readings'. In addition, however, previous measures may be deemed deficient either in terms of the original diagnosis of the 'problem' to be dealt with, or in the face of societal changes since the original measures, or in their expectations as to the responses by various actors upon whom the success of the measures was dependent. (Particularly noteworthy among such actors are likely to be the clients of the measures and the personnel of the agencies established to implement them). Third, the *public* character of policy-making may be merely symbolic, cloaking the power of particular groups to secure their social policy goals and 'readings'. It is therefore a matter for empirical investigation to what extent these public processes are also the *effective* processes of policy specification and evaluation, and the means of mobilising such popular support and cooperation as the policies may require for their effectiveness.

Neo-Marxist, liberal and Social Democratic writers typically give very diverse assessments of such policy development. For all of them, moreover, the dynamics of policy development cannot properly be appreciated except by looking also at its implications for social stratification and political order. We shall, therefore, be raising some questions in this chapter that only the discussion in chapters 5 and 6 can resolve.

For *neo-Marxists*, the ends of new social policies and the 'readings' of past policies are selected in the interests of capital. This may be by virtue of the hegemony that the values of possessive individualism enjoy in the society at large, or else through the pre-eminence of the propertied within the alliances they form with the makers and implementors of policy, or, finally, via systemic 'filtering' mechanisms that ensure that only social measures favourable to capital reach the forum of public debate. Such debate is hence so limited and uncritical of the existing distribution of power and advantage as to be of little effect, save as a means of quieting potential unrest among the populace at large. Nevertheless, continuing changes in the mode of production are likely to bring in their train increasingly sharp limitations on the effectiveness of social policies and these will be evidenced in growing 'crises' or 'contradictions' in policy implementation.

The *market liberals*, surveying the growing range of the state's social policies, contend that the ends in terms of which these measures have been justified and the 'readings' put on past measures either feebly cloak the selfishness of organised sectional interests or else manifest a myopic—and hence misplaced—social compassion. The democratic process whereby the populace is ostensibly enabled to participate in rational policy-making, if not a charade, is self-destructive, either because it renders policy-makers the more subservient to the greed of the articulate and organised, or because it so stimulates demands for state action that cannot be met that social harmony is imperilled. The *political liberals* offer an account of policy development that, while as historicist as many neo-Marxist accounts, avoids the expectations of catastrophe that they—like the market liberals—embrace. The ends and values used in specifying policy objectives are fairly well defined by changing societal dictates, although the latter are evident only to the welfare professional. The *public* character of policy-making is therefore at best epiphenomenal; at worst, it may engender socially damaging challenges to such expertise.

Finally, and in sharp contrast to this, for *Social Democratic* writers the mobilisation of the populace in an active and creative partnership with legislators is an integral part of social policy development. The degree of exclusion or inclusion of the citizenry in policy formulation significantly affects the implementation and impact of that policy. Hence no explanation of policy development in terms simply of the requirements of capital accumulation, the selfishness of sectional interests or the dictates of societal development can be adequate, in as much as any of these would presume an essentially reactive role for the mass of citizens. In a society of such active citizens, moreover, legislators will typically tend to pursue 'substantively rational' policy development, which will thus display its *sui generis* character as a process of collective learning and responsible choice.

These, then, are the theories of policy development with which we are concerned. As we shall see, however, their various political visions have often also served as the ideologies informing different post-war policies, depending on their appeal to different political leaders. We shall not, of course, deduce from the incorporation of some vision into policy the validity of the relevant account of social policy-making. It will be of particular interest, however, to trace how far the *outcome* of such a policy has differed from that anticipated by that account.

In each of sections II to V below, we investigate a fundamental issue in the recent development of one of the five main branches of social policy. There are two main limitations in our approach. First, we give only secondary attention to the private sectors of welfare and to state policies—such as tax relief—that affect their operation. Presumably in those sectors market power remains important; by excluding them from our main discussion, we risk bias against those analyses of our contemporary society—particularly the neo-Marxist—that see market power as continuing to mould policy development. Nevertheless, in chapter 2 we concluded that it was now incumbent upon neo-Marxist and liberal writers to address themselves to the state sector of welfare: no longer could developments here be deemed epiphenomenal to society at large.

Second, none of these discussions covers the whole range of questions raised above. Together, however, they span much of it. The limited scope of each individual section is not, however, especially alarming. For the various theoretical perspectives that are our governing concern claim global validity. To demonstrate serious weaknesses in their application to even one branch of social policy is logically sufficient, therefore, to force their proponents to engage in a general reappraisal of their case. We do not claim to make a major contribution to the sociology of individual areas of social policy. Rather, throughout this work, our concern is to draw on the already existing corpus of policy studies to inform our critical evaluation of the dominant contending macro-sociological perspectives on Western industrial society.

More specifically, our opening discussion of pensions, as part of social security, includes the ends in terms of which alternative proposals have been justified and their ideological bases, the divergent readings of deficiencies in past measures, and the significance of public debate and the mobilisation of popular support for specific reforms. We then proceed to consider how, in the recent reorganisation of the National Health Service, there have been sharply contrasting 'readings' of past deficiencies, even given broad agreement between the major political parties on the objectives to be sought. We explore the interests, values and political context that these differences express. In section IV we focus on the Seebohm reorganisation of the personal social services. Here is a coherent and major redefinition of objectives and of the criteria against which policy is to be judged. Here too, however, are important unanticipated consequences of policy implementation, exposing the essentially exploratory and innovative character of social policy development. Our fourth area is that of housing and redevelopment policy. We focus on the significance of property rights, both as a value informing policy formulation and as a power resource moulding its implementation. For such rights formed a focal value in the capitalist market society that we surveyed in chapter 2. Finally, in section VI we consider the dominant end or value in terms of which educational policy has long been legitimated and criticised and we trace the political implications of its progressive but exploratory implementation. We consider in what sense this process of policy development has been essentially public. In each section we unavoidably develop further lines of discussion. These are, however, governed throughout by our ultimate interest in the liberal, neo-Marxist and Social Democratic perspectives on policy development.

II SOCIAL SECURITY AND DESTITUTION

It was with the supposed abuse of outdoor relief—notably in the form of cash grants—that the 1834 Poor Law Amendment Act was chiefly concerned, although the reform failed to eliminate such relief. Indeed, the remainder of the century saw extensions of outdoor benefit to various specified categories of the population, contributing to what the Webbs saw as the 'break-up' of the Poor Law. Let us therefore start our investigation of contemporary social policy development with these benefits in cash.

Within the broad field of social security, space requires that we be highly selective. We therefore look at post-war pensions provision; for pensions reform has been one of the major recent areas of debate in social security. We focus upon pensions also because the resources they currently involve—both in private and in public schemes—are particularly large, relative to other areas of social security (Kincaid, 1973, pp. 82–3; Wilensky, 1975, pp. 47–8). We may, therefore, anticipate that the capitalist ruling class of the neo-Marxists and the various self-interested monopolies decried by the market liberals will be particularly concerned over the organisation and allocation of pensions. So, too, the demands of macro-societal evolution espied by political liberals and the partnership between social legislators and citizenry pictured by the Social Democrats will reveal themselves here, if not in more diminutive sectors. Third, pensions provision is focused upon a category of the long-term dependants who have left the labour market once and for all. Its beneficiaries stand, therefore, in a relationship to that market very different from that of the intended recipients of the 1834 relief. Here, therefore, we should be able to clarify how different are the ends of some contemporary social security arrangements from those of the Poor Law. On the other hand, a more balanced treatment would require equal consideration of those present-day measures—such as Supplementary Benefits, unemployment benefit and Family Income Supplement[1]—that seem to bear closer resemblance to the Poor Law provisions. Yet on these we can touch only in passing (and from a rather different standpoint in chapter 6).

The Beveridge scheme for pensions, enacted in 1946, is commonly portrayed as liberal in design and intent. For the level of benefits was to be set in terms of the basic requirements of living and was therefore at the same flat rate for all. It thereby provided the floor prescribed by the market liberal, although this floor had a universalist, rather than a selectivist character and was confined to those whose work record was adequate. Others—in Beveridge's view, soon to become a small minority—were to be raised to it by means-tested benefits. Above this, private initiative and responsibility would reign (Maynard, 'Social Security' in Cooper, 1973, esp. pp. 182–4; cf. pp. 51–2 above). Whether the experience of its implementation lends credence to liberal hopes for such a scheme is more questionable.

(i) Despite its proclaimed commitment to the Beveridge proposals, the post-war government failed to implement at least one key element of the scheme—the principle that pensions be at least equal to the levels of benefit granted under means-tested relief. Subsequent administrations have continued this neglect. Heclo explains this in terms of the politically unpopular burden that high flat-rate contributions would have imposed on the low-paid—together with Treasury opposition to an expanded Exchequer obligation (1974, pp. 256–9). With the early decision to reduce the qualifying period for full pensions—blanketing-in those close to retirement—the political limitations on the general level of pensions were probably even greater. The introduction of a graduated element in 1961 was seen by its Conservative sponsors as the politically least contentious method of raising contributions; yet the guaranteed minimum pension was barely affected, particularly in the short run (Parker, 1975, p. 62; Maynard in Cooper, 1973, p. 186). Thus real or imagined limitations on the capacity of policy-makers to mobilise political support have meant that significant—if not increasing —numbers of pensioners have remained elegible for means-tested relief (Atkinson, 1969, Ch. 3). The typical liberal confidence in the ability of the enlightened administrator to re-fashion society through rational argument within a general consensus is demonstrated naive.

(ii) The individual funds of accumulated contributions, from which pensions are paid, were to be calculated on sound actuarial principles in money terms—even though the employee's contributions were matched by those of the employer and the Exchequer. Economic growth, however, has tended to reduce the value of pensions in payment, relative to national average standards of living; and, with the officially defined 'poverty line' rising broadly in line with the latter (Atkinson, 1969, p. 17), has tended to increase the proportion of pensioners in poverty. Moreover, inflation has tended to erode the real value of pensions in payment, while its effect upon contributors to such a funded scheme has been to favour those whose earnings peak late in their careers, typically the middle- and upper-income groups. In practice, therefore, Exchequer supplementation of pensions in payment involved early departure from the strict actuarial principle. Only with the reform proposals of the 1970s, however, has allowance been made for the differential effects of inflation upon contributors with different earnings careers.

Here, then, three further assumptions within the liberal account of social policy invite criticism. First, Beveridge's liberal scheme failed to embrace a notion of poverty and of the basic requirements of social existence that is defined in terms relative to the standards of living of the society concerned. The associated conceptual weaknesses have often been rehearsed (see, for example, Townsend, 'Poverty as Relative Deprivation' in Wedderburn, 1974). Second, the redistributive consequences of inflation—and the political choices these pose over the degree of compensation to be granted pensioners and other dependent fixed-income groups—testify to perennial social conflict over the allocation of resources, with no 'natural' equilibrium pattern of rewards to judge the merits of the contestants and to permit apolitical, technical resolution of that struggle (cf. Kincaid, 1973, pp. 73–81). Third, actuarially determined funded schemes are shown to have no obviously greater security in real and relative terms than politically determined pay-as-you-go schemes; and politically articulated collective obligations to pensioners are shown unrealisable through the exercise of civil rights within the legal framework of the market place.

(iii) There have been considerable—but not entirely visible (Kincaid, 1973, Ch. 8) or anticipated—developments in the occupational pension arrangements permitted and envisaged by Beveridge. Yet their development has involved a tension rooted in the differing significance they have for employer and employee. For the former, occupational pension rights—and, more particularly, employers' contributions to them—may typically be seen as inducements to the recruitment and retention of employees, to be rescinded if the latter depart. For employees, however, accrued pension rights may instead be seen as deferred earnings, in which the employee's rights are absolute. Given such contested definitions of the situation, the occupational pension arrangements that have developed seem to express the varying power of employees *vis-à-vis* employers. It is in those segments of the labour force where collective organisation is weak, where workers are easily replaced, where loyalty and stability of personnel are unimportant, that pension benefits are typically poor and non-transferable (Parker, 1975, pp. 58–60; Kincaid, 1973, pp. 143–8; see too Government Actuary, 1972, Section 3 and paras 11.2, 13.4). Again, liberal confidence in the formal equity of private welfare arrangements is shown naive (cf. pp. 51–2 above).

The late 1960s and 1970s have seen a variety of proposals for pensions reform. They seem to be predicated upon what the two main political parties broadly agree are the shortcomings of the Beveridge scheme: the inadequate state provision, even after 1961, for continuity of incomes after retirement—or even for the mere prevention of destitution; the progressive erosion of pensions in payment, relative to national average earnings; and, finally, the failure of occupational schemes to supplement the state pension at all adequately, save among the middle- and higher-income groups. The 1975 Social Security Pensions Act became operational in April 1978. This measure superseded the Conservative Act of 1972, and was aimed at removing those aspects of the latter that the incoming Labour administration found politically objectionable or deemed technically inadequate. Yet it differed also from the Labour Bill of 1970. Let us consider, then, how diverse were the proposed schemes and the terms in which they have been publicly justified. Then we investigate more briefly who have been the principal protagonists and what forms of power have been successfully or unsuccessfully mobilised in the process of policy formulation.

Proposals for pensions reform

The Conservative scheme of 1972 reaffirmed Beveridge's liberal view of the limited responsibilities of the state. It judged that encouragement to a more vigorous private sector was both the technically most efficient and the politically most desirable orientation of reform. Thus the prime concern of the state remained the provision of a basic pension for all—albeit one that was inflation-proofed during payment and financed in part by graduated, not flat-rate, contributions. In supplementation of this, earnings-related occupational provision was to be encouraged—not least through tax relief (Department of Health and Social Security (DHSS), 1971a, paras 31, 70). The alternative was compulsory membership of an earnings-related state reserve scheme of modest proportions. All would thereby enjoy continuity of income as well as protection against destitution, without, however, becoming the wards of a politically capricious state.

Such a reform was propounded as sufficient to overcome the limitations that the Conservatives acknowledged within the post-war implementation of the Beveridge scheme. First, it was assumed that employees would more readily pay high contributions into private occupational schemes than they would into those of the state, for the dependence of individual benefit upon those contributions was more clearly guaranteed by the terms of the individual contract. Second, it was to be required of approved occupational schemes that they provide inflation-proofing during payment, while the reserve scheme would, through prudent investment of its funds, secure for its members an increase in pensions in line with national prosperity. The earnings-related element of pensions would, therefore, broadly retain its real value, if not necessarily its value relative to the living standards of the working population. Finally, statutory guarantee of the transferability and retention of pension rights accumulated under different employers would suffice to ensure that significant occupational pensions were no longer a privilege of a minority but instead the new property of the mass of the employed (DHSS, 1971a, paras 57–8, 75, 63–5 and Appendix 2).

The Labour scheme of 1970, in contrast, had redefined the state's concern as the provision of a universal earnings-related pension. The new scheme would operate on a pay-as-you-go basis, with the level of current contributions being set recurrently by political decisions over the general level of pensions in payment. That level could be adjusted to take account of inflation and economic growth. It would, moreover, be in terms of the 'dynamised' historic contributions of pensioners that their benefits relative to one another would be calculated, thereby avoiding the discrimination against manual workers that rising money earnings during the period of contribution tend to promote within funded schemes. Finally, some element of redistribution was incorporated, with contributions over the lower band of earnings being given preference when calculating benefits (DHSS, 1969, paras 32–4, 66, 31). In short, the new benefits would be aimed not only at the preservation of destitution but also at the promotion of income continuity and the preservation of the value of that income relative to the standards of the society at large. Moreover, certain forms of interruption to work record were more generously than hitherto to be credited with notional contributions—notably in respect of sickness and unemployment, although women were not to enjoy similar credits for periods of voluntary unemployment while raising families (DHSS, 1969, paras 69, 72 and Appendix 1, paras 24–8).[2]

Here, then, and in contrast to its Tory predecessor, it was assumed that the working population would be willing to pay the higher contributions that the state scheme would now require, even where the general level of contribution was indicated by the politically—rather than actuarially—defined level of pensions in payment and by the generosity with which notional contributions were credited to those with an interrupted work record. Indeed, the 1970 scheme included generous arrangements for 'blanketing-in' those shortly to retire and thereby involve a once-for-all additional contribution burden upon those in early or mid-career (DHSS, 1969, para 61 and Appendix 1, paras 20–1). Second, it was assumed that occupational schemes would be unable in general to guarantee inflation-proofing unless underwritten by the state; yet this would involve an open-ended commitment of public funds that was politically unacceptable to the Labour administration as a long-term proposition. Consequently, while occupational schemes were admitted as partners, with partial contracting-out, the conditions imposed on them were much more stringent than in the 1972 scheme. It was anticipated that this would result in their gradual—although not complete—phasing out, as their members opted for full membership of the generous and sounder state scheme (Atkinson, 1970, and Crossman, 1972a, p. 21). Finally, the 'reading' of past provisions on which the 1970 scheme was predicated involved little confidence that private occupational schemes could become universal among the employed: the retention of a multitude of rights under different employers was unlikely to be administratively feasible for many of the more mobile unskilled in particular (DHSS, 1969, paras 112–18).

These contrasting schemes seem more clearly, perhaps, than any of the measures we shall discuss in later sections of this chapter to raise again the classical liberal–socialist debate over the adequacy and proper role of the market as a distributive system within an urban–industrial society.[3] Yet the 1975 Act, which has superseded both schemes, must surely be judged a compromise—ignoring or denying the basic conflict of principles articulated by its two forerunners. It retains the basic pension of 1972 and looks to occupational provision of the second tier of earnings-related pensions for much of the employed population. On the other hand, it imposes more stringent conditions for contracting-out and it replaces the Conservatives' funded reserve scheme with one on a more generous pay-as-you-go basis. Many of the 1970 provisions are retained for 'blanketing-in', for 'dynamising' contributions and for crediting with notional contributions those whose record is incomplete (DHSS, 1974a, paras 58–61, 10, 14, 20, 44; these credits include those at home caring for children and invalids).

In this comparison we have followed most commentators in emphasising the distributional aspects of the various schemes. Yet they differ no less in their intended relational consequences—that is, the mode of social integration and distribution of power that they seek to promote. First, it will have been evident in the foregoing that the Crossman and Joseph schemes in particular enunciated two very different visions of social discipline and obligation and of individual freedom. That of the Joseph scheme was close to the liberal portraits of the good society expounded in chapter 3. Individual freedom and responsibility were to be exercised primarily through the market and the family. The state's role in expressing non-market obligations among citizens was limited to the prevention of destitution, at a level in effect less eligible than that provided by even the least generous of existing occupational schemes. The Crossman plan, in contrast, expressed some of the central elements of the Social Democratic writers' vision of social relationships in an advanced urban–industrial society. Social rights and obligations between the working population and the retired were to differ fundamentally from those of the market place and the individualistic contract, and might, indeed, be expected to have wider integrative consequences for a society that was overly dominated by the values of acquisitive individualism (see above, pp. 63–5).

Second, each of these two schemes took as one of its aims the limitation of socially irresponsible concentrations of power; yet each has also been attacked for promoting such concentrations. The Conservative scheme saw state domination of the pensions stage as a monopoly with minimal accountability to members. The sovereign choice of the consumer in the market place was replaced by the compulsion and uniformity of an omnipresent state. The Crossman plan, in contrast, was sympathetic to the view of such analysts as Titmuss that the growth of the private insurance companies in the post-war period had created an 'irresponsible society' of concentrations of power that were minimally visible or accountable (Titmuss, 1963, Ch. 11). The 1975 Act allows such private companies a greater role, but has been accompanied by moves for their increased accountability to the membership (see Prime Minister's Office, 1976). This has, in turn, provoked opposition from the companies, who see these proposals as tending to increase trade union power.

Third, in attending to the preservation and transfer of occupational pension rights, all three schemes may put in question the prevailing relationships of authority and social control between employers and their employees. Indeed, the Joseph plan seemed concerned lest the graduated state pension promoted criticism of the less generous of the private schemes—with possible challenges to the organisational hierarchies in which they were situated. How significant the 1975 changes will prove for collective bargaining strategies, labour force control, etc., must however remain a matter for future empirical investigation.

The 'social politics' of pensions reform

How, then, are we to account for these changes in pensions policy? Who were the principal protagonists involved and what forms of power did they mobilise? The studies available take us little further than the development and fate of the Crossman plan. Yet they at least suggest how, in principle, investigation of the more recent developments might proceed. Heclo provides a major study of the 'social politics' behind pensions policy in Britain (1974, esp. Chs

5–6). He argues that since pensions have been of only secondary interest to such wider interest groups as the trade unions and since their form has been politically peripheral (both to electoral contests and to overall governmental strategy), their development has been largely moulded by the initiatives of administrative and academic entrepreneurs and by consensual readings of the deficiencies in past measures. Such development, he argues, can be portrayed as a process of learning—a process governed largely by the clarification of past endeavours and future possibilities in which these entrepreneurs engage.

Thus Titmuss and his colleagues at the LSE are said to have provided the original idea of—and justifications for—national superannuation; Labour politicians such as Crossman seized upon the socialist principles it appeared to express, promoted it in Cabinet and secured Civil Service agreement on its administrative viability; and the occupational pensions schemes had some success in modifying the final proposals, in an accommodation to their interests. Yet the politically peripheral place of pensions also meant that with the Conservative election victory of 1970 an alternative reform could be proposed by other entrepreneurs. In brief, then, Heclo seems to assume that the 'politics of pensions' typically involve the periodic and behind-the-scenes mutual 'accommodation' of directly interested political groups, notably public administrators and private pensions interests; but he also sees a central catalytic role for the purposive actions of intellectuals and political sponsors. Yet with these emphases, he tends to play down the diversity of the objectives and social values embodied in competing reform proposals and the variety of 'readings' of past measures. Power and conflict are neglected in favour of processes of mutual 'accommodation' of interests and collective 'adjustment' to changed circumstances.

Consider, therefore, two specific aspects of Heclo's account that invite criticism. First, Crossman himself has portrayed the power mobilised by the private pensions interests in terms that go well beyond such processes of adjustment. He argues that the original Labour proposals for national superannuation, dating back to 1957, had envisaged still less of a role for those private schemes than did the 1970 plan. Not to have undertaken this modification, in the face of hostility from such schemes, would have been electorally damaging; for private employers and the occupational pensions industry would have used their economic power and organisational position *vis-à-vis* employees to mount extensive publicity campaigns hostile to Labour. Crossman therefore argues that the power of such interests extends even to the conditions of popular support and legitimation for government policy (1972a, esp. pp. 20–1; see too Crossman, 1977, p. 616).

Second, Heclo sees the trade unions as having had little interest in pensions. In collective bargaining, individual unions have concentrated on wages; while the TUC has in general failed to articulate any coherent view on pensions reform and to play any creative role. He infers their passivity in the development of the plan for national superannuation. Yet the evidence he provides is consistent with a very different interpretation (1974, pp. 262–9, 299–300). First, the academic and political sponsors of the reform considered it essential to mobilise TUC support if the measure was to be a success. Second, the lack of any 'creative' role by the TUC in the field of pensions seems to have sprung from its inability to. define its long-term collective interest and to perceive the likely distributional and relational implications of national superannuation, rather than from any lack of concern. This points, then, more to an explanation of policy development in terms of popular mobilisation by political leaders articulating collective interests and defining societal futures, rather than to an explanation that disregards social and political action within the wider system of social stratification.

Theoretical implications

What implications, then, do these policy developments hold for our competing perspectives on policy development? We have already indicated flaws that the implementation of the Beveridge scheme exposed in the approach adopted by liberal writers—more particularly, *market liberals.* In our subsequent discussion, we have found no evidence that the extension of the state's pensions role has been promoted by powerful self-interested groups in the manner they portray. Instead, indeed, we have seen how the private insurance companies and employers have been eager to restrict the role of the state, in their own self-interest. This lends support to a major thesis in the Social Democratic writers' critique of the market liberals: namely, that the market must be seen as an arena of conflict and contest rather than harmony, so that sectional greed may express itself, not in attempted reduction in the sphere of the market, but rather in its preservation and even *extension* into new areas of social life.

Against the *political liberals*, the foregoing offers at least two lines of criticism. First, we have argued that the Joseph scheme of 1972, like that of Beveridge, was predicated on broadly liberal assumptions as to the proper role of the state, while the 1970 Crossman plan was largely the brainchild of Titmuss and his associates—the Social Democrats. In the former, pensions were in large measure dependent on the permissive individualistic exercise of civil rights; in the latter, upon social rights politically guaranteed both in real terms and (less firmly) relative to the quality of life in the wider community. Two of the schools of thought we have hitherto taken as alternative analyses of social policy here appear as the rationales—indeed, the ideologies—of alternative political futures. Admittedly, the 1975 Act seems a compromise that, political liberals might claim, demonstrates that practical constraints preclude real political choice. Yet our discussion of the pensions protagonists suggests that such constraints must be seen as an expression of the existing distribution of power and as contingent upon the patterns of social and political action that political leadership is able to mobilise in the wider society.

Second, then, the significance of power differentials for policy development and implementation has been a repeated theme—from our discussion of the implementation of Beveridge to that of the development of the Crossman plan. Part of this lacuna in liberal accounts is their assumption that fairly apathetic adjustment by the mass of the population to the proposals and decisions of experts is exemplified by trade union passivity in pensions debate. We, however, have argued that, instead, such responses can be understood only by reference to the typical orientations of political leadership and mobilisation. These will be major themes in chapter 6.

At first sight, our account may seem to afford some comfort to the *neo-Marxists*. We have alluded to the post-war expansion of private pension schemes, reinforcing the power that 'finance capital', in the form of insurance companies, can exert in industrial and commercial life. So, too, our account would be consistent with any neo-Marxist claim that capitalist employers see pensions bargaining as a relatively attractive way of securing a quiescent labour force, with the real costs of such benefits postponed and likely eventually to be borne largely by state subsidies designed for inflation-proofing. We have also seen that at least some of the recent pensions proposals seem oriented to the higher earning groups; indeed, some neo-Marxists have argued that—in part because of its modification in face of opposition from those groups—even the Crossman plan would have had little redistributive impact among different classes (Kincaid, 1973, pp. 131–41). Such writers conclude that the range of policy options even considered within the capitalist state is strictly limited to those carrying no threat to capitalist interests (see above, pp. 44–6); incremental social reform is exposed as impotent to effect major change.

Two lines of criticism may, however, be developed. First, the foregoing hardly demonstrates the existence and enforcement of any long-term 'collective interest of capital'. It indicates merely how various advantaged groups and organisations may bring their interests to bear on policy formation. Our discussion suggests that the differences among them and variations in the types of power they wield are as significant as their similarities in explaining how policy has developed. It is far from certain that they had a common interest in the Joseph plan—or even the Castle plan—as compared with that of 1970, especially in conditions of continuing inflation (see Atkinson, 1970). Indeed, the very concept of a collective interest of capital appears nebulous.

Second, we may indeed not have demonstrated that, relative to the 1972 *Strategy for Pensions*, the Crossman plan was likely to have had an egalitarian impact as among social classes (but see Atkinson, 1970, and Lynes, 1969, Ch. 4)—even though it would have given a better deal to manual workers, especially the unskilled, the non-unionised and women. Yet we *have* shown that the two schemes involved fundamentally different relationships of the state to the private sector of pension provision and similarly different definitions of pension rights. For under the Conservative scheme these derive from the exercise of civil rights, while in the Labour proposals they are redefined as integral to the social rights of citizenship guaranteed by the state. Thus the two schemes do differ fundamentally in the degree to which life chance outcomes—and their determinants—are to be of immediate political concern. The Labour scheme might in consequence also have brought under closer political scrutiny the patterns of inequality within which the work and market careers of pensioners—and of current contributors—are pursued (see above, p. 89); although what action might have developed out of this scrutiny—by the trade unions for example—remains a separate question. Here, then, is potential significance for social policy developments in promoting the immanent practical critique of the wider distribution of power and advantage: a significance disregarded by the neo-Marxists but central to the Social Democratic position.

If these criticisms of liberal and neo-Marxist accounts are consistent with those that *Social Democratic* writers might voice, the latter exhibit weaknesses also. (Some of these, as we saw in chapter 3, are admittedly less evident in the later Social Democratic writings than in those of the immediate post-war era; see above, p. 66). First, we have seen how inequalities in private occupational welfare reflect and reinforce wider inequalities of power and advantage and demonstrate the resistance of the latter to modification by the social rights of universalist social services alone. On the other hand, it was partly in recognition of this division of occupational welfare that Crossman, under the influence of Titmuss, promoted his scheme of national superannuation, and that such researchers as Sinfield have followed Titmuss, albeit only recently, in widening their attention beyond the more visible provision of welfare through the social services (Titmuss, 1963, Ch. 2; Sinfield, 1978).

Second, we have traced some of the concentrations of private power that mould social policy development—most notably the pensions interests. We also pointed to the authority hierarchies within which private pension provision has been offered and of which such provision has been a support. In both cases we are touching on the dependence of such life chance distribution upon the wider distribution of power in our society: a dependence that operates, however, largely invisibly and beyond popular control. Again, as we saw in chapter 3, this has only slowly been recognised by Social Democratic writers as a major obstacle to their hopes for reform.

Third, we have pointed to the problems that these writers sometimes overlook of mobilising civic obligations among the citizenry at large. The trade unions, for example, have been less than eager partners in an intergenerational social contract of national superannuation. Neither rational argument nor citizen participation in policy development suffices to guarantee the pursuit of fraternity. Instead, the Conservative assumption, echoing Beveridge, that private self-interest could alone evoke the popular compliance required for any expanded pensions provision, remains at least plausible. The Social Democrats must, therefore, take more seriously the task Weber assigned to the political leader of defining political values and mobilising action in their pursuit: a task that is unavoidably constrained by the values held forth by other authoritative actors and by prevailing traditions of collective action (see above, pp. 35–6).

Finally, then, and bringing these points together, our account suggests that, for the Social Democratic approach to remain plausible as an intellectual scheme and a political programme, its proponents must combine a clearer recognition of the resistance to change of existing stratification patterns with a more specific and historical analysis of the opportunities for political leadership to create and engage the support of groups and collectivities having both the will and the capacity to effect major social change by democratic means. To these themes we return.

III THE REORGANISATION OF THE NHS: READING THE PAST

The development of the NHS in the post-war period seems to provide a particularly clear illustration of the process of rational policy-making with which our opening section commenced (cf. Ryan, 'Health: Policy and Administration' in Cooper, 1973): 1946 saw the legislation setting up the service and 1974 saw the culmination of a process of re-evaluation, with a major reorganisation of health care and a re-articulation of objectives. Thus the *Second Green Paper*—the principal document setting out the rationale for reform—took as its starting point a reiteration of the main objectives of the 1946 Act: notably the provision of treatment free to the user and of a uniformly high quality for all (DHSS, 1970, para. 1). It also reaffirmed the 1946 commitment to the clinical freedom of the medical profession, and, organisationally, to the centrality of the General Practitioner in the delivery of health care. The Green Paper then offered a survey of the principal changes in health needs and techniques during the post-war period, an identification of the deficiencies in the provision of treatment and the specification of new measures intended to achieve contemporary policy objectives.

The concern that illuminates most clearly the rationale of the debates over reorganisation was probably the reallocation of resources away from hospital-based intensive care for the acutely ill towards community care for the chronically sick and the long-term disabled, particularly the elderly, which involved greater emphasis on preventive measures and long-term supportive services. It seems to have been predicated upon certain demographic trends, notably an ageing population, and upon the success of hospital-based treatment in dealing with acute illness (DHSS, 1970, para. 7; Chester, 1973, esp. pp. 43–6).

Consideration of the treatment of such needs in the post-war period thus provides an especially fruitful vantage point from which to summarise the deficiencies identified by the Green Paper and other critics of the unreformed service. The concentration of resources on hospital-based care—with low priority going to those non-hospital services upon which the treatment of chronic illness is particularly dependent—was permitted by the retention, in 1948, of an administrative separation of the hospital service, the family practitioner and the local health services. For, in decisions on resource allocation, the fragmentation permitted the prestige of the hospitals and the power of their consultants to prevail over considerations of equity and efficiency. Thus, for example, the underdevelopment of non-hospital services had contributed to the inappropriate and inadequate treatment frequently received by the chronically sick, as compared with the acutely ill, and had also meant that often only high-cost institutional care had been available. As the Green Paper concluded, this tripartite service had its origins in 'earlier patterns of services, ... developed to meet particular needs or to establish particular priorities not all of which are still relevant today' (DHSS, 1970, paras 11–12, 106). Moreover, within the hospitals the medical profession had tended to accord low prestige—and few merit awards—to such specialisms as geriatrics: 'in this, and other respects, the profession's own structure of power and values often runs counter to those of policy-makers' (Klein, 1974, p. 6). Finally, it was the same health needs that were most affected by mal-coordination of the health and personal social services; a mal-coordination, as we shall see, due in part to dissimilarities in decision-making structure between the two services (DHSS, 1970, paras 22–3).

It was on the basis of this articulation of contemporary objectives in health policy and this identification and 'reading' of the inadequacies in past measures, that proposals for reorganisation of the NHS were then developed by the framers of the Green Paper. Unification of administration was intended to promote efficiency in the allocation of resources and improved coordination of different forms of care. Devolution was to ensure that such integration was no less real at local than at national level, to facilitate coordination with local authority services,[4] and 'to involve each community in the running of the services of its district'. Such reorganisation, moreover, seems in particular to have been aimed at improving treatment of the chronically sick, not only by facilitating exposure of the inefficiency of hospital-based care for such needs, but also by promoting 'effective central control over the money spent on the service' and hence over priorities (DHSS, 1970, Ch. 2; paras 62–4, 69–77; Ch. 4; paras 6–7).

However, these reform proposals raised certain contentious administrative and political issues that led to their modification by the incoming Conservative administration of 1970–4. For the Green Paper sought a redefinition of the lines of authority and political control in the health service. Most explicit was its commitment, on the one hand, to democratisation of a devolved service—for example through district committees, staffed in part by local professional and lay members, ensuring that 'the area health authority is exposed to the full vigour of local opinion', and, on the other hand, to central control, planning and the specification of policy (DHSS, 1970, paras 54, 60–1, 90–1; see too DHSS, 1974b, para. 7). The less explicit obverse was a reduced role for the regional tier and, by implication, diminished powers for the hospital consultants (Abel-Smith, 1971).

The Conservatives' *Consultative Document* of May 1971 defined areas of disagreement. In the first place, it proposed a much stronger regional tier, in the belief that 'direct supervision of some 80 to 90 area authorities by the Central Department . . . would not make managerial sense' (DHSS, 1971b, para. 6). Instead, regional health authorities 'will generally plan the regions, have building departments, and allocate the money to and supervise the area authorities beneath them' (Abel-Smith, 1971, p. 191). They would also appoint a majority of the members of the area health authorities, for the representational proposals of the Green Paper 'would have led to a dangerous confusion between management on the one hand and the community's reaction to management on the other (DHSS, 1971b, para. 20). Likewise, the *Consultative Document* largely dispensed with the Green Paper's proposals for district committees; instead, Community Health Councils would fulfil a consultative role. Abel-Smith argues that this two-tier system of responsibility was likely to mean that 'while the GPs will keep their eyes focused on their separate and special committee at area level, the consultants will continue to exert their influence at the [key] regional level'. This hierarchical separation of the GP and consultant interests, he continued, would vitiate local integration of the medical services and their coordination with local authority personal social services. As for Community Health Councils, they were likely to be 'a charade of local consultation'.[5]

In the event, the new Labour administration of 1974 strengthened the councils' managerial role and increased the proportion of elected representatives on the area authorities (Klein and Lewis, 1976, pp. 22–3). It thereby reaffirmed its view that 'to embark on total separation [of management and representation] is to challenge in a fundamental way the essence of democratic control' (DHSS, 1974b, para. 5). Indeed, the early experience of the councils has demonstrated the impossibility, in practice, of maintaining any such separation (Klein and Lewis, 1976, pp. 21–2, 158).

Thus the Labour proposals were justified in such terms as efficiency in resource allocation, equity in the treatment of different needs and democracy in decision-making. The Conservative critique had as its rationale the supposed dangers to managerial efficiency of lay control and the need to leave considerable decision-making power in the hands of senior medical professionals, as a precondition for clinical freedom and professional autonomy. In a full investigation, it would be necessary to identify the relationship of these contrasting proposals to the goals of the various interest groups involved and to trace the relative power of the latter. For indeed, the plethora of consultative policy documents preceding the 1974 reorganisation has itself been cited as a 'visible demonstration of the power which interest groups exercise in our society'. The medical profession is at most 'a loose coalition of conflicting interests'; and administrators, paramedical staff and advocates of patients' interests constitute additional 'contenders for the power to control the destiny of the nation's health service' (Abel-Smith,

1971). One would need also, for example, to consider the significance of the change of government for the apparent success of senior hospital doctors in obtaining a desirable form of reorganisation; and to explore whether, for example, the Conservatives adopted these more favourable proposals as a result of greater susceptibility to pressure from such an interest group or because they accorded with their managerial ideology. (Such a study might follow the lines of Gill, 1974.) One would need also to take note of the constraints imposed by wider contextual changes, such as the reorganisation of local government.

Here, however, we simply note that these diverging proposals involved competing diagnoses of past deficiencies in health care. The proposals actually implemented thus presuppose the selection and official triumph of one particular 'reading'. The deficient treatment of the chronically sick and disabled was partly attributed by both Labour and Conservative schemes to demographic change, excessive concentration of resources in the hospitals and mal-coordination of health and other social services. The Labour diagnosis, however, also stressed the different degrees of devolution in health and the personal social services and the consequent obstacles to effective professional partnership, the status of the hospital sector and the power of its consultants over the greatly expanded resources made available under the post-war NHS, and the absence of conscious specification of priorities and programmes by central government.

Theoretical implications

To conclude this discussion, let us reflect on its relevance to the various theoretical perspectives that are our ultimate concern.

(i) The Labour and Conservative schemes broadly concurred in at least one of the principal objectives of reorganisation: a shift in resources towards the chronically sick and disabled. The proclaimed aim, then, was that such conditions should no longer suffer inferior treatment, and that the original NHS goal should be achieved of providing high-quality treatment for all, as of right. Moreover, the designation of the measures to be undertaken proceeded, as we have seen, broadly according to the model of rational policy-making with which this chapter started—although we have indicated the disagreement over what those measures should be and its political context.

This gives little comfort to the *market liberals*. They portray consumer outcomes, not as the active concern of policy-makers, but rather as the mere by-product of the activities of powerful welfare bureaucracies. Thus as Lees, for example, argues, 'the British health industry exists . . . in the interests of the producer groups who make it up. The welfare of patients is a random by-product, depending on how conflicts between the groups and between them and the Government happen to shake down at any particular time' (1976, p. 12). Nor is there any obvious sense in which this redirection of policy could be seen as an adaptation to the technical requirements of our advanced urban–industrial society—even though it has in part been justified by reference to secular demographic trends and the slower technical advance of community-based care for the chronically sick, relative to hospital-based clinical techniques. Rather, it seems to have been an essentially political or moral choice, among alternatives really available, aimed at realising that equity in health care proclaimed as a social right under the NHS.

This concern to reallocate resources towards the long-term chronically ill is likewise hardly what the *neo-Marxists* would predict. For they commonly depict state health care as a form of human investment serving to promote expansion of the privately appropriated surplus; the chronically sick and disabled, however, are precisely those least likely to serve such an end. There is, then, little sign of the active selection by the state of those measures in the 'long-term collective interest of capital'—unless the aim of the reform is more one of legitimating the status quo through a show of social concern (cf. pp. 44–5 above).

(ii) We have explored how the divergent 'readings' of past policy and consequent prescriptions for reorganisation have important implications for the distribution of power among different medical professionals, their political masters and the consumers. We have seen how the interests of the most powerful medical professionals have tended to coincide much more with those of the acutely ill than of the chronic. Hence the definition of such professionals' role and legitimate concerns is itself an essentially political matter.

Market liberals tend to assume that the interests of the bureaucratised welfare professional within 'socialised medicine' will inevitably be in conflict with those of his client, and that a market organisation of care provides the model of a harmony of professional and patient interests, wherein no producer group obtains excessive rewards and against which other forms of organisation must be judged. We, however, have indicated that the pattern of such interest conflict and harmony is essentially a matter for empirical investigation. For example, Klein and Lewis, in their study of the Community Health Councils, conclude that 'it would be wrong to imply that the producer interest necessarily clashes with the consumer interest. . . . The CHC's . . . are themselves actors in a shifting world of coalitions, where there are a great many groups seeking allies and advocates for their particular interests' (1976, p. 133). The managerial, technocratic orientation of the Conservative reorganisation had obvious affinities with the account of power and interests that the *political liberals* would advance. Our criticisms of the Conservative scheme serve, therefore, also to indicate weaknesses in those liberals.

For the *neo-Marxists*, arguing that the 'reading' chosen of past policy will be such as to justify an organisation of health care that favours capitalist interests, our discussion poses the question of just how such interests are made effective. Is it, for example, through constellations of interest among the propertied, the senior medical professionals and the political leaders of at least the Conservative Party—who together form a self-conscious elite in which the first-mentioned are dominant? This is broadly the case argued by the neo-Marxists Waitzkin and Waterman in respect of the American 'medical–industrial complex' (1974, esp. pp. 90–1, 109). Berlant, in a comparative study of the United States and Britain, argues similarly that in both countries the medical profession has been able to expand its powers because of its harmony of interests and ideology with those of other elite groups; although it is more in the United States than in Britain that 'development of the medical profession has been closely tied with the development of stratified relationships between social groups, so that quality medical care has tended to be a prized scarcity and an object of class behaviour' (1975, p. 305). Whether this difference arises from the 'socialised' character of British medicine would merit investigation—and illustrates, indeed, the limitations that are imposed on the present work by its focus on a single country. However, it still remains to investigate the pre-eminence within this elite of the propertied, the institutional arrangements for securing its cohesion and endurance and the strategies available to medical professionals and political leaders in conditions where this constellation of interests dissolves. Alternatively, neo-Marxists might argue that we have given a misleading account of the power that medical professionals can wield, neglecting the wider systemic constraints that guarantee their subservience to capitalist interests. If so, it behoves such writers to spell out the character of those constraints—heeding the methodological canons of chapter 3, section V.

Our account of the process of reorganisation tends, in contrast, to vindicate *Social Democratic* arguments that social policy development has something of a *sui generis* character, in which the deficiencies of past measures are consciously evaluated and political choices made among alternative societal futures. Nevertheless, we have also seen that the boundary between political and professional decisions has been strongly—and perhaps even essentially—contested, with the power of the medical profession tending continuously to undermine this substantive rationality of policy development, to an extent not anticipated in at least the earlier of post-war Social Democratic writing. As Weber bemoaned the Social Democrats' failure to recognise the irresponsible powers of the bureaucratic administrator and the pretensions of their legal–rational authority (see above, p. 36), so today Social Democratic writers have been slow to recognise those of the bureaucratised welfare professional and his claims to professional authority (cf. Halsey's Introduction to Dennis, 1970).[6] They have to this extent inadequately realised that the substantive rationality of policy development requires continuing political reassessment of authority and its legitimation.

IV THE UNIFICATION OF THE PERSONAL SOCIAL SERVICES: IMPLEMENTING A DESIGN

The Seebohm design

At the risk of considerable over-simplification, we might suggest that the debates over reorganisation of the NHS broadly reaffirmed the original objectives of an established service, with conflict focussing on the effectiveness and political acceptability of alternative administrative means for achieving those objectives in a changed world. In turning to the Seebohm reforms, however, we encounter a more radical redefinition of objectives and an exploration of its multiple and extensive implications. Indeed, to study the Seebohm proposals is to confront a new arm of social policy *in statu nascendi*.

The various constituent services, previously administered by a variety of local authority departments, included among their origins the Poor Law provisions for such vulnerable groups as pauper children and the aged. Yet for Seebohm, their history demonstrated the inability of these various services to achieve their proper objectives save within a unified and reorganised personal social services department (1968, Ch. 4). First, mal-coordination of services was increasingly common when, with growing recognition of the complexity of need, clients were being treated by a multiplicity of agencies, as also when different members of families under stress received treatment from different agencies. Second, each service tended to deal only with individuals who came to its attention via particular well-defined avenues. The consequences were that (a) individuals in similar conditions of need might receive significantly different forms of treatment, as a result of entering the purview of the local authority by different channels; (b) some individuals in need might be the specific responsibility of no particular service; and (c) there might be an overemphasis upon remedial, rather than preventive, measures. The result was inaccessibility, insufficiently prompt recognition of need and unclear lines of responsibility and accountability (1968, paras 79, 98–100, 83–5). Third, Seebohm echoed the Younghusband Committee, set up in 1955, which pointed to the scarcity of trained workers and recommended professionalisation of the health and welfare departments, partly as a means of encouraging recruitment (see Parker, 1965, pp. 70ff). Seebohm argued that the fragmentation of the personal social services inhibited their attraction and career development of trained personnel. Together, these deficiencies inhibited also the attraction of resources and militated against attempts at overall planning (1968, paras 78, 88–95, 74–5, 86).

It was, then, in such terms that Seebohm argued the necessity for a unified personal social services department, if the objectives of the various services were to be achieved. In addition, however, but not fully explicit, was a redefinition of their common objective—or, equivalently, of the basic type of need with which the new department was properly to be concerned. Following our account of the threefold deficiency in the previously existing services, three aspects to this redefinition may be highlighted. First, the need requiring treatment was a property, not of the individual in isolation, but rather of his social and community network. It was the support or, if necessary, the replacement of weakened family and community networks that constituted the fundamental and unifying concern of the new department. One corollary was a greater emphasis on preventive work and community care (although lack of resources for institutional care had been no less important an incentive to the latter). Another was that the new department and the social network in which an individual is located should properly be seen, not as alternatives in meeting his needs, but rather as partners. Thus Seebohm argued for a 'much wider acceptance of the idea of shared responsibility and a greater development of mutual cooperation between parents and those social services with special responsibilities for helping parents with the upbringing of their children'.

Second, the needs with which the new department was to be centrally concerned were universal. That is, the services 'should be readily accessible and available to all families'. Indeed, 'the greater simplicity and accessibility of a unified department is likely to expose many needs which have hitherto gone unrecognized or unmet'. Likewise, in order that no needs should be neglected merely because of inadequate categorisations, 'the availability of different forms of help should not be closely defined in terms of particular kinds of behaviour or the means through which children with difficulties come to the notice of the local authority' (Seebohm, 1968, paras 80, 311, 186, 150, 188). Here, then, was at least partial recognition that in a rapidly changing urban–industrial society, no social network is invulnerable to attenuation rendering it inadequately supportive in times of crisis; and hence all individuals are potentially at risk.[7] Again the corollary was an increased preventive orientation.

Third, these needs were esoteric and *sui generis*: their diagnosis and treatment required an expertise no less than—but distinct from—that of the medical professional or the educator. This is the obverse of Seebohm's argument that 'no really effective family service is possible unless the staff receive a sound basic training followed by opportunities to develop their skill in the light of new knowledge and changed circumstances'. Moreover, partly in recognition of the scarcity of such essential skills and the need to husband them, Seebohm proposed the allocation of services among local authority departments according to the principal skill involved (1968, para. 528 and Part III; cf. DHSS, 1970, para. 31).

It was then in terms of such a redefinition of need that Seebohm presented the case for a unified, accessible, professionally staffed service, capable of attracting increased resources, engaging in overall planning and meeting individual and community needs comprehensively. Seebohm went on, however, to clarify the fundamental change in the social significance of the personal social services that is implied by this redefinition of objectives. He saw his proposals 'not simply in terms of organisation but as embodying a wider conception of social service, directed to the well-being of the whole of the community and not only of social casualties, and seeing the community it serves as the basis of its authority, resources and effectiveness'. Here the notion of community 'implies the existence of a network of reciprocal social relationships, which among other things ensure mutual aid and give those who experience it a sense of well-being'.

The encouragement of citizen participation in local communal activities was thus integral to the work of the personal social services. In this way, the latter would be able to encourage 'community development . . . seen as a process whereby local groups are assisted to clarify and express their needs and objectives and to take collective action to attempt to meet them. It emphasises the involvement of the people themselves in determining and meeting their own needs.' Such local groups would play an essential role in 'the identification of need, the exposure of defects in the services and the mobilisation of new resources'. In these ways, the new department would 'enable the greatest possible number of individuals to act reciprocally, giving and receiving service for the well-being of the whole community'. Seebohm concluded: 'Above all, the development of citizen participation should reduce the rigid distinction between the givers and takers of social services and the stigma which being a client has often involved in the past' (1968, paras 152–4, 474, 476, 480, 491, 2, 492). Kogan and Terry comment: 'Hence "community" under the Seebohm rubric will concern itself not only with the extirpation of deprivation but also with *the creation of new social forms*, which derive their power and strength from the widest base of social support both for reasons of compassion, and to reinforce national resources as well' (1971, p. 10).

Such a concern with community development carried with it, therefore, participation by users in policy formulation and service decentralisation. Consumers should be included on area committees, which would help 'in strengthening the lines of communication between the social service committee and department on the one hand and local communities and local organisations on the other hand'. To be effective, then, the social service department needed to work through 'area teams, drawing support from the communities they serve . . . and able to call on the more specialised resources, advice and support of the departmental headquarters'. Not, however, that conventional resources alone would be sufficient; mobilisation of voluntary resources and the catalysis of mutual aid were essential (Seebohm, 1968, paras 594, 191).[8]

Finally, however, Seebohm recognised that the processes of urbanisation and industrialisation mean that to define what is to be a community or neighbourhood is 'increasingly difficult as society becomes more mobile'. The reintegrative task of the social services is greatest 'in areas characterised by rapid population turnover, high delinquency, child deprivation and mental illness rates and other indices of social pathology'. He therefore advocated the designation of priority areas, which 'should receive extra resources comprehensively planned in cooperation with services both central and local' (1968, paras 476–7, 487). The adequacy of such official portrayals of deprived neighbourhoods will be scrutinised in chapter 5.

Theoretical implications
Let us reflect upon the implications of the foregoing for the theoretical perspectives that are our main concern. First, observe that the goals of the new service presented fundamental differences from those of the 1834 Poor Law. There was a concern, not with the 'less eligible' treatment of a sub-group of the population defined in terms of its destitution, but rather with a high-quality provision to the community as a whole. Moreover, there was increasingly a preventive orientation—with the service anticipating emergent needs and preventing their exacerbation by supportive aid to attenuated networks in times of crisis and by giving priority treatment to those

areas most prone to such attenuation. In these respects, the personal social services depicted by Seebohm depart from that essentially reactive view entailed by the *political liberals'* perspective. We have, admittedly, seen that social disintegration in areas of high mobility occasioned Seebohm's proposals for priority treatment. This can hardly, however, be cited as illustrative of the way in which societal dictates constrain and mould social policies. For, on the one hand, public knowledge of such 'dictates' is mediated through various groups of experts and is not, therefore, unproblematic; furthermore, the actual *extent* to which the areas so designated are granted priority over others remains a political or value-judgement.

The *market liberals* deny the possibility of rational justification for progressive extensions of state activity. We have, however, traced the coherent rationale presented by the Seebohm Committee, on the basis of its retrospective identification and diagnosis of deficiencies in the existing services, for a wider and more preventive service. Indeed, economic considerations formed part of this rationale. For example, 'expenditure of time, effort, talent and money on children . . . is, above all, an investment in the future. It makes no sense . . . in terms of sheer economics . . . to allow young children to be neglected physically, emotionally or intellectually.' (Seebohm, 1968, para. 191). Second, the market liberal assumes that the needs with which social policy is concerned are of such a character as to be capable of articulation in the market place. Social policy formulation is then interpreted as a partitioning of such needs between market and state provision. We have, however, seen that Seebohm's proposed personal social services were also to be concerned with needs that are hidden to the individuals concerned and that can be discerned only through the expertise of the professional.

In some respects, however, the Seebohm reorganisation does seem to conform to the market liberals' explanation of state intervention in terms of the self-interest of powerful groups. The Report has been portrayed as a 'Social Workers' Charter' (Sinfield, 'Which Way for Social Work?' in Townsend, 1970, pp. 23–4, 40–1). It aroused considerable hostility from the medical profession and local government officials, jealous of their powers (Hall, 1976, Chs 5–6); and it was only by glossing over 'the really important issues . . . [that] a precarious consensus' politically was achieved (Townsend, 1970, p. 15). Nevertheless, the market liberal is, surely, arguing that it is upon the interests of individuals and groups in the wider society that the expansion of any arm of state policy intrudes; of such an intrusion we have found no clear evidence. Rather, the necessary mediation of the welfare professional to which we have just alluded may involve a coincidence between his interests and those of his client. Under what conditions this coincidence does not arise—and what implications follow for our view of the market liberals—will be a recurring theme in subsequent sections and chapters.

Further lines of criticism can be suggested. Community development, we have seen, was integral and explicit to the proposals accepted for reorganisation. Immediately, however, a problem is posed for one strand in *political liberalism*—the portrayal of the political system as a market place to which established and therefore legitimate interest groups have free access and achieve success in proportion to their political weight (see above, pp. 55–6). Such legitimacy is taken as unproblematic; there is no formal provision for inclusion of new groups that may develop in society at large. Here in Seebohm, however, we find an explicit and central commitment to the goal of helping hitherto inarticulate communities collectively to voice their objectives within the policy-making process; by implication at least, the 'legitimacy' of established and traditional channels of representation is rendered fragile. As for the *market liberals*, this commitment must be viewed in highly negative terms. For it exemplifies the more general attempt in the state's social policies to engender forms of social relationship other than those of the family and the market; such attempts cannot but produce social conflict, involving as they do interference with individuals' autonomy (see above, pp. 49–50). Here, however, we have traced a very different notion of autonomy. For Seebohm, guaranteeing of the citizen's autonomy required a supportive partnership between his community networks and the personal social services, and would find its expression, in part, through his participation in the clarification of collective needs and in mutual aid for their collective provision. To this we return shortly, while in chapter 6 we investigate whether community development indeed produces conflict and discord. Concluding this point, it is perhaps rather less clear what are the implications for *neo-Marxist* accounts of policy-making. For our investigation thus far is not inconsistent with the view that social policy developments are initiated in part as a means of diverting the attention and activity of underprivileged social groups from fundamental class determinants of deprivation. Whether community development proves in practice such an opiate, and whether the values and perspectives it inculcates promote the stability of the dominant capitalist order are issues we must again leave to chapter 6.

Finally, does not Seebohm's redefining as universal the needs with which the personal social services were properly to be concerned implicitly enunciate a particular view of man-in-society? More specifically, the redefinition of these needs as community needs presented man as essentially a social being, whose needs could be articulated and whose self-realisation was possible only within a context of community networks, which were not, indeed, to be thought of as given. Rather, the Seebohm concern with community development made the continuing re-creation and transformation of such networks constitutive of man's self-realisation. The redefinition of needs as esoteric, on the other hand, is antithetical to any view that man's needs are given and self-evident to the individual in pre-social and abstract terms. At the same time, the concern with community development also incorporated the notion that the identification of need emerges out of a cooperative partnership between the appropriate professionals and the community in which the individual is located. This philosophical anthropology has clear points of difference with the classical *liberal* perspectives presented in chapter 2, where man is seen in pre-social terms, manipulating social arrangements in the interests of independently given, self-evident individual objectives. As for the *Marxist* perspective, man is historical and social, creating himself and his world through cooperation with his fellows in the productive process (see above, p. 29). For Seebohm, however, while man's autonomy, needs and self-knowledge are socially created and are, indeed, the concern of social policy, man's social being is not narrowly rooted within the production system as presented in orthodox Marxism. Rather, it is also derivative of the individual's relationship to his domestic and neighbourhood community and of his political relationship to such organisations as social policy agencies (cf. Rex, 1970, pp. 62–5). Yet this notion of man does seem wholly consonant with that implicitly used by *Social Democratic* writers. To the empirical significance of these contrasts between the notion of man-in-society implicit in Seebohm and those presupposed by these various theoretical perspectives we return in chapter 6.

Implementing the design

It may, nevertheless, be objected that since the Seebohm Committee was dominated by those of Social Democratic persuasion, it is hardly surprising that the Report's proposals were broadly consonant with the vision held by our Social Democratic writers. It is therefore desirable to examine also the outcome of the attempt to implement these proposals through the 1970 Local Authority Social Services Act. The processes whereby Seebohm's recommendations were translated, with modifications, into law have been the subject of a recent study by Hall. She points not only to the changing alliances among interested pressure groups, but also to the significant role played by individual politicians and advisors and by such external factors as the forthcoming General election (1976, Chs 5–6).

Here, however, let us look briefly at just two aspects of the implementation of the reforms.

(i) Some commentators have argued that, because of the wider context within which the service operates, the new department has perforce adopted an orientation very different from that which Seebohm espoused. Thus Jordan (1974) argues that the new service has become increasingly an appendage to the Supplementary Benefits Commission, with its major task the discretionary distribution of emergency and extraordinary claims for means-tested benefits in cash and kind. Jordan points to at least two causes of this reorientation. First, there have been significant moves over the last decade towards a centralisation and standardisation of the administration of Supplementary Benefits. These have been aimed in part at a reduction in the stigmatisation of claimants—and have, perhaps, been prompted by pressure from, *inter alia*, the Child Poverty Action Group and welfare rights movements. Only the personal social services have been left to deal with claimants locally, personally and promptly. Admittedly, personal social service professionals had themselves sought powers to distribute cash in exceptional circumstances, as part of their preventive concern. Yet in practice, many families with exceptional financial need alone have been referred to the new department. Pursuit of the Seebohm objectives has thus been swamped by the Supplementary Benefits Commission's shedding of some of its erstwhile responsibilities (Jordan, 1974, pp. 72–4, Chs 6–7). It follows that in the study of

social policy implementation, we must attend to the consequences—whether intended or otherwise—of one area of policy
development for the needs and demands for resources presented to
others.

Second, Jordan points to the way in which differential class usage
of the public sector—for example, the greater ability of middle- and
upper-income groups to make use of private care for children at risk
and the aged—may encourage policy-makers and professionals to
see low incomes and social need as tightly linked (1974, pp. 120–1).
Whatever may have been Seebohm's concern to define the distinctiveness and universality of such social needs, therefore, low
incomes continue to be widely taken as their indicator. Seebohm's
advocacy of positive discrimination towards areas of high social
need has been taken as justifying a focus upon areas with particular
dependence upon state cash benefits. Here, then, it is evident that in
the study of social policy implementation we must attend to the
perceptions that practitioners hold of the pattern and aetiology of
needs, dependent as these perceptions may be on differential class
access to the private sector.

Thus Jordan is, *inter alia*, arguing that the personnel of the new
department are being significantly restricted in their treatment of
those esoteric needs that Seebohm defined as their proper concern.
Equally, they are discouraged from seeing their concern as a
universal one. Finally, as we shall see in chapter 6, Jordan argues
that the main consequence of the processes outlined above is that
the service takes on, not a supportive role of partnership in meeting
community needs, but the repressive and stigmatising role of traditional destitution agencies. Thus we need to study not only the
aspirations of legislators but also the actions of practitioners.

(ii) It is not always clear which innovations of the 1970s may
properly be seen as the fruit of Seebohm. The late 1960s saw
proposals for government-sponsored Community Development
Projects (CDPs) as part of the Urban Aid programme (cf. Batley and
Edwards, 'CDP and the Urban Programme' in Lees and Smith,
1975). Such projects would tackle the deprivation of priority
areas—in part through better field coordination of the personal
social services. They would mobilise community participation, on
the lines advocated by Seebohm, in programmes of mutual aid and
self-help. Yet whether they may properly be seen as part of the

implementation of the Seebohm vision is unclear. Mayo indicates how early advocates of the CDPs saw them as 'a convenient form for the government's immediate response to the Seebohm recommendations' ('The History and Early Development of CDP' in Lees and Smith, 1975, pp. 7–8)—recommendations that, it was feared, might meet with politically embarrassing delay, if taken *in toto*, on account of their likely cost and wider administrative implications. Other commentators, however, have seen such early advocacy of the CDPs as an attempt to pre-empt the Seebohm reforms (Specht, 1976, pp. 7–8). Yet, like Seebohm, the projects received political support not only from those concerned with social deprivation, but also from the Home Office, concerned at the apparent lack of social control of the young in the inner cities, as evidenced by vandalism and truancy. This was, moreover, mixed with fears of racial tension and a concern to ensure effective social regulation in plural neighbourhoods (see, for example, Coventry CDP, 1975b, Paper 1, paras 1.1 and 2.2–3).

The implementation of this particular innovation will receive greater attention in the next two chapters and will suggest what would typically be the fate of the wide-ranging programmes of community development proposed by Seebohm. In chapter 5 we shall consider the research findings of the CDPs and, in particular, the change in their diagnosis of deprivation. From an initial dual concern with the supposed social pathology of poor neighbourhoods and with the technical malfunctioning of their public services, the projects have shifted to a diagnosis in terms of wider distributive processes. This has brought a reorientation of their action—with calls for much wider institutional change than initially officially anticipated (Mayo in Lees and Smith, 1975, pp. 15–16). In the view of many of the CDP personnel, it has been this politically contentious reorientation that has contributed to a winding-down of the national experiment. Not all the projects have been allowed to complete their lives and new programmes, such as the Comprehensive Community Projects (for accounts of these, see 'CDPs writ larger' *New Society* 17 July 1975, p. 122), have been substituted. The central information and advice unit has been closed, and thus, although officially sponsored, there may never emerge an official account and evaluation of the overall experience of the CDPs (Cantor, 1976).

Thus, as we shall later argue at greater length, the community development that was central to Seebohm's proposals may typically promote not only mutual aid and the community's control of its members but also the politically more contentious community criticism of wider social processes. Whether or not that criticism is too high a price to pay for the resuscitation of community is then the unanticipated dilemma typically posed for policy-makers. In the case of the CDPs at least, it seems to have been resolved by retreat from the Seebohm reorientation.

Theoretical implications
What are the theoretical implications, then, of these obstacles to the effective implementation of Seebohm? They give some comfort to the *neo-Marxists*. The fate of the CDPs is what the latter would presumably anticipate; in chapter 6 we therefore investigate this in much greater depth. Likewise, Jordan's findings might be interpreted as indicating, first, that within a capitalist society the brute fact of financial poverty will invariably prevent welfare agencies from dealing with other sources of human misery; and second, that differential class access to private services will equally invariably mystify the perceptions of human need held by the personnel of public agencies. To these issues in the professional identification and mediation of needs we return in section VII.

Stronger reservations appear in regard to the *political liberals*. First, Jordan is tracing the substantive irrationality (in Weber's sense) that can arise in social policy, with the implications of developments in one branch for the operation of another unforeseen by the policy-makers in either. Here are indeed constraints and 'necessities' imposed on the concerns of the personal social services; yet they are not so much technical as the (unanticipated) fruit of political decisions. Second, Jordan exposes the dependence of expert perception upon the social context in which it takes place. The welfare professional is not the objective discriminator of individual and societal needs; his own assumptions are socially constructed and reinforced. Finally, the CDP experience—which, to repeat, we consider in much greater detail later—throws doubt on the political liberals' broadly positivistic view of how social science and rational enquiry feed into policy development. Instead, the official response to the CDP findings gives stark contemporary expression to the perennial debate over objectivity and political values in social science and policy research (cf. pp. 189–90 below).

Equally, the foregoing demonstrates how necessary have been some of the modifications in the views of *Social Democratic* writers that we noted in the previous chapter. For example, Jordan's discussion points to the inadequacy of universalism as a vehicle for securing equal realisation of social rights (see above, p. 66). Still further deficiencies in the Social Democratic standpoint are evident, however. First, these writers expect universalist social policies to promote not only social integration but also, *contra* the political liberals, criticism of wider social processes (see above, p. 65). Our discussion of the CDP experience, however, suggests that their optimism over the capacity and willingness of political leaders to heed such criticisms has been misplaced. So, too, they perhaps underestimate the ability and readiness of even Social Democratic political leaders, once they (in Weber's phrase) come to live *off* rather than *for* politics (see above, p. 35), to substitute the 'symbolic uses' of politics[9] for political leadership proper: that is, looking merely for public quiescence rather than for the implementation of a particular societal design. Second, in our discussion of the NHS we concluded that Social Democratic writers have inadequately recognised how the definition of the bureaucratised welfare professional's role and legitimate concerns is itself an essentially political matter. Here we have gone further, pointing to the social construction of his assumptions and perceptions and to the dependence of this construction upon processes of bureaucratic change elsewhere in the Welfare State. Third, as Sinfield (1978) has recently noted, Social Democrats such as Titmuss have tended to neglect the significance of social policy as an instrument of social control. This is a theme on which we concentrate more in chapter 6, but already here we have seen that regulation and direction of the potentially disaffected have been an important concern of those implementing policy, if not always of those initiating it.

V PROPERTY RIGHTS AND SOCIAL VALUES IN HOUSING POLICY

The social security system is concerned principally with the distribution of cash benefits; the NHS, the personal social services and the educational system with the provision of expert service. Housing policy, in contrast, centres upon the allocation of a physical good—capable of constituting a marketed commodity, desired less for its use value than its exchange value. Moreover, its 'distinguishing features ... as compared with other goods are its high capital costs and its extreme durability' (Cullingworth, 1966, p. 15). These, together with its fatefulness for a wide range of life chances, encouraged Weber to see the ownership and control of domestic property as being potentially as important as ownership of industrial property in defining the class structure of a community or society (Gerth and Mills, 1948, pp. 181–2).

Given our general concern with the contemporary role of social policy in a society historically organised in capitalist market terms, i.e. a society in which private appropriation and control of property are accorded fundamental importance, let us focus on some of the implications of recent housing policies for access to such domestic property. For a broad range of *liberal* writers, owner-occupation is a key element in making modern advanced society a property-owning democracy. If diffusion of property ownership and control is no longer possible in respect of the means of production, such diffusion is both possible and desirable for the means of accommodation. For *neo-Marxist* writers, the various housing sectors are organised as a hierarchy, access to which reflects and reinforces class membership. Owner-occupation confers rights from which working-class households are in general excluded (Clarke and Ginsberg, 1976). For *Social Democratic* writers, the multiplicity of housing sectors invites investigation of the possibly contrasting values and objectives embodied in official policy towards them, and of the possible challenge that these policies may pose to traditional definitions of the privileged property rights of the owner-occupier.

Housing policy must be taken as including the state's policies towards each of the three main sectors—owner-occupiers, local authority tenants and private tenants, although, as we shall see, such policy has been far from coherent; rather, policies towards different sectors have developed to some extent independently. As far as privately owned property is concerned, the major change over the last century has been the decline of the private landlord and the rise of the owner-occupier. This change has, moreover, been in considerable measure the fruit of state policies, some involving deliberate discrimination. Rent controls, for example, have reduced the attractiveness of housing as an investment; while tax privileges have encouraged the development of a credit system based on the building societies that caters to the owner-occupier (Nevitt, 1966, Ch. 5; cf. Holmes, 1975).

The development of local authority housing before the First World War was in general confined to the rehousing of families displaced by slum clearance. The provision of working-class housing through a generous system of subsidies introduced in 1919 was intended as a temporary measure, but gradually assumed an increasing role in the total housing market. The most rapid growth of local authority building for general needs was in the post Second World War decade, and was geared to provision for the average family, although the subsequent decade saw the restriction of the local authority programme to particular needs, e.g. slum clearance and rehousing, old people's dwellings and the relief of overcrowding and overspill.

With our initial interest in the significance of private property rights, consider the qualifications for access to these various sectors and the extent to which legal ownership grants unconditional and exclusive control over use. Owner-occupation seems to conform most closely to classical notions of private property rights to ownership and use. An adequate capital deposit, a secure and sufficient income and a life style sufficiently respectable to gain the confidence of a building society serve as the principal criteria for access; rights of use and disposal are extensive. In contrast, the private landlord, in addition to recurrent rent controls, has been subject to growing restrictions on his rights of free disposal of occupied tenancies—most recently in the 1974 Rent Act (see *Legal Action Group Bulletin*, 1975, pp. 211–16). Such restrictions alert us to the continuing redefinition of property rights, with the rights of the tenant to retain his accommodation receiving stronger guarantee from the state at the expense of the owner's civil rights to dispose freely of his property.

In local authority housing, we again find that criteria additional to financial resources seem to determine access and use. Most notably, a wide variety of 'points schemes' are in operation, under which various aspects of the housing circumstances of different households are expressed in terms of an index whose value defines their priority within the queue for council housing. Moreover, provisions for exchange and transfer have served to promote a congruence between changing household needs and the accommodation occupied (Cullingworth, 1969, paras 130–2 and Ch. 5).[10] Here, then, in principle, is a form of access to and movement among houses fundamentally different from that defined by the property rights of owner-occupation. It serves, again, to alert us to the problematic and historically changing definition of rights *vis-à-vis* domestic property. More particularly, it demonstrates the relevance of the distinction drawn by the Social Democratic writers between civil rights and social rights as principles of life chance allocation. While, however, housing may thus be distributed among council tenants on the basis not primarily of their incomes but rather of their housing need, it remains the case that council properties tend in certain important respects to offer inferior accommodation to that of the owner-occupier sector (see Parker, 1975, pp. 110–13)[11] and that such tenants are drawn principally from the lower social classes (Cullingworth, 1965, Table 9)—notwithstanding moves away from a 'working class only' philosophy of public provision (Cullingworth, 1969, para. 48). To this extent, neo-Marxist claims in regard to the class distribution of housing retain plausibility.

If, however, we take some of the Cullingworth Report's recommendations for reform of local authority housing policy as defining the continuing agenda for policy formulation and choice,[12] the significance of this distinction between the values embodied in the promotion of owner-occupation and those informing council house allocation becomes clearer—as does the contrast between the exercise of civil and social rights. First, Cullingworth argued that in its housing policy the local authority should take an overall view of housing—attending not only to such traditional concerns as slum clearance and overcrowding, but also to changing needs and provision in all housing sectors in its area. Moreover, 'unlike the private sector, which is concerned with immediate market demands, local housing authorities should be looking for hidden needs, for needs which are not being met elsewhere and for needs which may arise in the future (1969, paras 32–3, 39).[13] Second, Cullingworth clarified the relationship between housing provision and individual choice. He argued that allocation procedures frequently remain unpublicised, and that housing officials who visit prospective tenants tend to evaluate them in terms of their likely behaviour patterns and suitability for different qualities of house, rather than seeking to inform clients of the range of choice open to them.[14] The citizen's choice is to this extent unnecessarily—and, in Cullingworth's view, undesirably—restricted and controlled. Here, then, is a policy debate that can hardly be propounded in terms of civil rights of property ownership and control, as liberal and neo-Marxist writers would typically claim. Rather, it concerns the definition of what the Social Democratic writers would term social rights—with the content of the latter in practice, however, depending crucially on the degree of participation granted to citizens in the decision-making processes that affect them.

Lastly, Cullingworth urged a rationalisation of the fragmented and varied methods of rent determination. He went beyond many other proposals for reform in urging that such a rationalised system should take account not only of tenants' incomes, but also of the quality of the houses they occupy, so that tenants may have some choice over the proportion of their incomes they pay on housing (1969, paras 75, 87–105). Yet such rationalisation, as attempted in the Housing Finance Act of 1972, has highlighted certain further issues of central relevance to any discussion of contemporary policy-making in housing. This Act has been described as 'the most ambitious attempt . . . to recast the country's fragmented, and often capriciously inequitable, housing system, according to consistent, logical principles' ('Housing Finance Act 1972: A Guide' *New Society* 28 December 1972, pp. 734–7).[15] It followed the main lines of the scheme proposed by Nevitt (1966, Ch. 10)—conspicuously omitting, however, her advocacy of a reduction in tax relief to owner-occupiers and housing associations as a precondition for equity among tenure groups (cf. Crouch and Wolf, 'Inequality in Housing' in Townsend and Bosanquet, 1972, pp. 32ff.). In particular, it extended the principle of 'fair rents', already operating for many private tenancies, to local authority housing and 'controlled' private tenancies. All tenants were to be eligible for a means-tested allowance; differences and inequities would thus be eliminated between the treatment received by tenants in the public and private sectors. Such attempted rationalisation, however, served to expose the conflicting values hitherto coexisting in different branches of a fragmented housing policy.[16] *Contra* the political liberals, this suggests that the rationalisation of fragmented social measures cannot typically be portrayed as a purely technical matter. In retaining the tax privileges of the owner-occupier and in promoting a general rise in rents (notwithstanding the new allowances), it constituted a mode of rationalisation that gave emphasis to market power as against housing needs—and to civil as against social rights—in determining housing provision (Parker, 1975, p. 120; Haddon, 'A New System of Housing Subsidies' in K. Jones, 1973).

The implications of contemporary housing policies for domestic property rights can be further explored via two case studies in redevelopment.

1. *Property rights and professional interests in Sunderland*

Dennis, in his study of Sunderland (1970; 1972) enquires into the processes whereby decisions are reached over the demolition of urban areas and the rehousing of their residents. He is particularly interested in the sources and types of information used in policy formulation; in the processes of legitimation of decisions; and in the relationships among professionals, local politicians and citizens. He first clarifies the implications for these various issues of a commitment to the more adequate provision for residents' housing needs; second, he examines in what respects the actual planning process involved significantly different forms of information, modes of legitimation and political relationships; finally, he teases out the actual objectives of the planning process underlying the latter.

(i) Dennis starts, then, by seeking to characterise housing needs. First, housing conditions affect residents' health. In the 1930s, slum clearance decisions were predicated principally upon public health criteria of habitability. Such decisions were legitimated in terms of the ability of the public health official, on the basis of his professional expertise, to make a judgement on houses' habitability (1970, pp. 150–2);[17] and there was little or no place for residents or local politicians in the decision to demolish. Yet in the programmes of the 1960s, habitability neither was, nor could have been, invoked in justification of many of the demolition programmes (1970, Chs 12–14, 18). Consequently, Dennis argues, if the latter were indeed oriented to residents' needs, it must have been to needs other than physical health—such as the social networks and the privacy whose quality is crucially affected by housing conditions. Yet these needs are far more subjective than are health needs; 'and the decision-maker has no way of knowing anything at all about the social values which are embedded in the situation except by familiarising himself with them through the words and other symbolic behaviour of the people concerned'. This, in turn, 'connotes control of the decision-maker to ensure that the values which are incorporated in any scheme'—in terms, for example, of that scheme's effects on neighbourhood networks and on the inter- and intra-household privacy people enjoy—'are those of the people affected by it'. Moreover, Dennis argues that long-term planning decisions cannot be portrayed as mere technical forecasts of what is required for smooth adjustment to changing external conditions; rather, they involve essentially political choices among alternative housing—and hence social—futures. Here, then, are certain requirements that must be met by the policy-making process if its results are to be legitimated as rational means of promoting residents' housing needs. Among the types of indispensable information are not only the objective and technical 'knowledge of the externally observable structures' but also households' varied social preferences; among the required political relationships is effective participation by residents and their political representatives (1970, pp. 353–4, 74, 107–11, 269, 291). Dennis here demonstrates that active citizenship and (substantively) rational policy-making not merely can coexist, but are moreover mutually indispensable partners. He thereby vindicates and refines a major thesis of the Social Democrats (see above, p. 80).

(ii) Dennis goes on to examine the actual planning process in Sunderland during the 1960s, and the way in which, for example, choices were made between demolition and rehousing (involving dispersal to new estates) on the one hand and maintenance and redevelopment *in situ* on the other. To start with, the recognition of the resident as a necessary commentator upon essentially subjective needs seems to have been absent—even though the planners sought to legitimate their programmes in terms of people's housing needs. Consultation was seen by decision-makers as irrelevant to rational policy-making: 'if expertise and democracy were at variance, so much the worse for democracy' (1972, p. 244). Likewise, the planners viewed interference by political representatives as implicitly challenging their scientific expertise. That expertise was sufficient, they considered, to legitimate their decisions scientifically and politically.[18]

The result was a violation of residents' civil, political and social rights. First, lack of consultation and apparently capricious postponements of publicly declared demolition dates exacerbated planning 'blight'. The publishing of demolition proposals is bound to reduce property values; yet periodic postponement meant that houses that eventually were allowed to stand sufficiently long to have been eligible for maintenance grants, had this 'life' been anticipated from the start, failed to qualify and suffered unnecessarily rapid deterioration and loss of value (1972, Ch. 4). Many residents in the area studied were owner-occupiers; here we observe how their civil rights to use and freely dispose of their property were crucially dependent upon the planning process and could not be abstracted from the residents' political rights *vis-à-vis* that process. Second, however, Dennis shows how those political rights were themselves usurped—with the planners denying any role to the citizens themselves or their political representatives. Finally, the social right to enjoy certain standards in relation to the needs that housing serves was in many important respects compromised. For example, many of those rehoused (or facing rehousing) faced a loss of internal space and hence ability to accommodate guests and maintain former social networks, the break-up of well-established community networks through dispersal, and reduced privacy (1970, pp. 258, 262–8).

(iii) Towards what goal, then, were the Sunderland programmes *actually* oriented? Why were demolition and rehousing favoured far more than residents would themselves have wished and why were the planners' 'projections . . . systematically biased in the direction of a much larger population than careful examination would allow'? Dennis argues, *inter alia*, that such grandiose programmes were selected because they meant 'improved prospects of departmental growth, with the associated benefits of . . . more rapid promotion' (1970, p. 75; cf. pp. 336–7). To the pursuit of such ends, participation by local politicians and citizens is essentially irrelevant and potentially threatening; while apparently capricious rescheduling of programmes makes sense only when they are seen as a means to departmental growth. Thus the definition of the function and competence of the professional—in this case, the planner—is itself a political question, for it concerns their authority, discretion and legitimate activity.

Theoretical implications
It is, perhaps, to the arguments of the *political liberals* that Dennis's

study is most obviously relevant. It stands as a direct critique of their belief, for example, that policy-making can be reduced to a purely technical process in which democratic participation by citizens and political value choices by politicians have no essential place. At least at this local level, it suggests that a variety of futures was available; the constraints defined by changes in the wider society could hardly be said to be so tight and clearly defined as to render political judgements obsolete. Some *market liberals* have hailed Dennis's study as justifying their claim that welfare state bureaucracies serve principally the interests of their staff, as a vested interest group. Yet their claim is surely more specific than this—namely, that the concern of such groups is with obtaining an excessive share of narrowly economic rewards, where 'excessive' is judged by reference to some hypothetical equilibrium distribution. Dennis's discussion in no way supports the meaningfulness or usefulness of the latter criterion, and it reveals the significance of such goals as departmental growth and professional status as against merely economic concerns. As against the *neo-Marxists*, there is little evidence here of any propertied class moulding policy; indeed, their arguments seem remarkably irrelevant for Dennis's perspicacious and highly critical investigation. As for the *Social Democrats*, Dennis's investigation develops further the analysis of political rights and other rights of citizenship begun by Marshall, exploring the various possible roles for active participation in policy development. At the same time, however, he provides a further corrective to the Social Democrats' tendency to treat the bureaucratised welfare professional as benign and their relative neglect of social policy as a potential instrument of social regimentation and control.

2.   Property rights and industrial interests in Coventry

The main thrust of our discussion so far has been the implications of recent housing—and rehousing—policy for the rights of residents. We have argued that analysis of access to and use of housing requires that we recognise, with the Social Democratic writers, the significance of social and political as well as civil rights. Moreover, the definition and exercise of even such civil rights cannot be portrayed as absolute and unconditional, but have come, rather, to be significantly and unavoidably dependent upon the professional and political activities of policy-makers. Thus an investigation of contemporary housing policy reveals its essentially political context, with the powers and rights of citizens and policy-makers irreducible to explanation in the terms commonly employed by liberal and neo-Marxist writers. Our second case study goes further, however, in exploring *inter alia* the relationship to such powers and rights in domestic property of those in industrial property. It, too, centres upon redevelopment policies at the local level—even though it emerges out of the research concerns of one of the Community Development Projects referred to in the previous section. The Coventry team has been especially concerned to investigate the development of land use policy in an inner city area where competition for space is intense. Their findings provide interesting parallels—but also contrasts—with those of Dennis.

Just as Dennis's interest was initially aroused by the discrepancy between the ostensible goals of redevelopment policies and their actual consequences, so too the Coventry researchers started with the paradox of redevelopment in the neighbourhood of Hillfields. The Corporation has undoubted management and planning skills, which have been used in drawing up a succession of 'sophisticated plans for the comprehensive physical renewal of the area'; such plans have been presented as a top priority for the city throughout the post-war period. Yet the achievement has been protracted, piecemeal and puny in the face of the area's social and economic decline (Coventry CDP, 1975a, para. 6.22; cf para. 7.38). Benington and his colleagues therefore seek to clarify (i) the constraints that may have impeded the translation of programme into actuality, (ii) the possibly covert goals of policy-makers within these constraints, and (iii) the implications for redevelopment programmes of the prevailing relationships among professional planners, local politicians and industrialists.

(i) First, then, rapid population growth over the last half-century, induced by rapid industrial expansion, has 'put enormous pressure on the city's housing and basic services'—particularly in such central areas as Hillfields. Such pressures were greatly exacerbated by war-time bomb damage and problems of reconstruction. Growth in the rateable value of the city, however, has been reduced, first by war-time damage to property and second by the exodus of middle- and upper-income groups beyond the city boundaries. Furthermore, recurrent economic crises have induced periodic central government restrictions on urban redevelopment and house build-ing. Still, within these tight constraints the renewal of Hillfields has remained high on the list of publicly affirmed priorities (Coventry CDP, 1975a, paras 7.30, 7.33, 7.39).

(ii) Benington goes on to argue that, in their programmes for Hillfields and similar areas, policy-makers have in practice pursued three related objectives. First, in their forward plans for land use and capital expenditure they have been concerned to provide a 'calculable' economic environment for the private construction industry. More generally, the local authority has provided 'social capital [including] the basic infrastructure . . . needed by industry to support its phenomenal and profitable expansion'. Second, Hill-fields has provided prime land, the scarcest economic resource in the inner city. Redevelopment programmes have therefore increas-ingly been informed less by the housing and other needs of the Hillfields residents than by the Corporation's participation in the competition for its increasingly valuable land. Finally, rescheduling of redevelopment programmes has proved a politically uncontentious—or at least uncontested—and technically simple way of responding to fluctuations in the financial resources made available to the city by central government (Coventry CDP, 1975a, paras 7.41–5; 1975b, Paper 7, paras 3.1, 3.3).

(iii) The Coventry study, like that of Dennis, scrutinises the legiti-macy and status of professional judgements. More particularly, Benington focusses on the implications of introducing such new decision-making techniques as programme planning and budgeting.[19] The latter seems, *prima facie*, a particularly clear manifestation of the iterative model sketched at the start of section I, for it involves the clear choice of objectives, specified in terms of targets that can be operationalised empirically, a selection of par-ticular measures, chosen in part on the basis of what has been learnt in implementing previous measures, and continuing scrutiny and monitoring of performance. It typically carries with it the elabora-tion of medium- and long-term social plans, in which the choice of outputs and the weighing of alternative possible strategies for their attainment are made explicit. Its increasing use in central, as well as local, government policy-making has been a marked feature of the last decade (Self, 1975, pp. 178–87).

Yet, as Klein observes, 'the intellectual tools used will influence and may even determine the policies adopted' (1972, p. 270). This is Benington's concern. He scrutinised each element in the rational policy-making process that these new forms of corporate management supposedly promote. The specification of objectives and targets may, admittedly, be explicit. Yet, Benington argues, these are typically defined with little regard to any expressions of preferences and needs by the populations affected or their political representatives. Instead, targets are generally specified by reference to central government statutes and recommendations, which are more likely to express professional than consumer interests. Choice among objectives then tends to appear, not as a political decision over priorities and over the weight to be given to the interests of different affected groups in the city, but rather as a depoliticised designation of departmental targets. Likewise, the selection among alternative possible measures is indeed made explicit; yet 'the array of alternatives brought forward for political consideration will have been filtered already through professional presuppositions, stereotypes and value judgements'. Measures that threaten local authority professionals as a group are especially unlikely to reach the political agenda. Furthermore, while the monitoring of performance is integral to these modes of policy-making, it typically takes the form of measuring activity rates in different services. Just as the initial definition of needs and objectives tends to take little account of political priorities and consumer preferences, so too there is little monitoring of the receipt, quality and effectiveness of services on the ground. Lastly, the associated advocacy of long-term, large-scale and broad-grain social planning tends to conceal the conflicts of interest among different local groups, to impute a homogeneity of needs and preferences to diverse populations, and to limit the range of political choices to those that can be made at a macro level (Coventry CDP, 1975b, Paper 7, paras 6.3–6.6).[20]

Benington concludes, then, that the typical consequences of the intrusion of such managerial techniques into social policy-making are at least threefold. First, a spurious legitimacy is lent to what is no less than the usurpation of essentially political decisions by technically sophisticated experts. The general knowledge and technical expertise of the professional are given improper weight relative to the councillor's 'specialist knowledge about the ward he represents and about the overall needs of other groups whose interest he shares'. Second, these techniques tend not to clarify but to obscure the political implications of different policies. The major social, economic and physical consequences of the latter may then appear, like the decisions themselves, not as politically chosen but as technically necessary. Third, 'the removal of strategic issues . . . into the upper levels of metropolitan and regional government allows new sets of relationships to be developed between public and private interests'. Commercial and industrial interests are likely to attain privileged access to key decision-making (Coventry CDP, 1975b, Paper 7, paras 5.4 and 4).

Theoretical implications

What observations does this second case study provoke for our competing perspectives on social policy in industrial society? Dennis's critique of *liberal* writers here finds parallels too obvious to require further rehearsal. Benington's demonstration of the dependence of policy direction upon the degree of citizen participation is in line with *Social Democratic* arguments, although his analysis of professional usurpation of that participation goes beyond what such writers have often provided. Yet the study also suggests strengths in the *neo-Marxist* case that merit more extended attention (and that indicate that Dennis might with profit have investigated, for example, the relationships between industrial interests and redevelopment planners in Sunderland). Thus, in regard to housing, the team conclude that 'in spite of the Council's best attempts, the interests of private capital . . . cannot be challenged and controlled adequately by the present powers and procedures available to the Local Authority' (1975b, Paper 2, para. 3.13). Indeed, even if the latter had the will to mount such a challenge, it would not have had access to many key issues and decisions. For, as seen above, these are filtered before reaching the political arena or are camouflaged as technical matters, becoming easily influenced by industrial and commercial interests. Here, then, would seem to be clear demonstration of how the state apparatus selects only those social measures that coincide with the interests of capital. Moreover, with increasing competition for such scarce inner-city land as that of Hillfields, the gap between the local authority's public priorities for the neighbourhood and the policies actually undertaken has grown. Here is the increasing contradiction that O'Connor espies in the dual role of social policy—the facilitation of private accumulation and the disguising of the immiseration that results. A legitimation crisis is upon us (see pp. 44–5, 48 above).

Nevertheless, this vindication of the neo-Marxists is less than total. First, the Coventry team seem to exhibit an *a priori* commitment to this neo-Marxist position, in that while they concede that their findings admit of a variety of theoretical interpretations, it is the neo-Marxist case alone that they expound. For example, the role of the state—or in this case, the local authority—in providing a 'calculable' economic environment for industrial enterprise is taken as supporting such neo-Marxist economists as Baran and Sweezy (Coventry CDP, 1975b, Paper 7, para. 2.2; cf. p. 43 above); omitting to point out that the provision of calculability has been no less central to the analyses of the state offered by such political liberals as Galbraith (1967, Chs 26–27). Likewise, the gloss put upon local authority provision of social infrastructure is explicitly that of O'Connor—without, however, rigorous justification of this choice (Coventry CDP, 1975b, Paper 7, para. 3.1).

Second, one would wish to explore the alleged 'new sets of relationships . . . between public and private interests (see above, p. 126) before one could speak of some local ruling class based on common economic interests, as neo-Marxists would typically wish. For the policy developments that Benington traces, while they may have served local industrial and commercial interests, are mediated by welfare professionals and local politicians; the neo-Marxist must, therefore, make clear what guarantees the continuing allegiance of the latter to those interests. (The Liverpool CDP has been particularly critical of this view of local authority subservience—see below, p. 225.) Third, in pointing to the limited ability of the local authority to challenge and control the interests of private capital, Benington locates this incapacity within the context of 'the present powers and procedures available to the Local Authority' (see above, p. 126). He thereby places it within its wider national political and legal context; he leaves open the possibilities for, and the effects of, changes in those powers and procedures.

Finally, and perhaps most interestingly for our purposes, we should observe that the instigation of the CDP was itself an act of professional and political will and commitment, albeit predicated upon assumptions and involving strategies subsequently rejected by the CDP itself. The principal fruit of the project was a critique of the assumption that there was a wide community of interest between industry on the one hand and the residents of Hillfields on the other. Indeed, the critique extends beyond the residents of the project area to Coventry city at large, challenging the traditional assumption that 'what is good for industry . . . must be good for the city as a whole' (Coventry CDP, 1975b, Paper 7, para. 3.2). One may speculate, therefore, that if national and local political and professional concern over city 'black-spots' becomes a normal feature of social policy-making and is perceived by political leaders and welfare professionals as a precondition for legitimation of their authority (cf. chapter 6, sections IV and V below), and if the Coventry experience with agencies established to deal with such areas is at all typical, then such professional and political commitment will encounter, as a perennial dilemma for the relation of public to private power, the exposure of conflicts of interest between private national and international commercial and industrial interests on the one hand and the city's residents, resources and services on the other.

Admittedly, such neo-Marxists as O'Connor might claim that this is nothing other than the developing crisis of which they speak, with policy-makers engaged in continuing and growing efforts at legitimising the dominant capitalist order, but with decreasing success. Such efforts as the CDPs then epitomise the 'contradictions' of late capitalism, displaced into the state sector (cf. p. 48 above). Nevertheless, these neo-Marxists leave unclear how demystification of societal arrangements is supposed to proceed among the subordinate classes, promoting action directed at societal transformation. It cannot, moreover, be assumed that the conditions for retaining professional and political legitimacy coincide—or are even compatible—with those for legitimation of the wider socio-economic order. It is not, then, the legitimacy of a well-integrated 'system' that is under consideration, but rather that of diverse actors and their potentially rival claims to authority (cf. pp. 72–3 above). The patterns of likely action by welfare professionals and political leaders in such a developing crisis must therefore be made clearer; this is likely to make even an appeal to the 'relative autonomy' of the state insufficient to retain a recognisably Marxist analysis. Rather, it is the questions raised by such writers as Weber that are thrust to the fore: questions that as yet have been only superficially addressed by any of the main writers and schools discussed in chapter 3. To these issues we return in later chapters.

VI EQUALITY OF EDUCATION OPPORTUNITY: POLITICAL
IDEOLOGY AND PUBLIC KNOWLEDGE

As we saw in chapter 2, the later part of the nineteenth century saw
a shift within the dominant liberal ideology of British society
towards an emphasis upon the state's role in developing, through
education, an enlightened and rational citizenry able and willing to
exercise its new rights responsibly. Equal—but compulsory
—access to educational opportunities would promote both social
and economic progress (see above, p. 33). 'Equality of opportunity'
has, indeed, provided the goal, slogan and ideology in terms of
which educational reform has most commonly been espoused and
evaluated over the last century. Or, as a recent survey of educational policy in the twentieth century concludes, it has married the
dual commitment to equality and national efficiency: 'Efficiency for
modernity. Equality for efficiency and justice' (Halsey, 1972a, p.
6). As ideology or as myth, it has had its own momentum; yet its
elusive, ambivalent and pregnant character has permitted profound
changes in its referent and in the measures deemed necessary for its
realisation, as the pattern of interests shaping the educational
system has changed.

We focus on three post-war developments in the evolving redefinition of 'equality of opportunity'—each principally concerned
with a different tier of the educational system.

(i) The 1944 Act established universal free compulsory education
up to the age of 15. It aimed to provide, within this framework,
equal opportunity for each child to develop his or her capacities; the
requirements of social equity and national economic efficiency
would thereby simultaneously be met. The contemporary
psychological literature suggested that children's inherent abilities
could be reliably measured at an early age and that such ability
could in general be classified in terms of three categories. In the
implementation of the Act, this encouraged a tripartite educational
system in most local authorities and the use of selection—in general
on a once-and-for-all basis—at age 11. Children of academic ability
were alone to be sent to grammar schools; the latter's technical
education functions were largely to be removed, and the variation in
their pupils' intellectual abilities reduced. Bureaucratic criteria of
measured ability were to be the sole overt determinants of alloca-

tion in the public secondary education system, in the hope of achieving 'a dominantly selective system of education based on equality of opportunity [which] denies the relevance of class in education while satisfying the requirements of a complex division of labour' (Halsey, 'The Sociology of Education' in Smelser, 1973, p. 260).

The aim of the 1944 Act was that each secondary sector 'should have such parity as amenities and conditions can bestow. Parity of esteem cannot be conferred by administrative decree . . . ; it can only be won by the school itself' (quoted in Banks, 1955, p. 14). Yet in two complementary respects the tripartite system—and its real-isation of equal opportunity—came under increasing attack. First, educational psychologists questioned whether children's abilities can be reliably measured on a once-for-all basis at age 11 and also the evidence for three types of ability, corresponding to the three sectors of secondary education. Second, it became evident that the prestige of each sector derived not so much from the adequacy with which it developed its pupils' capacities, but rather from the prestige of the occupations to which it granted access. Banks argues that the grammar schools remained associated with the prestigious occupa-tions; 'and while that association continues, both administrators and educators will fail to equate parity of conditions with parity of esteem'. Thus because 'the driving force in the demand for educa-tion has been the desire for status rather than for education as such' (Banks, 1955, pp. 203, 4), status inequalities among secondary educational sectors reflected those among occupations in the wider society. Such prestige differences, moreover, tended to attract teachers to the grammar schools, further compromising equality of opportunity (Halsey, 1972b, Table 6.11).

Here, then, was a twofold challenge to post-war equality of opportunity that was central to the cases made out for comprehen-sivisation. The latter was meant to permit continuous re-evaluation of children's abilities and educational needs, and to extend to all children in secondary education the opportunity for recruitment to the coveted higher levels of the social and economic hierarchy. The foregoing discussion has, however, more general implications for our conceptualisation of 'equal opportunity'. For it suggests a conflict, within a hierarchical society having wide differentials of authority, material reward and prestige, between the provision to each child of opportunities to develop his or her capacities and the

provision of equal opportunity to gain access to advantaged positions within the wider society. It also—a closely related
point—points to some of the ways in which the wider society may
constrain and mould what is counted as a worthwhile and legitimate
concern of the educator; for we have traced how the perceived
fatefulness of pupils' formal credentials for their subsequent life
chances has tended to reduce the priority given in schools to
pursuits that are not of an orthodox academic character. More
general investigation of the organisation and control of what is
counted as knowledge and of its dependence on wider societal
processes has provided the central theme of the recently developing
'new' sociology of education (see, for example, Young, 1971).

(ii) The investigations by the Robbins Committee and others of the
effects of the 1944 reforms indicated persisting strong class gradients in educational achievement within the state system (Robbins,
1963, esp. Appendix 1).[21] The 1944 Act had not eliminated the
influence of personal economic circumstances on educational
achievement: for example, high rates of early leaving by working-
class children were partly caused by the inadequacy of maintenance
grants for the 15–18 age group. It was also increasingly accepted
that class inequalities in 'cultural resources', rather than in inherent
ability, were largely responsible for class variations in education
attainment.[22]

In consequence, the Plowden Report (1967) recommended that
priority areas be designated for positive discrimination, especially
at pre-school and primary stages.[23] In defining such areas, the
Report 'suggested a tentative list of significant factors relating to
occupation, family size, the receipt of state benefits, housing conditions, poor school attendance, the proportion of handicapped children in ordinary schools, incomplete families and children unable to
speak English' (Halsey, 1972a, p. 32). The devotion of extra
educational resources to such areas was intended to counter class
variations in 'cultural resources', thereby ensuring greater equality
of educational outcomes between priority and non-priority areas.
Here, then, was a second challenge to the 1944 notion of equal
opportunity and its assumptions as to the appropriate path to such a
goal. Equality of average outcomes among the members of broad
non-educationally defined categories was to be the *ex post* indicator
of whether equality of opportunity had truly been enjoyed by the

individuals concerned (Halsey, 1972a, pp. 8, 31). It was, moreover, *this* redefined notion of equal opportunity that was required by the dual commitment to social equity and optimal utilisation of national manpower resources.

The commitment to positive discrimination constituted the apogee of post-war official hopes that educational measures could by themselves serve to effect a major shift towards a more equal society and towards the elimination of deprivation: towards a fundamental modification, that is, of the prevailing patterns of power and advantage. These were expectations common to many political liberals and Social Democrats. Experience of implementing such reforms has tended, however, to promote pessimism as to the impact of positive discrimination alone. Halsey, admittedly, concludes from his evaluation of positive discrimination in Britain that 'pre-schooling is the outstandingly economical and effective device in the general approach to raising educational standards in the E.P.A.s' (1972a, p. 180); and joins Smith and Little (1971) in challenging the conventional view of the failure of American programmes such as Head Start (1972a, Ch. 2). Nevertheless, these American views have been reinforced by such subsequent studies as Jencks' *Inequality* (1975),[24] although the policy inferences drawn from the latter range from a resurgence of geneticist accounts of educational achievement[25] to demands for social reform on a much broader front than the merely educational.

On the other hand, the British experience has pointed, more positively, to the 'community school' as 'the *essential* principle along with that of positive discrimination in a policy for educational priority areas'. Rather than such areas having schools that, as Plowden proposed, would be the best within a nationally uniform system, 'the community school seeks almost to obliterate the boundary between school and community'. Indeed, it becomes 'the organisation and process of learning through all of the social relationships into which an individual enters at any point in his lifetime' (Halsey, 1972a, pp. 189, 31). Such an additional element is 'essential' in priority education in the sense that only thereby, as experience within the EPA action–research projects demonstrates, can the objectives of priority education, as originally specified by Plowden, be achieved. It carries the idea, not of 'compensating' for a background seen in essentially negative terms, but rather of complementing and partnering those local community institutions and learning situations (Midwinter, 1972, esp. Chs 1 and 7; Bernstein, 'Education Cannot Compensate for Society' in Rubenstein and Stoneman, 1972). It points, then, to the implementation of social policy as being essentially dependent upon the active involvement of the citizens concerned; and questions the viability of 'reform from above' as espoused in political liberalism and the Fabian strand of Social Democracy (see above, p. 38).

In turn, however, the question is then posed of the wider quality of life in the community concerned—and hence of the wider social and economic policies to be pursued. Community education thereby raises fundamental political questions over priorities and participation—questions more suitably explored in chapter 6, where our concern is with social integration and conflict. Let us simply note Halsey's conclusion, fundamentally relevant to any discussion of the meaning, implementation and fruits of equality of educational opportunity:

> The schools cannot accomplish important social reforms ... unless social reforms accompany the educational effort. [Indeed], the schools are hampered in achieving even their more traditional and strictly 'educational' purposes when in societies changing rapidly in their technologies and in the aspirations of their populations, a comparable effort to make the required change in social structure and political organisation is lacking. [1972a, p. 8]

(iii) Our discussion so far has been of educational reforms that have actually been implemented and evaluated. Yet with the most recent major official enquiry into equal opportunity, the Russell Report of 1973, we encounter a further redefinition that has yet to be implemented. On the other hand, the report's proposals are rooted in an analysis of existing educational measures and cannot therefore be disregarded as mere recommendations for policy development.

Thus Russell starts by highlighting still further barriers to equity and efficiency in our existing educational provisions. First, it has become evident that not only individuals' desires, but also their abilities, to profit from post-secondary education may be delayed into adulthood; on pedagogical grounds education should not be the preserve of the young. Second, inter-generational equity dictates that contemporary expanded resources and new techniques be made available to the young of previous decades as well as of the present. Finally, the continuous technological change characteristic of modern society emphasises the need for life-long re-educational opportunities for all, as a counter to technological unemployment and monopoly by the young of the most recently developed skills, and as a means to optimal overall programmes of human invest-ment (Russell, 1973, paras 8, 26, 46.1, 34).

Russell therefore concludes that equal opportunity properly requires that post-secondary education no longer operate on a strict year and grade basis. This would involve 'a new kind of citizenship right adjusted to the realities of a rapidly changing society'. For each citizen would be granted 'a claim on education . . . which . . . he may choose to fit into his own life cycle and his preferences for patterns of work and recreation', rather than having to demonstrate, through possession of recognised credentials, his meriting access to highly standardised selective educational programmes. This contrasts markedly, then, with such meritocratic equality of opportunity as that of the 1944 Act, which tended to promote 'extreme inequality in the allocation or resources between the educationally successful and the unsuccessful', in accordance with its dominantly selective function *vis-à-vis* the occupational hierarchy (OECD, 1971, p. 17).

No less than in the case of community election, recurrent educa-tion would be dependent for its success on a commitment to wider social, political and economic reform. At an organisational level, for example, the individual's choice of his educational biography would depend on the flexibility and responsiveness not only of the educa-tional system, but also of the occupational, to his successive entries and exits.

Not, however, that the cases made out for such reform are limited to a redefined equality of opportunity. Russell portrays recurrent education as the natural complement to community education and development. It is likely to promote educationally informed homes, most fundamentally by inculcating 'a positive belief in the value of learning', as parents find it 'relevant to their chosen aspirations and the quality of their lives'. This adult education is also necessary if the voluntary action to which Seebohm looks as a partner to profession-al provision is to be equipped with 'skill and understanding based on firm knowledge'. More generally, however, 'the cohesion and sense of identity of a local community depends largely on the vitality of the groupings that compose it; and one of the functions of adult education will be to form and sustain such groupings and to promote their interraction' (Russell, 1973, paras 46.2, 38, 64).

Theoretical implications

(i) To the extent that these educational reforms *have* been implemented, to what end is policy directed? If the 1834 Poor Law was predicated upon a conception of the ideal citizen as an able-bodied adult legally free to offer his labour power and goods for sale in a universal market place, recent educational policy seems predicated upon an alternative conception—that of an individual choosing a life path of personal self-development through social, political and economic institutions. Nationally uniform application of 'less eligibility' and the workhouse test enforced progressive realisation of the former ideal. Promotion of the latter is the fruit of a resource allocation for equality of outcome among a variety of non-educationally defined groups, and of pedagogical facilities and agents responsive to individuals' particular needs and preferences. As therefore, in our discussion of Seebohm (see p. 109 above), here is the enunciation of a view of man-in-society that differs significantly from that of the liberals and neo-Marxists but is consonant with that implicit in the Social Democratic writers.

(ii) Our account suggests a process of learning-by-doing, in which the evaluation of existing measures and of the changes they have wrought provides a basis for reforms aimed at more adequate realisation of objectives. The Robbins, Plowden and Halsey Reports exemplify this public evaluation, in which there is an officially legitimated redefinition of the political alternatives facing the society—in this case, in respect of education—and of the measures appropriate to each. It is, indeed, the growing incorporation of social scientists' expertise that most dramatically expresses this learning process (see Halsey, 1972a, esp. Chs 1 and 13; Halsey, 'Government against Poverty in School and Community', in Wedderburn, 1974). With such learning integral to developments in education policy, any ahistorical systemic approach—such as is often implicit in liberal and neo-Marxist accounts—is put fundamentally in question. Rather, it is the Social Democratic account of contemporary policy development, in terms of a process of collective learning and responsible choice, that is lent some credence (see above, p. 80).

Not, of course, that this process of learning-by-doing is free from the oft-rehearsed problems of objectivity and political values. Indeed, the incorporation of social science into state policy-making may have significant effects on its concerns and approaches (Karabel and Halsey, 1977, pp. 5–8). Here, however, it is on another qualification that we focus. This process of learning may indeed have promoted perennial redefinition of the political agenda, with the key question being 'the willingness and power of ... society to define education imperiously in relation to the other social organisations which carry educative or culturally transmitting functions' (Halsey, 1972a, p. 5). Yet that willingness and power cannot be taken for granted; the learning process in political debate and public scrutiny cannot be assumed effectual in policy implementation. Rather, as we have noted in earlier criticisms of the Social Democratic account, it is necessary to identify what groupings of actors are available as potential vehicles to press effectively for such changes as may be highlighted in this public debate, and the conditions under which political leaders are likely to live for—rather than merely off—politics (cf. pp. 95, 114 above).

(iii) Three further questions thus arise—although we can only touch on them here. First, to what extent *have* reforms thus revealed as necessary in the educational system and the wider society actually been implemented? Comprehensivisation has been slow and is as yet incomplete; positive discrimination remains paltry and the Halsey recommendations on community education have yet to receive government backing; Russell's proposals seem to have little prospect of implementation, at least during the present austerity.

Second, how is this implementation or non-implementation to be explained politically—that is, in terms of the power mobilised by interested groups and organisations? One would properly need, for example, to investigate the interests advanced by the teachers' unions and local authorities, the social, economic and political constraints upon successive governments, and, not least, the political reverberations of the professional and social unrest that has been generated by—or anticipated from—such reforms as comprehensivisation, the community schools and recurrent adult education.[26] The last of these will form one of our concerns in chapter 6. In principle, the results of this investigation could be related to the political liberals' appeal to the technical necessities of social development, the market liberals' appeal to sectional interests and the neo-Marxists' citation of capitalist interests as the effective determinants of policy development. Against all these accounts stands that of the Social Democratic writers, claiming that policy development has to some extent a *sui generis* character, with the learning process we discerned in public debate effectual because the continuation of popular support depends upon the lessons learned being implemented.

Third, what have been—and are likely to be—the consequences of such non-implementation? Halsey points to some of the likely implications of failing to extend community schooling: continuing under-achievement and low parental involvement. Only in chapter 6, however, will we investigate whether non-implementation of officially sponsored lessons can also pose threats to the political legitimacy of policy-makers—and, indeed, the political system as a whole—in the eyes of the population affected. Here is a range of questions that seem in general to be neglected by neo-Marxist and liberal writers; and that, while more consonant with the concerns of the Social Democratic writers, have hardly been explored in any depth.

For example, we are alerted to the relationships between political leaders and their supporters and hence to the possible role of political leadership in mobilising support for new policies. It likewise encourages enquiry into the relationship between the significance of social policies for the legitimation of the economic system—a central concern of neo-Marxists—and their significance for the legitimation of the political order. For example, it may be that not only the official and public evaluation of positive discriminatory measures (the Halsey Report) but also politicians' *responses* to the Report's findings—notably in respect of community schools—carry crucial implications for the political legitimation of policy. In this case, our earlier discussion suggests (see above, p. 133), the continuing political legitimacy of the policy-making process would require the choice of policy options whose likely consequence is a challenge to the legitimacy of wider distributive arrangements, including the economic and occupational. Nevertheless, such questions can properly be answered only when we have considered the patterns of group formation and action that social policy strategies evoke—the theme of chapter 6.

VII CONCLUSION

In this final section, we do not recall our findings in detail, but simply draw out some of the more important implications for the competing theories of social policy development in Western industrial societies.

(i) As *neo-Marxists* would claim it is, first, true that this development seems to have been significantly oriented to the interests of the powerful and advantaged. Yet the latter include those welfare professionals who are themselves the creation of social policy and the political leaders who are its nominal instigators. It is far from clear that self-interest or external constraint secure their subservience to the interests of the propertied ruling class of the Marxist tradition. (Indeed, we have questioned whether there can be said to be any long-term collective interest of capital to which the state's policies can, even in principle, be oriented.) Our discussion has, admittedly, impinged on this only partially (see, for example, pp. 101–2 above). It would, for example, be of interest to investigate empirically how similar are the patterns of selection and how close the social intercourse between the propertied and managerial elite of private industry and commerce and the public policy-makers and agents we have encountered here.[27] Nevertheless, we have argued that developments in social policy may typically—but in unanticipated ways—render such constellations of interest fragile, disrupting rather than cementing them (see, for example, pp. 127–8, 137 above). (Such has also been the American experience recounted by Marris and Rein—Rein, 1970, Ch. 11; Marris and Rein, 1974, Ch. 6.) The patterns of action by welfare professionals and political leaders in relation to the owners and controllers of industrial property cannot then be subsumed under any simple, *a priori*, generalisation. Rather, they must be matters for empirical investigation; and this we shall attempt further in subsequent chapters.

Second, for neo-Marxists the continuing pursuit of private profit remains the dominant orientation of social action. The social policies of the capitalist state involve no contrary objective. We, however, have pointed to certain recent policy developments that would hardly seem aimed at providing the social infrastructure for capital accumulation or social control of the population. For example, a major aim in the 1974 reorganisation of the NHS was a shift of resources to the chronically sick; while current pensions reform includes attempts at a redistribution of power to employees (see above, pp. 99–100, 89). (On the other hand, these may as yet be little more than statements of intent; and the winding-down of other developments that tend to challenge the wider social order have loomed as large in our discussion: see above, pp. 112–3, 136). Further, we have argued that even if and where social measures *are* undertaken in the interests of capitalist industry, they typically modify the goals, powers and expectations of the various groups involved, promoting—or at least permitting—reorientation of the measures concerned. Equal educational opportunity may indeed in part have been pursued because of its role in promoting economic efficiency; yet its further pursuit may now be both a precondition for popular legitimation of the political order and corrosive of wider distributive arrangements (see above, pp. 136–7). Lastly, of course, even the instigation and adaptation of social measures for industrial expansion and economic growth—such as the human investment of chapter 2—leave open whether or not such expansion is dominated by the pursuit of exchange value, as in classical Marxist portrayals of capitalist development; although we have perforce left this issue untouched.

Third, central to neo-Marxist accounts of societal development is the role of the working class—including the trade unions; although, as we argued in chapter 3, it is at times unclear how actively and effectively it is seen as having instigated social measures. As to the *effects* of social policies upon working-class formation and consciousness, neo-Marxists seem equally unagreed (see above, pp. 45–8). Given this lack of clarity we have, perhaps, been justified in limiting our explicit mention of working-class organisations to the area of pensions reform. There we argued that interests advanced by such organisations have tended to be inchoate in the absence of properly political leadership; it is again inadequate, therefore, to portray the political as essentially secondary and derived (see above, p. 91; cf. p. 34).

(ii) While recognising the way in which changing socio-economic conditions have provided material for debate over policy development, our studies have also posed serious problems for the *political liberals'* view of policy development. First, our findings question whether societal demands dictate the policies chosen and their specific orientation. We have offered several historically oriented studies of policy choices among a variety of options where there does seem to have been a real 'openness' to the situation, and where it is meaningful for subsequent policy evaluation to trace out significantly different consequences that would have followed had an alternative policy been chosen.[28] For example, our analysis of the NHS suggested that the retention of a tripartite system was fateful for the subsequent treatment of the chronically sick, especially dependent as these are upon efficient coordination of the various health services. If it is argued that in the circumstances of 1948 no abandonment of the tripartite system was feasible, it must be recognised that this infeasibility sprang, not from a lack of techniques or from broader demands of societal functioning, but rather from the political pressures of interested groups of medical professionals. Likewise, Dennis retrospectively exposes an alternative possible orientation for planning policy from that actually adopted, and the significantly different treatment of people's housing needs that would have ensued. He argues that, far from such an alternative having been infeasible as a result of wider technical constraints, its availability was obscured as a result of usurpation by planners of an essentially political role. More generally, the policy options we have encountered seem to involve widely differing societal futures. For they have concerned the rights and obligations of citizenship, the relative priority of market valuations and human needs in determining the level of provision to be made, and the definition of the individuals whose needs are to be taken as the direct concern of the state.

Second, the political liberals seem confident of the professional and the expert as the guardians of society, and of their capacity to perceive and implement such systematic social policies as may promote comfortable adjustment to societal dictates. We, however, have argued that social policy increasingly involves not a reactive but a creative and transformative activity *vis-à-vis* the wider urban–industrial society. Exogenous development of this society can no longer suffice as an explanation of developments in social policy. Furthermore, the apparently technical systematisation or rationalisation of policy has frequently tended to promote increased awareness of the perennial conflicts in social policy (see, for example, p. 118 and Note 16 above). Moreover, the welfare professional's knowledge and prescriptions, far from being objective and neutral, are socially constructed and located, while his proposals and action must be understood as in part oriented to his own power and advantage (see above, pp. 101–2, 113–4).

(iii) The activity of the welfare professional is no less central to the *market liberals*' perspective on policy development: he is one of the principal actors in terms of whose self-interest state welfare has supposedly been substituted for market provision. However, recent social policy developments exhibit a growing emphasis upon optimal utilisation of scarce professional resources, involving continuing redefinition of skills as techniques change, the organisation of services among different agencies according to the main professional skill involved and, finally, coordination of these various professionals for the effective and efficient treatment of frequently coexisting needs. This is a rationale of resource allocation and organisation that is powerfully oriented to the effective provision of outputs and treatment of needs (DHSS, 1970, paras 13–17, 31, 42–52; Seebohm, 1968, paras 226, 303, 325–8, 414–23; Cullingworth, 1969, paras 106–16). Professional self-aggrandisement can hardly suffice as an explanation. Additionally, and *contra* the market liberals, we have argued that sectional greed may express itself in the attempted *extension* of the sphere of the market (see, for example, pp. 91–2 above); that professional status and the control of resources may be as prized goals of bureaucratised welfare professionals as an 'excessive' share of extrinsic economic rewards (see, for example, pp. 107–8, 122 above); and that rational justifications of increased state intervention in social policy have often centred on the collective interest and on considerations of economic efficiency (see, for example, p. 107 above).

Admittedly, we have seen that the mediation of needs by professionals puts in question the coincidence between their interests and those of their clients. It also renders problematic the proper lines of authority and political control, and makes the direction of policy implementation crucially dependent upon the manner in which these professionals use their autonomy and discretion. Yet in previous sections we have hardly found such professional interests and action readily explicable in terms of liberal—or, indeed, neo-Marxist—accounts (see above, pp. 100–2, 107–8, 121–2, 127–8).

Concluding these criticisms of the market liberals, three conceptual weaknesses merit recall. First, the social policies of recent decades display a concern with needs that could not, even in principle, be surrendered to market distribution—for they are esoteric, hidden to the individuals concerned and requiring the mediation of the professional expert. Second, various of the ahistorical and abstract notions typically used by the market liberals, especially in their frequently normative writings, have proved of doubtful relevance; a properly historical perspective on such categories is necessary. This we found in the case of individual autonomy, freedom and needs, as also in our definition of property rights of ownership and control (see above, pp. 109, 116, 122–3). Finally, recent social policies seem increasingly concerned with the creation and development of the capacities of all citizens, rather than with the mere repair of damaged capacities; the traditional liberal assumption of the abstract individual possessing given initial endowments thereby loses verisimilitude.

(iv) In contrast, this chapter has lent some support to the *Social Democrats*. They propound social policy development as a process of collective learning and action on the part of the populace as a whole, who are involved in active partnership with legislators. Such development is therefore *sui generis*, not wholly reducible to explanation as the derivative of wider social forces, to which citizens merely react. Against such writers as Heclo (see pp. 89–90 above), however, they portray this process of learning as irreducibly political: different groups and organisations mobilise various forms of power to secure acceptance of their readings of past, and their justifications of future, measures (see above, pp. 60–1); the lessons learned are an immanent critique of wider social, political and economic arrangements; and, as we shall consider more extensively in chapter 6, the mobilisation of popular support is dependent upon the justification of policy by reference to what has been thus publicly learned (see above, pp. 136–7).

However, our investigation has also displayed qualifications to this view.

(a) The readiness of political leaders to implement these collective lessons must not be taken for granted; for they may instead pursue the 'symbolic uses' of politics, aiming simply at public quiescence. Indeed, the visibility of the lessons themselves is subject to manipulation by the powerful and may, again, be deliberately restricted in the interests of maintaining popular passivity (see above, pp. 112–14). Citizens are here excluded from policy formation and allocated a merely reactive role. What such excluded groups 'learn' is therefore merely their own incapacity to influence the social policies that impinge upon them. The typical responses to such a realisation and the conditions under which such reactive quiescence can be effected—in short, the possible uses of social policies as means of social control (see above, pp. 114, 122)—will be explored in chapter 6. Only there, therefore, shall we be able to complete our evaluation of the significance of popular debate and acquiescence for policy development (see above, pp. 79–80).

(b) We have touched on all three of the practical disappointments and theoretical weaknesses met by Social Democracy since its heyday in the 1940s and noted in the previous chapter (see above, p. 66). First, we have traced the failure of the universalist policies to secure equal appropriation of social rights; instead, their exercise seems at least as much to reflect and reinforce, rather than to reduce, wider inequalities of power and advantage (see above, pp. 94, 114). Second, we have pointed to the concentrations of power exercised by public and private decision-makers, including bureaucratised welfare professionals, that reduce citizens' capacity to enforce the substantive rationality of policy development through exercise of their political and social rights (see above, pp. 94, 102, 114, 119ff.). Finally, we have touched on individuals' reluctance to subordinate their self-interest to the obligations of citizenship, especially where individual acquisition of property and educational qualifications is authoritatively prescribed in the wider society—and even within such spheres of universalist social policy as the educational system (see above, pp. 94–5).

(c) We have argued that in consequence of these two sets of weaknesses, the Social Democrats have been over-optimistic as to the acceptability of their societal designs and too little concerned with identifying social agents having both the will and the capacity to implement them (see above, pp. 95, 136). They have, moreover, failed to spell out sufficiently how those social policies must, to be realised, reach far beyond the social services into the reproduction and transformation of social stratification and political order as a whole (see above, pp. 95, 133–4). To these issues we return.

Finally, our discussion has raised questions for treatment in chapters 5 and 6. We have seen how social policy-making has typically involved recurring evaluation of past measures, notably in terms of the inequalities in life chances among different social groups and in treatment of different needs by various social policy agencies. Such inequalities are the focus of attention in chapter 5. We have also referred to the dependence of policy outcomes upon the responses not only of social policy personnel but also of the individual citizens and communities with whom the policies are concerned. We must investigate the typical patterns of such response—and, not least, the way in which they depend upon past, present and proposed future social policy strategies. Indeed, this helps to justify our attention in this chapter to policy alternatives and futures currently mooted but not yet implemented. For in clarifying the policy innovations currently proposed—albeit with varying enthusiasm—by competing political leaders, we prepare to consider how, in a relatively 'open' situation, the pursuit of a particular social policy strategy—and hence, as we have argued, the promotion of a particular societal future—may be dependent upon the articulation by political leaders of hitherto unvoiced possibilities and upon the mass response that such articulation may mobilise (cf. Goldthorpe *et al.*, 1969, pp. 187–95). It is with these issues, *inter alia*, that we are concerned in chapter 6. There we shall also take up a further theme touched on here: namely, the legitimation of social policy-making and the implications of social policy developments for the legitimation of the wider socio-economic order.

NOTES

1. In addition, of course, developments in one branch of income maintenance policy may have important implications for the other branches: see, for example, Hall *et al.* (1975) Ch. 14.
2. Although in other respects women received improved treatment: see, for example, Lynes (1969) pp. 7–8.
3. On the other hand, French arrangements for occupational or 'complementary' pensions show that the alternatives enunciated by the Crossman and Joseph plans cannot be regarded as the only two broad directions open to an advanced Western society: see Lynes (1967) esp. Ch. 6 and pp. 153–4.
4. Amalgamation of the health and personal social services was rejected, in part as endangering the clinical freedom of the medical professionals (DHSS, 1970, paras 18–19, 65–8).
5. Townsend (1974) in the immediate aftermath of reorganisation, surveys the power of hospital consultants and the social and occupational background of members of the regional health authorities and finds Abel-Smith's fears amply justified.
6. For an American study of the conflicting interests of bureaucratised health administrators and medical professionals, see Alford (1975) esp. Ch. 5. Their contentious interrelationship was a principal concern of DHSS (1972) and has recently been briefly investigated in Heller (1978).
7. This is, of course, a major theme of the sociological tradition—see, for example, Durkheim's continuing concern with egoism and anomie (see above, pp. 36–7).
8. Townsend, however, criticises Seebohm for failing to explicate fully the political and other implications of such community development—for example, 'is the social worker an agent of social control or an articulate representative of minority

interests and views?' (1970, pp. 15–16). We shall take up such questions in chapter 6.

9. The phrase is Edelman's (1964). For an application in the sphere of health policy, see Alford (1975).

10. For discussion of the continuing relevance of the policy issues highlighted by Cullingworth, see M. Smith (1975).

11. In regard to basic amenities, however, see Cullingworth (1965) Table 3.

12. Department of the Environment (DoE) (1977) echoes many of Cullingworth's themes.

13. Notable among these emerging needs are single people and young adult households (Cullingworth, 1969, paras 26, 309–11), who have been especially affected by the decline in the private rented sector, with its substantial number of one-bedroom dwellings and its wide variety of sizes and types (Cullingworth, 1965, p. 22). See too DoE (1977) Ch. 12.

14. For an empirical study of such 'grading' by housing visitors, see Jacobs, 'Rehousing in Glasgow' in Jones and Mayo (1975).

15. For fuller discussion of the Act's provisions, see Spencer (1973).

16: Cf. Goldthorpe's argument that the search for agreed principles in incomes policies may well serve to clarify the conflicts of interest over the distribution of life chances and rewards, hitherto confused and obscure ('Social Inequality and Social Integration in Modern Britain' in Wedderburn, 1974, esp. p. 228).

17. Although Dennis does point to the wide variation among local authorities in the criteria of habitability (1970, Ch. 7)—the latter is not wholly objective and unambiguous.

18. Dennis also discusses critically the exaggerated claims advanced by the planners in regard to the reliability of their forecasts, which they saw as inviolable to challenge by 'lay' people. See too Dennis (1978).

19. A similar concern has been marked in the Liverpool CDP: see National CDP (1974) para. 5.29.

20. For a parallel discussion, see Edwards (1975).

21. For education as a whole, these gradients were even stronger, owing to the virtual exclusion of the working class from the private sector of education (Halsey, 1972b, Table 6.22).

22. Cf. Halsey and Floud (1957) on the contribution to class gradients of teachers' assessments and other culturally loaded tests.

23. This was imitative of such American programmes as Head Start: see Halsey, 1972a, Ch. 2.

24. For reviews and critiques of Jencks, see 'Perspectives on Inequality' *Harvard Educational Review* February 1973, pp. 37–164.

25. Such is, at least, the expectation of some of Jencks' critics: see Edmonds *et al.* in *Harvard Educational Review* February 1973.

26. Some recent attempts at these questions are available. Kogan (1975) looks at the expansion of higher education and comprehensivisation over the period 1960–74, identifying the various interest groups involved and their access to consultation by government.

27. For a review of the literature, see Goldthorpe and Bevan (1977). From a neo-Marxist standpoint, see Nichols' investigation of the cohesiveness of such propertied and managerial elites (1970, esp. Chs 10–12), Harris's account of the Conservative Party's enduring role in securing the recruitment and cohesion of these various elites (1972, esp. pp. 263–8), and Westergaard and Resler (1976) pp. 252–61.

28. Cf. Weber's discussion of the use of counterfactuals in historical explanation (1949, esp. Ch. 3).

CHAPTER 5

The Social Division of Welfare

Arithmetic has its uses, but neither the injuries inflicted by inequality nor the benefits conferred by diminishing it can be reliably ascertained by sums in long division. [R. H. Tawney Equality p. 219]

I INTRODUCTION

Classical liberal and Marxist analyses of the cash nexus and of its role in defining group interests provided a second theme in Part I. It is the constrasting sets of propositions advanced by contemporary liberals, neo-Marxists and Social Democrats on the relationship of social policy to the cash nexus that we now investigate. In chapter 2 it was, moreover, seen how classical analyses of group interests led on to a concern with group formation, social integration and social transformation—the third theme of Part I. The present chapter will likewise lead on to the empirical investigation in chapter 6 of the impact of social policies upon group formation and conflict.

These various schools of thought agree in recognising the 1834 Poor Law as epitomising a social policy supportive of laissez-faire capitalism. As a distributive system, it was to rely on the twin principles of 'less eligibility' and the abolition of outdoor relief. This reformed system was intended to be not the challenge to the dominant market order its predecessor had been, but, rather, subordinate to that order: the gradient of life chance outcomes between employed and idle would be restored; the elimination of the possibility that those in employment might secure outdoor relief ensured that market valuations of different employed individuals would likewise be restored to the pre-eminence that was properly theirs. Nor did the Poor Law challenge the disregard by the cash nexus of variations in the number of dependants of a bread-winner, and its disregard of the very existence of the unemployed. For, on the one hand, it did not acknowledge the possible failure of the dominant market order to guarantee adequate employment opportunities at a wage level sufficient for subsistence needs; on the other hand, it did not recognise that there might be any contradiction in principle between providing each pauper family with its subsistence needs and ensuring that the cost of the latter was less than the labour market rewards which the family's chief breadwinner could earn in independent employment. Thus, the overall pattern of distributive outcomes in the society as a whole would express and embody the values of the market place: those values would not only reign unchallenged over the life chances of the employed, but would also define the parameters for provision of relief to the destitute.

Neo-Marxist writers typically view contemporary social policies as a distributive mechanism no less subordinate to the dictates of the dominant market order than was the social policy legislation of 1834. In the criteria of eligibility, in the level and quality of benefit granted and in their impact upon distributive outcomes, such social policies reflect and reinforce market values. Moreover, following Marx's immiseration thesis and his more general view of the inequities suffered by the proletariat, neo-Marxists argue that it is precisely the section of the population—namely the working class—experiencing disproportionately the depradations of capitalism that *also* receives least favoured treatment. Social policies and the market place constitute a single, well-integrated distributive system, within which access to life chances is, for the mass of the population who own little or no property, heavily dependent upon the market value of their labour power. An individual's position within the social division of welfare therefore remains derivative of his position within the social division of labour, which continues to define individual and class interests. Moreover, such subordination cannot but continue to prevail while there is private ownership and control of the means of production.

Contemporary *market liberals* propose a definition of need and a level of provision for social policies that accepts, like the 1834 legislation, the priority of the market as a distributive mechanism and measure of values. Their discussion of the distributive role of social policies is therefore often couched in normative terms, critical of what they see as the significantly different role actually played by contemporary policies. We may, however, in part re-state their arguments in terms that appear in principle amenable to empirical investigation. First, they postulate that a sufficient criterion of need for state aid, in cash and in kind, is a specified low level of income. Unlike the Poor Law provisions they do not, of course, advocate entry to the workhouse as a condition of relief that will deter those not truly in destitution; rather, they typically favour rigorous means-testing. Here, then, as in the 1834 legislation, the cash nexus and the valuations of the labour market are to be pre-eminent: an individual's money income from that market is taken as indicating either his inclusion among the minority of the population requiring state assistance or else, in the case of the majority, the life chances distributed by the market to which he, on grounds of equity and social efficiency, is entitled. As for the level of provision that state social policies should ensure, market liberals advocate a basic minimum or 'safety-net': an argument harking back to the 'less eligibility' principle of the Poor Law. Expressed in less normative terms, market liberals are arguing that for any of the benefits distributed to individuals through social policies, it is possible to distinguish—and to justify this distinction—between that basic level of provision strictly necessary for social existence and supplementation of the latter. Finally, in regard to the overall pattern of distributive outcomes in such a market-dominated society, an optimism prevails as to the long-term consequences of economic growth in a capitalist market system. In particular, such growth may be expected to eliminate need and poverty without the aid of redistributive social policies; the safety-net provided by present-day Welfare States will be required by a declining proportion of the population. Some writers appear to go even further, arguing that such growth may additionally be expected to produce a more general trend towards equality in life chances.

Political liberals tend to be less concerned to demarcate the appropriate realms of the market and state social policies. The distributive justice that, for the market liberal, is the fruit of continuing dominance of the cash nexus, is seen by the political liberal as being the result of free access, not so much to the economic market place as to the political 'market place'. Moreover, such free access to the political arena is a sufficient condition for the elimination of political value-judgements from social policy definitions of need and of the appropriate level of provision. As to the overall patterns of distributive outcomes in the life chances with which these social policies deal, an optimism is prevalent at least as great as that of market liberals. As barriers to meritocracy are progressively removed and an equality of opportunity realised, a trend to greater equality in life chances may confidently be expected and is, indeed, already apparent. By neither group of liberals, therefore, are the social policies appropriate to a modern advanced urban–industrial society seen as involving distributive principles fundamentally and necessarily in conflict with the wider market society. They are, rather, seen as subordinate or complementary to it. As such they promote and reinforce an identity of interests among all citizens, who enjoy free access to the economic and/or political arenas.

For the *Social Democrats*, it is neither methodologically sound nor empirically very illuminating to treat the distribution of life chances in our society as being dictated by a unified, coherent distributive system. Rather, the overall pattern of distributive outcomes must be understood and accounted for as the net result of individuals' access to, and outcomes within, a variety of distributive institutions. These include two of particular importance: the market and social policy agencies. Within the former, individuals exercise their civil rights; within the latter, their social. The subordination of the exercise of one set of rights to exercise of the other—and hence the existence of a unified and relatively well-integrated overall distributive system—cannot be assumed *a priori*, but must, rather, be a matter for empirical investigation.

What then, are the principal differences in perspective and argument from the neo-Marxist and liberal standpoints summarised above?

(i) First, it must be conceded that Social Democrats have been somewhat uncertain and varied in their reactions to the neo-Marxist claim that class gradients in distributive outcome have not been reduced by the advent of the Welfare State. They seem in general to have held optimistic expectations at its institution; but subsequent investigation and evaluation suggested that, notwithstanding an apparent egalitarian trend, 'ancient inequalities had assumed subtler and more sophisticated forms' (Titmuss, Introduction to Tawney, 1964, pp. 10–11). Thus as we saw in chapter 3, over the post-war period they have tended to lose confidence in the *sufficiency* of universalist services to reduce inequalities, while continuing, however, to insist on their necessity (see above, p. 66). Over the last fifteen years, theirs have been among the foremost investigations that have furnished ammunition for the neo-Marxist case (see, for example, Titmuss, 1962).

Nevertheless, their arguments do differ significantly and fundamentally from those of the neo-Marxists. One difference concerns the criteria by which the significance of inequalities in life chance outcomes is to be judged. In classical Marxism, such inequalities derive their significance principally from their implications for individual and class interests. The immiseration that accompanies capital accumulation ensures that this conflict of objective interests progressively increases in intensity. For the neo-Marxist, it is sufficient to point to the continuing class gradients in outcome as evidencing at least no reversal of the process of immiseration. For the Social Democrat, in contrast, the significance of these persisting inequalities is more problematic: they are the net result of individuals' experience of a variety of distributive agencies, whose systemic integration cannot be presupposed. Consequently, it becomes necessary to explore the definition of individuals' interests and the loci of conflict in these various milieux. The free exercise of civil rights, whose peculiar domain is the market place, may indeed tend to promote an increasing conflict of objective interest between those owning property in the means of production and those whose only marketable commodity is their labour power. In respect of social rights, however, a fundamentally different delineation of interests may in principle be possible. More particularly, the Social Democrats argue that universalist social policies establish areas of common interest. In this case, the inequalities deriving from individuals' differing market and work situations will not necessarily have the same significance as inequalities in the enjoyment of social rights.

Second, the Social Democrats affirm, no less than the neo-Marxists, the desirability of the distributive principle 'to each according to his needs'. They argue, however, that the prior socialisation of the means of production is neither a necessary nor a sufficient condition for the realisation of this principle. Rather, it is through the attempted extension and enrichment of social rights that the specific character of market-imposed obstacles to its realisation are laid bare and a programme for such socialisation and public control as may be necessary is actively developed. Hence, such attempted enrichment represents the immanent practical critique of market values and distributive principles demanded by classical Marxism, avoiding the utopian tendencies of many neo-Marxists.

(ii) The Social Democratic arguments also contrast with those advanced by liberals. First, Titmuss has been a particularly strong critic of liberal expectations of the elimination of need through the automatic development of a market-centred urban–industrial society (1968, Chs 11, 12). He argues, on the one hand, that the inequalities of income and wealth generated by the market appear to have diminished little in this century (Introduction to Tawney, 1964), and, on the other hand, that the depradations and social costs generated by accelerating socio-economic change are likely to be increasingly fateful for individuals' life chances. Without preventive and redistributive social policies, therefore, he sees no evidence that greater equality of life chances is likely (1974, Ch. 5). Yet he also fears that even such policies tend to be accompanied by the expansion of 'fiscal welfare' distributed through the personal taxation system and of 'occupational welfare' enjoyed unequally by different categories of employee. Both tend to be regressive in their impact (1963, Ch. 2).

Second, the Social Democrats deny, *contra* the market liberals, that need for state aid is sufficiently and validly indicated by criteria of income; and, *contra* the political liberals, that need and merit in respect of access to social services are sufficiently indicated by apolitical, technical criteria. The political liberal errs in neglecting the value-judgements implicit in the unavoidable ranking of different needs; the market liberal fails to make explicit the value-judgement implicit in surrendering this ranking to the dictates of market power. Finally, the Social Democrats refuse to accept that some basic minimum level of provision can, even in principle, be defined in absolute terms as the appropriate standard for state aid, in contrast to the market liberals in particular. They argue, rather, that the substantive content of social rights is unavoidably determined by continuing political value-judgements over the quality of that common life to which all citizens should be guaranteed access.

The first line of enquiry appropriate to this chapter is, therefore, an exploration of the distributive principles and outcomes in different branches of social policy, although for reasons of space, we must confine ourselves to detailed examination of only one, namely health care. Extrapolation of our conclusions must therefore be cautious. However, a second line of investigation is also relevant. Instead of focussing on some branch of social policy, we consider the overall life chances typically enjoyed by individuals variously situated in our society. More specifically, it was the poor—or, more strictly, the destitute paupers—whose overall circumstances of life were the particular concern of the Poor Law. Since, therefore, all the schools of thought in which we are interested take the 1834 policy as a criterion for evaluating that of today, in section III we focus on the overall life situation of the poor in the contemporary Welfare State. We leave to the start of that section any rehearsal of the competing perspectives on such poverty and its treatment.

II THE SOCIAL DISTRIBUTION OF MORBIDITY AND MEDICAL CARE

Health policy has preventive, ameliorative and curative functions. There may be inequalities in the extent of need, i.e. in morbidity, as well as inequalities in the treatment of need, i.e. medical care. The former may be affected by preventive and promotive measures, such as environmental improvements and health education. The latter, on the other hand, concern ameliorative and curative measures. The health of a particular individual or group, and thus the extent of his or their continuing need for medical care, will depend, first, on the morbidity of that group and, second, on access to, and quality of, treatment for that particular morbid condition.

There is an extensive literature on the distribution of health needs and treatment but we do not attempt any extended review (see Halsey, 1972b, Ch. 11; Parker, 1975, Ch. 5). Rather, we limit ourselves to the empirical evidence of relevance to the contrasting arguments set out in section I on the definition of needs, the level of state provision and the overall pattern of distributive outcomes. This then permits some evaluation of these various theories' analyses of the implications of contemporary social policies for individual and group interests. Two principal impressions emerge from such recent surveys: (i) the data available are of only limited use and do not permit confident and reliable judgements to be made;[1] (ii) there appear to be continuing marked class inequalities in morbidity and care, notwithstanding several decades of a National Health Service. Both points are relevant to our present concerns.

(i) Three main types of information on the pattern of morbidity are available (Morris, 1964, has here been a seminal work). In the first place, mortality statistics provide relatively reliable information on the age, sex and class distributions of death from various specified causes. However, by themselves such data are likely to be of only limited use as indicators of the general morbidity of different social categories, for many diseases and disabilities can of course vary greatly in their severity and in fatalities. Second, information (collected principally by the various branches of the health service) is available on the use of health service facilities—for example, General Practitioner consultation rates among different social categories. Yet such data may be unreliable as indicators of morbidity: different social groups may have different self-medication practices, different abilities to recognise symptoms, different tolerances of pain and different attitudes to the available National Health Service facilities—or even knowledge of their existence. Programmes of multiple screening of the general public have revealed considerable unrecognised morbidity (Cooper, 1975, p. 13). Furthermore, there may be medically irrelevant factors influencing consultation rates: for example, working-class patients are more likely to need sick notes for employers. Moreover, studies that rely on information concerning the use of a single branch of the health services (e.g. GP consultation rates) will have their reliability further reduced if different social groups differ in their preferences among these various branches. That these two measures, morbidity and consultation rates, have little systematic relationship to one another is suggested by Rein's comparison (1969), for diseases with a class mortality gradient, of the death rates and consultation rates; his results indicate no clear pattern whatever. Neither of these two indices, therefore, seems adequate by itself; possibly some combination might be of value (Cf. Culyer *et al.* 'Health Indicators' in Shonfield and Shaw, 1972, pp. 100–2). Third, surveys have been undertaken to ascertain people's own assessments of their morbidity. Yet again, the reliability of this information will be vitiated to the extent that members of different social groups vary in their typical perception of symptoms and their tolerance of pain.

The information available on health care and its distribution among different social categories is of similarly limited reliability. The quality and effectiveness of treatment would appear intractable to reliable direct measurement. Instead, studies of the distribution of health care typically rely upon measures of inputs of various kinds—medical personnel, hospital beds, etc.—and assess input variations among different specialisms and medical conditions and among different regions and social classes (Parker, 1975, Ch. 5).

(ii) Two main aspects of inequality in morbidity and treatment have received particular attention in the literature: those among different regions and those among different social classes. In addition, the relative resources devoted to different morbid conditions have been of concern. It is the differences among social classes that are of initial interest here, given the criteria of relevance developed in section I. We consider in turn the available measures of differential class morbidity and of treatment received.

Morbidity

It seems clear that different disabilities exhibit different class distributions: there are 'diseases of the rich' as well as 'diseases of poverty' (Arie, 1966). The latter, deriving principally from economic and environmental deprivation, include ulcers, hernia, bronchitis and pneumonia. The 'new' diseases of the rich, such as coronary disease, in part owe their increasing prevalence to increased life expectancy: chronic degenerative disease is more common in the upper and middle classes, with their older age structures. In addition, however, occupational stresses of men in these classes—in particular, nervous strain and sedentary work situations—seem to be a contributory factor. (This is suggested also by the fact that middle-class women suffer coronary disease relatively little, yet at an increasing rate, paralleling the rising female labour force participation ratio.) For some disabilities, the class pattern appears to vary markedly among different age groups. Logan, for example, finds that the class gradient for mental illness involves higher rates for lower social classes in younger age groups, but a reversal of this gradient above the age of sixty-five (Logan and Cushion, 1958–62; cf. Rein, 1969); which suggests—perhaps not

surprisingly—that the principal causes may be significantly different for these different age groups. Morbidity, therefore, must be
recognised as a multi-dimensional phenomenon, with class gradients varying a great deal for different disabilities. Nevertheless, as
already noted, it is the older age structure in higher socio-economic
categories that accounts in some measure for the concentration of
degenerative conditions in these groups. That classes differ in their
patterns of morbidity does not, therefore, necessarily imply that for
any given age group the class gradients for these various forms of
disability exhibit similar variations.

The foregoing generalisations may be supplemented and supported by reference to findings based on the various indicators of
morbidity discussed earlier. Parker finds significant class gradients
in mortality for several major forms of disability; although for
coronary disease, no clear gradient appears.[2] Overall mortality
rates exhibit marked class gradients, although the change in these
since the 1930s is a matter of dispute (Parker, 1975, pp. 73–4,
covering the period 1930/2–1959/63).[3] So also do infant mortality
rates (Parker, 1975, p. 74, for the period 1949–64; cf. Halsey,
1972b, Table 11.9) and stillbirth rates,[4] and the latter gradient
appears to have widened in the post-war period (Parker, 1975,
p. 74, citing evidence on the period 1949–64). In contrast, the
social class gradient in childhood deaths narrowed considerably
during the period 1930–50 (Arie, 1966).

Evidence of differential class usage of health services—such as
General Practitioner consultation and hospitalisation rates—serves
to supplement such comparisons of mortality, although problems of
interpretation and validity are especially great. The establishment
of the National Health Service involved the formal elimination, but
for the retention of a small private sector, of the cash nexus between
patient and doctor. Among the reformers' intentions was that
consultations should henceforth reflect medical need rather than
ability to pay. In addition, therefore, to investigation of class
consultation rates and changes in these over recent decades, there
has been a continuing debate over the extent to which the reformers' intention has indeed been realised, with consultation rates
providing valid indicators of morbidity. This debate has led on to
investigations of the social processes whereby such validity may be
undermined even in the absence of a cash nexus. For the moment,
however, we simply record some of the broad conclusions on

consultation rates, as an indicator—of greater or lesser validity—of morbidity.

For General Practitioner consultations, highest rates in the mid-1950s seem to have been among members of social class III (Parker, 1975, p. 76; Halsey, 1972b, Table 11.17). However, fifteen years later it was the lower social classes that exhibited the highest rates (Parker, 1975, p. 76, citing the *General Household Survey*).[5] Class gradients in consultation rates vary among disabilities. They are marked in the case of bronchitis and cancer, where lower social classes consult considerably more frequently than the upper, but are not in evidence for various other complaints (Halsey, 1972b, Table 11.18).[6]

Hospitalisation rates are another indicator of facility use whose relationship to morbidity is debatable. During the first decade of the NHS, Abel-Smith and Titmuss found that hospitalisation rates corresponded to social class proportions in the population (1956, p. 149). In contrast, Carstairs' data on Scotland give a strong class gradient both for admission rates and for mean stay. Carstairs argues that this greater use of hospitals by lower social classes reflects a lack of home amenities and/or greater prevalence among the lower social classes of certain *chronic* diseases—hospitals become a substitute for better housing, etc. (1966; the data refer to 1963). The influence of such non-medical factors upon need for and use of hospitalisation is also highlighted by Abel-Smith and Titmuss, when they argue that for the aged and mentally ill 'the existence or otherwise of surviving husbands, wives or children is perhaps the most important single social factor governing the amount and distribution by age and sex of demand for hospital care' (1956, pp. 146–7). That is, hospitalisation rates for these categories are especially high for the single, widowed and divorced.

Finally, the morbidity of different classes is to some extent revealed through surveys of people's own assessments of their state of health. Over a wide range of chronic illnesses, the *General Household Survey* indicates strong class gradients in reported disability. Resulting absenteeism exhibits similarly strong gradients (Gough, 1970, p. 213). Overall, then, notwithstanding the inadequacies of the available information, there are grounds for suggesting that, while the morbidity of each age group has been reduced for all social classes over recent decades, class gradients have changed little in respect of many major disabilities. Without giving any detailed treatment, because of their limited relevance to our present concerns, we may observe that regional variations in morbidity are also marked and persistent—although in some measure regional and class variations overlap, inhabitants of the South and East suffering least debilitation (Parker, 1975, pp. 74–6).

Levels of treatment and allocation of health care resources
Prior to the establishment of the National Health Service, such resources were very inadequate and were maldistributed both geographically and functionally (Eckstein, 1958, Chs 2, 3). Hospitals and consultants were highly concentrated in metropolitan areas, accessible (at least geographically) to the lower classes; but General Practitioners and other non-institutional services were more concentrated in middle-class areas, partly because of their reliance on a private patient clientele for an adequate income. Functionally, there were shortages of hospital and specialist facilities for chronic illnesses, and surpluses in other fields. These defects were exacerbated by the lack of coordination of voluntary and public hospitals and many of the former were very small, unable to enjoy economies of scale. Moreover, such charitable foundations were unable to exploit to the full the rapid advances that were taking place in medical science, on account of their limited funds; public institutions were likewise constrained by the limitations of local authority funds. For the General Practitioners, few of whom worked in partnerships, the costliness of new equipment incorporating the latest medical advances meant that clinical conditions were often severely deficient. Reliable information on the class distribution of treatment is again limited and fragmented. Access to health care, however, was class dependent in two particularly obvious ways: first, the middle class was excluded from the National Insurance Scheme; and second, the voluntary hospitals, which included all the teaching hospitals, came to be associated with technical sophistication, a contrast being apparent between the standard of treatment they offered and that granted in public institutions to a predominantly lower-class clientele.

Attempts under the NHS to deal with such regional disparities appear to have met with only limited success. Designation of under-doctored areas produced some improvement in the 1950s, but this proved only temporary (Parker, 1975, p. 77; Butler and Knight, 1974); other resources have no better a record. In general, it is the South and South-East that are most privileged across a wide range of medical care resources: regional disparities in one resource appear not to be counterbalanced by compensating disparities in others, but rather reinforced (Cooper, 1975, pp. 60–72).

Within this general context of marked regional variations (which, favouring the South and South-East, probably also favour the middle and upper social classes), significant inequalities are evident in the treatment accorded to different morbid conditions, as also in the treatment received by members of different social classes suffering the same disability. Within the hospital service, long-standing inferiorities in geriatric and psychiatric medicine and mental care are especially glaring (Townsend, 1974). Of course, different forms of disability require different forms of treatment, which in turn require different combinations of health care resource. Strictly speaking, the relative extents to which different morbid conditions are being relieved are, therefore, intractable to objective comparison; particularly when those conditions are chronic and amelioration, rather than cure, is the most that can be achieved. Nevertheless, certain components of need, such as the quality of wards and food provided in hospitals, are common to patients with diverse medical conditions; and in these respects it is geriatric and mental patients who receive markedly inferior treatment (Crossman, 1972b). The relatively low numbers of skilled manpower devoted to them may then, perhaps, be plausibly interpreted as resulting more probably from a similarly low priority being accorded to the medical needs of these categories, rather than from their conditions requiring lower skills. Alternatively, it may suggest that many of these aged and mentally ill patients are being hospitalised *faute de mieux*—a dearth of community health services and personal social services hinders the community care that would be more appropriate. As seen in the previous chapter, it is in these terms that the development of community health services and cooperation with local personal social services has been emphasised in the recent NHS reform.

Finally, there is evidence that middle-class patients are more able to obtain desired treatment from NHS facilities than are members of the lower classes with the same need. Townsend (1974), for example, finds that among the geriatric cases to whom we have just referred, there is a marked class gradient in the quality of care. Feldstein undertakes a special study of the hospital treatment of maternity cases. He finds that this ability to manipulate the medical services sufficiently outweighs the poorer home conditions of lower-class mothers (implying a need for hospital delivery) for the higher classes to have a higher probability of admission, longer stays and greater likelihood of being in teaching hospitals. Even when Feldstein controls for the doctor and the hospital care, and for the woman's age and parity—the number of children she has already borne—duration of stay is found to decrease monotonically from the highest to the lowest social class (1967, Ch. 8). Howlett and Ashley (1972) investigate the higher quality of care available in teaching hospitals. They find that in the case of prostrate gland operations it is the older and the lower class patients who are least favoured. However, Carstairs (1966), while acknowledging that middle-class patients are more likely to enter small hospitals, and that their General Practitioners are more likely to have access to hospitals' diagnostic facilities, sees that as being largely a result of area variations in NHS facilities; little difference in treatment occurs while the patient is in hospital. But she *does* see the upper and middle classes as having a more positive attitude to elective surgery and preventive care. The need for further studies is agreed by all these writers.

The change in life chances as a result of some disease will depend on the success of the treatment, together with the opportunity cost of the disease for the individual (i.e. any cost of treatment, loss of earnings while ill and changes made in future occupation as a result of the disease). Cartwright's hospital study demonstrates the striking class differentials here (1964, Ch. 12). Thus 77 per cent of the middle-class heads of households obtained full wages while in hospital, as compared with 20 per cent in the case of working class; and only 12 per cent of the middle class received no payment from an employer—and presumably many of these were self-employed—compared with 55 per cent of the working-class patients. Few middle-class (10 per cent) but more than half of the working-class patients had suffered moderate to severe financial strain.

There was also a marked class differential in the proportions who felt that their work had contributed to their illness—especially in the case of long illness.[7] Yet more than half of these returned to the same job, owing to inability to find an alternative job or because of family responsibilities. Little help was given by hospital almoners.

Their class situation thus made likely the need for recurring hospital treatment. In those cases where recovery is incomplete, such a likelihood is increased; while if an easier—and probably lower-paid—job is taken, poverty may foster general health deterioration. Thus the chronic sick tend to be downwardly mobile. Here, then, are displayed some of the constraints upon the potential, even in principle, for a health service from which the cash nexus has been eliminated to render independent of class situation the consequences for an individual of succumbing to some morbid condition.

This discussion of the dependence of treatment upon class membership has been confined to the facilities of the NHS. The persistence of a private sector, however, particularly in the hospital service, appears to involve the perpetuation of the cash nexus for the highest quality of health care. The extent to which two standards of treatment indeed prevail is difficult to judge in the absence of adequate empirical studies; but the differential would seem to be not insignificant. The manner in which the elimination of the private sector would affect the total resources available to the NHS is even more difficult to gauge on the basis of available information—it would, of course, depend crucially on policy decisions by the government of the day. Nevertheless, that the private sector's persistence and current expansion reinforce the class gradient in treatment obtaining in the NHS can hardly be doubted (Parker, 1975, pp. 78ff.).

Theoretical implications

The foregoing discussion of morbidity and medical care in Britain may serve as the basis for an evaluation of the competing arguments summarised in section I.

Neo-Marxists
Neo-Marxist propositions pertain first to the distribution of disabilities and morbidity among members of the population, harking back to Marx's depiction of the proletarians' debilitating work situation and Engels' account of their living conditions (1969). That class membership continues to be significantly associated with morbidity lends some *prima facie* support to neo-Marxist contentions that relative immiseration of the working classes under capitalism can be reversed not by the health policies of the Welfare State, but only by the humanisation of living and working conditions

that socialisation of the means of industrial production would permit.

However, as we have seen, the relevant evidence is incompletely available; and where it is, closer examination prevents unqualified acceptance of these neo-Marxist arguments. First, it may indeed be the case that certain important disabilities are caused principally by characteristics of work situation, by poor housing conditions and nutritional deficiencies and by inadequate health education and improper self-medication practices. Nevertheless, our discussion suggests that the association between work situation and health can only very crudely and superficially be expressed in the neo-Marxist terms of class gradients. Likewise, when in the previous chapter we investigated access to adequate housing, the neo-Marxist assumption that civil rights to dispose of property in the market place were of overwhelming importance proved inadequate (see above, p. 117). Lastly, one can hardly infer from these occupational and environmental determinants of morbidity that no changes are possible without the prior fundamental changes in the ownership of industrial property that the neo-Marxists demand. Rather, these findings have encouraged increased attention to industrial and community health policies (Arie, 1975). Whether such policies must prove politically unacceptable to the powerful can hardly be decided *a priori*, but must be a matter for empirical investigation. While this is not an issue to which we shall directly address ourselves, we do explore, in chapter 6, the political acceptability of preventive social policies aimed at reducing the social costs of urban–industrial change imposed upon the powerless.

In regard to the personal health services, the neo-Marxists argue the continuing dependence of access upon class membership. Evidence that within the NHS middle-class patients obtain better treatment suggests that the formal abolition of the cash nexus has been of little significance. The mediation of the professional may determine the *type* of treatment, but not its *quality*. The indicators used in deciding the latter are in practice merely a surrogate for individuals' market power; and overall health outcomes among different social classes are no less clearly monotonic in gradient than is the hierarchy of rewards distributed through factor markets (cf. Westergaard and Resler, 1976, p. 183).

Nevertheless, our discussion again suggests that this is too crude and superficial an inference. First, class differences in treatment seem to arise in part from patients' own role in identifying their needs and prescribing treatment. Carstairs' study, for example, highlights the more positive attitudes to preventive care typical among the middle and upper classes. Douglas and his colleagues find, similarly, that working-class patients are less likely to seek out preventive services provided by local authorities for their children (cited in Arie, 1966). The empirical studies we have surveyed also suggest there are considerable variations among patients from different social classes, regions and age groups in tolerance of pain and expectations of health. Second, Arie (1966) argues that the '"social distance" between doctors and patients has important effects on the type of care that patients receive'. Together these points suggest, therefore, that we must think of the prescription of treatment as arising from negotiation between patient and doctor, with the patient seeking to put a 'health project' into effect, within the context of his more general life project. As Cooper comments, 'Probably the most important factors determining [treatment] are the patient's persistence, his ability to articulate his symptoms in a form understandable to the doctor and the resource constraints' (1975, p. 22; see also Stimson, 1976).

Here, then is a process of need definition fundamentally different from that obtaining under the Poor Law, which was meant to be 'self-acting' and unambiguous, deriving not from a negotiation between professional experts and patients engaged in the attempted realisation of their health projects, but rather from the clear valuations of the market place. In a modern socialised health service, the negotiation that appears to take place between professionals and patients over diagnosis and treatment requires that the resulting inequalities in treatment be accounted for, not in terms of the subordination of the definition of medical needs to the values of the market system, but rather in terms of differences in health projects and individuals' capacities to realise them.

To maintain a distinctively Marxist position, it would be necessary to demonstrate, first, that there are systematic differences in the health projects of individuals in different social classes, adequately accounted for in terms of their market and work situations; and, then, that individuals' differential capacities to realise their health projects may be accounted for in terms of their relationship to the ownership and control of the means of production. The available evidence is scanty. However, that individuals' life goals cannot adequately be seen as deriving from their work and market situations is a principal conclusion of the *Affluent Worker* studies. Moreover—to turn to the second of the above propositions—the final volume of the Luton studies includes discussion not, admittedly, of health projects but rather of the educational projects these workers have for their children (Goldthorpe *et al.*, 1969, Ch. 5; cf. Halsey *et al.*, 1979, Ch. 5). A principal conclusion is that differential capacities to realise these projects spring, not from the relationship of parents to the means of production, but rather from differential knowledge and understanding of the education system, of the selection mechanisms at work within it and of what constitutes a conducive home environment. As we shall see in the next section—and in chapter 6—the degree and social distribution of such understanding is itself in considerable measure an outcome of existing social measures. Health projects and the capacity to realise them may well be susceptible to modification through health education, with positive discrimination towards less articulate groups, or through the development of collective action that results in criticism of the professional and political organisation of health care and of the inequalities it reproduces (see below, p. 224). Thus serious doubt is thrown on the neo-Marxist theses rehearsed above.

Market liberals

In the opening section, we summarised the market liberals' arguments in a threefold form: (i) in respect of the definition of need for state aid, they postulate that a sufficient and valid criterion or indicator is a specified low level of income, applied through rigorous means-testing; (ii) they argue that, for each of the life chances distributed through social policies, there exists a basic level of provision necessary for social existence, which can be determined by objective study; (iii) they display a measured optimism as to the trends in the pattern of overall distributive outcomes generated in a market-dominated society and anticipate the elimination of need without the aid of redistributive social policies. Let us examine these arguments in turn.

(i) We saw earlier that the chronically sick are likely, in a private health insurance scheme, to be subject to increased risk-rating and premia by virtue of their chronic condition. This reduces the effective demand for the private sector to provide a quality of service for chronic degenerative disease superior to that of the state. At the same time, their probable downward mobility, in search of less demanding jobs, renders them decreasingly able to afford private treatment proportionate to their likely requirements; and, if a specified low level of income is taken as indicating need for state aid, these chronic and degenerative conditions will tend to become the concern primarily of the state's safety-net provision—as, indeed, was to a considerable extent the case in the inter-war years (for a personal account, see Aronovitch, 1974). Yet, as we saw in chapter 4, with advances in techniques for dealing with acute and infectious illness, chronic degenerative conditions have become increasingly prevalent, partly as a concomitant to increased life expectancy (see p. 96 above). Consequently, it is for no small number of the population that private medical care services cannot be expected to provide a high quality of treatment. Moreover, the accidents of chronic disablement would be at least as significant as the individual's taking out of health insurance policies in determining his health outcome. Such nullifying of the individual's 'responsible' choices in the market place is hardly consonant with the market liberal's own prescriptions for social organisation. Furthermore, this effect of a market organisation of health care could hardly be reversed by procedures for legal compensation from the agent responsible for the chronic disability; for, as Titmuss has frequently argued, it becomes increasingly difficult, in a complex and rapidly changing urban–industrial society, to identify such agents (1974, Ch. 5; 1968, p. 133).[8]

(ii) These liberals affirm that there exists a basic level of health care provision that can be determined by objective study and that they prescribe as the limit of the state's proper role; above this, a market organisation ensures equity, efficiency and individual choice. Our earlier empirical analysis suggests a fourfold criticism. First, the very definition of health and health needs is recalcitrant to precise specification and cannot but be seen as a social construct. The probability that different social classes and age groups have differing tolerances of pain and health expectations was noted earlier. Moreover, as medical techniques advance and increased resources are made available, medical conditions hitherto regarded as untreatable become susceptible to alleviation. We might, therefore, say that demand and need for medical care are, in principle, unlimited, and that as new techniques and additional resources become available, so expectations as to standards of health are likely to rise (Cooper, 1975, Chs 2, 3). Among the empirical studies cited earlier, this is, for example, a principal conclusion of Feldstein's analysis of hospitalisation: 'in health care, ... appropriate standards of provision cannot be determined by reference to levels of "need" inherent in or manifest by the community' (1967, p. 201).

This insatiability of need also has implications for the likely distribution of health care resources between public and private sectors if health services were organised on the lines the liberals advocate. Jewkes and Jewkes, in their study of the NHS, while not denying that the immediate effect of an expansion of the private sector might be to redistribute resources towards the middle and upper classes, argue that in the medium and long term such a reform would call forth a sufficient increase in health care resources to produce an improved service for all groups. The queues in the NHS testify to the excess of demand over supply; and 'it may be that the NHS, because of its form, has positively discouraged the allocation of resources to the purposes of medicine'. If, however, private provision were encouraged as a complement to the public sector, 'everybody [would get] a better service. As more people move over to the private supply, the pressure on the public supply is reduced and waiting time there also becomes less' (1961, pp. 37-8). In contrast, our evidence on the seemingly unlimited character of medical need suggests that, whatever new resources may be called forth by the presence of a private sector, they will not satiate the effective demand emanating from that sector. Rather, the result would seem likely to be a starving of the public sector resources no less perpetual then the existence of unmet medical need. The traditional liberal thesis that the pursuit of individual self-interest within the market place cannot but promote the collective interest and the interest of others is here shown to be incorrect or even meaningless. This discussion also undermines liberal attempts to depict the process of health care allocation in a market system as a competitive equilibrium determined as much by actors' varied preferences as by their economic resources. Rather than some harmonious systemic equilibrium being attained, what is apparent in our foregoing empirically oriented discussion is a power contest in which actors' economic resources are of crucial significance in determining an outcome that can in no meaningful or useful sense be termed an 'equilibrium'.

It is convenient at this point to examine a related argument advanced by some market liberals in recognition of this potentially unlimited demand for medical care. This is that a market organisation of health care services discourages excessive demand by imposing an opportunity cost upon the potential patient: prescription charges render less likely the wasteful use of drugs; consultation fees prevent pressures upon medical professionals building up intolerably. The introduction of the NHS fostered a debate over the consequences for consultation rates, etc., of the elimination of the disciplines of the cash nexus. Titmuss agrees that in the early years of the new service, following the austerity of war and post-war reconstruction, it had to face a 'back-log of needs ... most vividly depicted by the demand for spectacles, dentures, hearing aids and other postponable adjuncts to better health' (1963, p. 153). However, he also marshalls evidence suggesting that the establishment of the NHS not only did not lead to any excessive demand for GP services, but that it saw, rather, an actual decline in GP consultations, as between the nationally insured labour force in the 1930s and the same age group of men in 1949–50 (1963, Ch. 9, pp. 171–4, 203–14). Cooper, moreover, observes that even in the absence of a cash nexus there do exist opportunity costs to seeking health care: 'Deterrents include the necessary expenditure of time and energy, inconvenience, travel costs, leisure forgone, the discomforts of the doctor's waiting room. . . .' (1975, p. 16). The more fundamental question that arises out of these considerations, however, is the distribution among different medical needs of the reduction in effective demand for health care, as a result of market allocation on the one hand or the costs mentioned by Cooper on the other. Only in the light of a value-judgement on the desirability of these distributions can either of these two methods of restricting effective demand be evaluated. The value-ladenness of the liberal argument we have been examining in this paragraph must, therefore, be recognised.

The final criticism of the second liberal proposition also derives from our empirical discussion of the character of need for medical care. The diagnosis of medical need, we saw, is essentially an esoteric task, notwithstanding the patient's participation in the pursuit of his health project. That a market organisation of health care widens the citizen's choice, as in the neoclassical economist's model of competitive markets, must therefore be questioned. The esoteric definition of need by professionals means, rather, that no realistic choice can be said to exist for the patient, as among different patterns of treatment, even in a market system (Abel-Smith, 1976, Ch. 4). True, each individual would be exercising choice as to the proportion of his income to be devoted to health care; yet the most significant choice that the market would introduce is for those with substantial financial resources to command equally substantial health care resources.

(iii) The market liberal typically anticipates that the 'natural' development of a laissez-faire market system will ensure the elimination of basic need without the aid of redistributive social policies. In so far as these market liberals expect this to result from a reduction in the occupational and environmental depradations of advanced capitalism, there seems only limited supportive evidence. It is true that over wide ranges of morbidity, rates for all classes have declined, even though class gradients have often remained broadly unchanged. That this is due to post-war prosperity may well be true. Nevertheless, this has of course been the era of state-managed capitalism, raising the much wider question of the viability of a laissez-faire advanced market system. Moreover, at least some of this reduction in morbidity must surely be attributed to preventive health policies and to the impact of other aspects of post-war social policy, such as housing.

However, market liberals also look to developments in the personal health services for the elimination of basic unmet need. That the objective specification of this 'basic' level of medical need is in principle impossible has, however, been argued above; and it renders this third liberal proposition somewhat vacuous. Second, we have also just argued that with a substantial private sector alongside the public, the latter would be starved of resources; it might be said to suffer probable immiseration, in relative if not absolute terms. Third, as also already argued, a market organisation of health care would seem likely to concentrate the chronically sick in a low-quality public sector. The chronically sick would be disproportionately represented among the objects of this immiseration.

Political liberals

The arguments of the political liberals recalled in section I related (i) to the meritocratic equality of opportunity that free access to the policy-making arena could be expected to promote; (ii) to the technical and apolitical character of the resulting indicators of need and merit; and (iii) to the greater equality of life chances that such meritocratic social policies—themselves increasingly guaranteed by the logic of industrialism—might be expected to produce.

(i) The first of these propositions may be criticised on three grounds. To start with, 'free access' is not, for those political liberals who emphasise it, an unqualified presumption. Rather, there is typically the caveat—explicit or only implicit—that such access be granted to all *legitimate* interest groups. Such legitimacy is itself problematic, of course, but is typically applied to established interest groups only, with no formal provision made for the legitimation and political inclusion of any new groups that may develop in the society at large (see Lowi, 1969, especially Ch. 3; Wolff, 1968, pp. 150–61). Interests not subsumed in the objectives of 'legitimate' interest groups are not, therefore, heeded in the bargaining process of which social policy formulation is supposed essentially to consist. Clearly a more general critique of such a political theory cannot be attempted here. Nevertheless, particularly in our discussion in chapter 4 of recent debates over consumer participation, we have seen that the question of the legitimacy of consumers as an interest group to be admitted to health policy formulation has been put into sharp focus. The Conservative government's *Consultative Document* counterposed efficient management to participation by consumers; and its modification of the Labour proposals on such participation must be seen as a refusal to admit advocacy of their interests, save by their 'legitimate' political representatives in Parliament and government (see above, pp. 97–9; cf. p. 108). Since reorganisation, the experience of the Community Health Councils has involved continuing challenge by medical professionals to the councils' competence and legitimacy to pronounce on consumer and community interests (Klein and Lewis, 1976, pp. 124–34).

This proposition may additionally be criticised in terms of its assumption that free access to the policy-making process is a *sufficient* condition for advocacy of the interests of all legitimate groups. Our earlier discussion highlighted the need to account for inequalities of treatment in terms of typical differences in health projects and individuals' capacities to realise them. Yet, consistently with this, it was also seen that it has been precisely those categories of patients most lacking in such capacities—namely the aged, the chronically sick and the mentally ill and handicapped—who have been accorded least favoured treatment of all the various morbid conditions. In a situation where such medical conditions seem to be growing in their prevalence, the insufficiency of equal access to the policy-making process as a condition of equitable treatment—however the latter may be defined—is especially evident.

A final criticism centres on the assumption that social policy formulation may adequately be conceptualised as a bargaining process in the course of which a systemic equilibrium is achieved, the just outcome of an interaction of group interests. On the one hand, the discussion, in chapter 4, of the evolution of health policy revealed some of the ways in which the struggle of diverse interest groups in pursuit of their goals has involved a perennial promotion of substantive irrationality in health care services (see above, p. 96). Similarly, to take an example from the inequalities discussed in the present chapter, 'the distribution of [consultant awards], associated as it is with high professional status, must surely influence the choice younger doctors make about the area of medicine in which they practice' (Parker, 1975, p. 82). On the other hand, to speak of a systemic equilibrium presumably requires that there be some central values to which policies increasingly tend, in the course of the bargaining process (see above, pp. 70–71). It is, however, the perennial diversity of values and conflict among them that is evident in our investigation—where by values one is here referring to the priority rankings of different health needs.

(ii) The political liberals suppose that political value-judgements may be eliminated from social policy formulation: criteria of need and merit, and decisions over the allocation of resources become increasingly the proper concern of scientific and professional expertise. That such a proposition has much plausibility in the field of health care follows from our earlier empirical survey. The esoteric nature of medical need, especially with the advance of diagnostic and clinical techniques, finds its obverse in the expertise of highly trained medical personnel.

However, our empirical discussion also revealed the existence of value-judgements in health policy irreducible to technical questions of medical diagnosis and prescription. As we have seen, the social construction of definitions of health and the seeming insatiability of needs for care render health care resources inherently scarce. But for such scarcity, it might in principle be possible to envisage a service meeting all health needs; decisions in health policy would be wholly of a technical and administrative character. Yet the inherent scarcity that in fact obtains requires that priorities be specified for resource allocation— whether it is through a market or through professional and bureaucratic criteria that such a ranking of priorities is achieved. Such priorities concern the relative treatment of different needs and, therefore, of different individuals. It is in this sense, then, that the ranking of priorities involves value-judgements in a most fundamental sense—judgements on the degree to which the needs of different individuals should constitute the ends or objectives of social policy. This unavoidable specification of priorities has been at least partly responsible for continuing friction between medical practitioners and the state, as a provider of resources, over the relationship between clinical freedom and service planning (Klein, 1977). Placing this discussion within the context of the more general view of urban–industrial society held by the political liberals, the question arises as to whether this set of value-judgements may be resolved in terms of society's evolving 'needs', i.e. by technical judgements, albeit not by *medical* experts. One of the conclusions of chapter 4 was that no such reduction was possible.

Likewise, it was evident in chapter 4 that the problems of, and the need for, improved planning and effectiveness have increasingly been felt in the NHS. Such recognition has grown *pari passu* with awareness of the need for more adequate information and data collection. Alderson argues that the integration of the three branches of the NHS permits the creation of a unified health information service, not service-oriented but 'population-based and problem-oriented', enabling *inter alia* a comparison of the costs of different methods of treating a given condition (in Maunder, 1974, section 7). Feldstein's study of the hospital service (1967) exemplifies the latter analysis. He first develops several production functions relating inputs to treatment. He is able to assess the cost-effectiveness of an input for any category of patient; this enables both the analysis of the efficiency of resource use, and rational decisions on changes in policy, if it is desired to change the weights given to various illnesses when allocating resources. Cooper surveys recent attempts to engage in cost–benefit analyses of different forms of treatment. Methodological problems are often substantial; nevertheless, he sees such investigations as promoting 'a very critical self-examination of current practices and a ruthless pruning out of the ineffectual' (1975, p. 124). Neither Feldstein nor Cooper, however, sees such technical analyses as removing the need for value-judgements and priority rankings in respect of different needs and different categories of patient; such investigations, rather, can properly serve only to *inform* these judgements.

(iii) The final argument of the political liberals is that the meritocratic social policies that are developing as part of the logic of industrialism may be expected automatically to produce greater equality in the overall distribution of life chances. However, our foregoing discussion suggests three grounds for doubt. First, we have argued that political value-judgements over the relative priorities to be accorded to different medical needs are perennial and are irreducible to technical judgements. No trend in the pattern of health outcomes can, therefore, be deemed 'automatic'; it will, rather, in principle at least, be or have been a matter of political will. Second, the trends in class gradient we have reviewed give no clear indication of growing equality. Lastly, as among different categories of medical need, our discussion suggests that the aged, the mentally ill and handicapped, and the chronically sick continue to receive poor quality treatment; and that, while recognition of this may have informed recent attempts to redefine the objectives and priorities of the NHS, there can hardly be said to have been any obvious trend in the post-war era towards equality of treatment among these various need groups.

Social Democrats
Such criticisms of liberals and neo-Marxists are broadly consistent with the position adopted by Social Democratic writers. For them, the NHS has provided perhaps the clearest example, in both its birth and its aims, of a universalist social policy making a reality of the 'needs nexus'. Nevertheless, within our discussion are pointers to the inadequacy of such universalism, requiring at least some modification of the Social Democratic position as enunciated in the euphoric 1940s. First, we have traced persisting inequalities in realising the right to equal treatment—reflecting the priorities and perceptions of medical professionals, patients' varying expectations and tolerance of ill-health and the historical patterns of resource distribution and institutional organisation. Whether positive discrimination—for example in health education and resource

allocation—is technically and politically feasible, as a means of reducing such inequalities, is at best an open question. Second, it has become increasingly evident that for social inequalities in morbidity to be reduced, preventive policies are necessary that involve new social controls on industrial and urban milieux— and hence upon those enjoying power there. A social right to health—rather than merely to treatment when ill—cannot be realised by universalist social services alone. Third, this universalism may indeed compensate unconditionally the victims of urban–industrial change, recognising that the agents of depradation are often invisible. However, as neo-Marxists affirm, it may also thereby discourage investigation and preventive social control of such agencies. Equally invisible socially are the costs, in terms of poorer treatment, that the articulate and informed are able, through their manipulation of medical professionals within a universalist service, to impose upon their socially less competent fellows. The conditions under which the visibility of such processes and outcomes may be increased will be a major theme of chapter 6.

Consider now the implications of the foregoing for the definition of interests.

Liberals
For contemporary liberals, free access to either the economic or political arenas suffices to define an identity of interests among citizens, irrespective of social class. Such free access ensures that the pursuit of self-interest will not conflict with, but will rather promote, the collective interest; distributive outcomes will be determined through the establishment of a systemic equilibrium. However, our empirical criticisms of both market and political liberals included a demonstration that such 'free access', as conceived of by these writers, cannot be seen as establishing a value-free 'equilibrium'. Rather, our discussion revealed that within any health care system there is bound to be perennial conflict over the priority rankings of different medical needs, and that a market organisation of care resolves such conflict only by subordinating its outcome to differentials in market power. This lends support to the Social Democrats' criticism of liberal analyses of individual interests. For, *contra* the liberals, the Social Democrats argue that an advanced urban–industrial society cannot, even in principle, be organised in

such a way that individuals' pursuit of their self-interest need not necessarily be mutually opposed.

Neo-Marxists

Contemporary neo-Marxists, while admitting the absolute improvement that may well have occurred in the life chances of manual workers, affirm a continuing trend to relative immiseration, and deny that contemporary social policies affect the implications of this threat for the definition of class interests. The earlier empirical discussion suggests at least three lines of criticism.

(i) Consistent with the Social Democrats, there are certain respects in which there exists a common interest among all classes in state interference with the market. (Marx himself acknowledged the common interest of different social classes in such measures. Yet this acknowledgement, far from demonstrating that such measures are consistent with the capitalist market economy depicted by Marx, shows rather that such an economy was taken by Marx as an ideal type, and that he saw such community-oriented measures as representing a movement of English society away from that ideal type; Avineri, 1968, pp. 159–62). Thus we have referred to the impact of preventive policies upon morbidity and the new importance ascribed to community medicine, particularly its preventive aspects, in recent reforms of the NHS. However, it cannot be assumed that all preventive measures will significantly benefit *all* social classes, still less that such benefits will be perceived as *evenly* distributed. We have, for example, seen that the lower socio-economic groups tend to be inarticulate and lacking the understanding required to appropriate the treatment that the middle classes obtain. Therefore, measures aimed at health education and early presentation of symptoms or at enabling medical professionals to overcome cultural barriers of class and ethnicity may tend, in the absence of significant increases in overall health care resources, to threaten the standards of care that those middle classes have come to expect. This in turn threatens the Social Democratic confidence that such measures will typically and immediately evoke widespread popular acquiescence. Or, alternatively, it makes especially clear how different their approach must be from the liberal reliance upon self-interested acquiescence in societal functioning: emphasising, instead, not only that such acquiescence must involve some subordination of this self-interest to the common interest, but also that imperious definition of this common interest is a matter for political leadership. However, these considerations (central to Weber's concerns) have been left implicit or only superficially explored by our Social Democrats (see above, pp. 63, 143).

A further area of common interest among social classes is apparent when one considers the prevalence and consequences of chronic illness of various kinds. Under a market distribution of health care, we argued earlier, such illness is likely to receive low priority in the allocation of resources. No private insurance scheme will guarantee members full cover against the risk and costs of chronic illness of unlimited duration. To the extent, therefore, that the risk of chronic illness or disablement is significant through all social classes, and to the extent that the resource costs of providing the quality of treatment technically available are high, there is defined a common interest among the members of all social classes in the establishment and promotion of services free to the user. The growing costs of medical care, apparent in this section and chapter 4, together with the growing prevalence of chronic illness among different social classes, suggest that such a common objective interest is today not insignificant.

We may, therefore, recognise that such common interests do objectively exist and that class interests are not wholly opposed. Nevertheless, these counter-arguments might meet with a twofold rejoinder from the neo-Marxists. First, such areas of common interest in universalist social policies extend only to the lower- and middle-income groups; the wealthy, encouraged by tax relief on private health insurance schemes, have no such interest. This, then, suffices merely to support the thesis of the 'proletarianisation' of the middle classes. Second, we have failed to make explicit the more fundamental common interest that the mass of the population shares in eliminating the substantial ill-health that is the fruit, directly or indirectly, of a capitalist organisation of the division of labour. Against the latter retort, however, we have conceded that politically contentious changes may indeed be required; but we have insisted that their form and their manner of realisation cannot be defined *a priori*.

(ii) A second criticism of the neo-Marxist analysis of class interests is that the processes of care allocation within the NHS create common interests that transcend considerations of class. We earlier argued that the treatment an individual receives appears typically to depend upon his health project, upon the negotiation between doctor and patient over the definition of need and the prescription of treatment, and upon the priority granted to that need category by political decisions on resource allocation. For those with a common need, as defined by the medical professionals, there is therefore a common *immediate* interest in altering the priority ranking of that need within the political resource allocation process. Admittedly, for certain wealthier individuals receiving NHS treatment, they might prefer to 'opt out' of the NHS, paying less taxes and taking out private health insurance. Their objective interest is class related. Once, however, health care is distributed in accordance with medical need, as a social right of citizenship, and charges are levied upon the healthy as a social duty of citizenship, the common interest is created that we have just delineated. Thus as Titmuss argues, 'the middle classes . . . have not contracted out of socialised medical care . . . their continuing participation, and their more articulate demands for improvements, have been an important factor in a general rise in standards of service' (1968, p. 196). As argued by Social Democrats, the pattern of immediate interests generated by social rights may therefore be fundamentally different from that generated by the exercise of civil rights. It follows, then, that the Social Democratic critique of the neo-Marxists here depends on the readiness of even the wealthy to embrace the social rights and duties of citizenship that such a universalist service embodies. These writers have, perhaps, increasingly acknowledged the fragility and vulnerability of such readiness in face of the acquisitive individualism enjoined by other social milieux. This will be a major theme in the next chapter.

(iii) The neo-Marxists imply that while the working class may have an immediate interest in the extension of social rights realised through universal social services, such extension has little prospect of major success; for it comes into conflict with the interests of the dominant capitalist class. The trade unions and the labour movement cannot, therefore, reasonably see the extension of such social policies as a new means to their long-standing aim of withstanding the threat of immiseration and even establishing a socialist distribution of treatment according to need. We have, however, argued with the Social Democrats that, at least in the case of health policy, it has been through the attempted extension and realisation of common social rights that the immediately necessary modifications of free exercise of civil rights have been revealed, in an immanent practical critique of market influences. An essentially historical conception of the realisation of social rights is necessary, rather than the relatively static systemic approach of the neo-Marxists, with its utopian tendencies.

It may, of course, be that, as the neo-Marxists predict, such efforts lead to authoritarian reaction by the ruling class, if such may be said to exist. For the Social Democrats, however, this is essentially an empirical question. Moreover, they would argue that it is through attempts at social policy reform that such potential areas of conflict are revealed; that since such revelation is in the interests of the working class, so too is such attempted reform; and, finally, that such revelation promotes a subjective appreciation of objective interests. On the other hand, as we have noted elsewhere, the Social Democrats have insufficiently explored what social groups are available—or can, by appropriate political leadership, be created—having both the will and the capacity to voice and implement this critique.

Finally, in bringing our empirical findings to bear upon the liberal, neo-Marxist and Social Democratic arguments, we have laid bare important differences in the significance they attach to the social division of welfare. For liberal writers, the distribution of life chance outcomes is of only secondary interest. What is of primary importance in judging distributive processes—and in predicting their implications for group formation and action—is their formal equity among individuals enjoying free access to the economic or political market place; although liberals do use evidence of distributive outcomes as indicators, first of how meritocratic in some objective sense—and hence how equitable—our society is, and second of the elimination of need defined in some basic or absolute sense. For Marx, the investigation of trends in inequalities was significant in indicating the development of the objective conditions of immiseration that, as they were subjectively apprehended, would impel the working class to active transformation of capitalist society. Yet many contemporary neo-Marxists seem, in contrast, to see the documentation of continuing inequalities as serving primarily to demonstrate the continuing validity of Marx's portrait of capitalism. Indeed, both liberal and neo-Marxist writers sometimes seem content to take measures of such inequalities as sufficient evidence of wider social processes—for example, some automatic trend to meritocracy or a hardly less inevitable immiseration. Or they may even take these measures as adequate indicators of the 'species' to which our contemporary society belongs. In both cases they betray the ahistorical systemic view of society that we criticised in chapter 3. For Social Democratic writers, the elucidation of inequalities—of an 'abnormal' social division of welfare—is significant primarily for continuing redefinition of the state's role in enunciating and realising the social rights of citizenship: a role that is necessary for social cohesion in particular (see Terrill, 1974, pp. 217, 275; see above p. 37).

Following this comparison, note that neo-Marxists commonly take class gradients in, for example, morbidity, as the significant measure of inequality. This seems consistent with their inherited interest in immiseration: they are comparing the proportions of the lower socio-economic categories suffering debilitation relative to society in general and to the upper categories in particular. However, with such class gradients unchanged, a reduction in the absolute rates of morbidity for all social classes logically implies that for the lower social classes the proportionate increase in those *not* suffering ill-health is greater than in the case of the middle and upper classes. It is *this* definition of inequality that liberal writers seem commonly but implicitly to embrace; it is consistent with their interest in progress to a society of competent and self-sufficient individuals—with incompetence or incapacity conceived of in absolute terms. Social Democratic writers seem ready to take the improvements in the health of all classes as indicating, in part and *contra* the neo-Marxists, the efficacy of social policies, and to take the persisiting class gradients in ill-health as indicating, *contra* the liberals, the need for further intervention including, for example, positive discrimination and preventive measures, if the appropriation of these social rights is to be universal. What might appear, then, as a merely technical problem of defining indicators of inequality turns out to involve fundamental value-judgements and theoretical interests.[9] What measures of inequality are most appropriate will, therefore, depend upon the ability of the theories utilising them to provide adequate explanations of the empirical consequences of inequality. Among such consequences, we have argued, the implications for group formation and action have been accepted by all schools as particularly important; these form the subject of the next chapter. There we shall investigate the influence of inequalities in the social division of welfare upon the values and goals to which individuals and groups orient themselves.

There are, however, at least three major limitations to the approach we have adopted in this section. First, for reasons of space we have investigated the pattern of needs and outcomes in only one branch of social policy. Had we considered educational inequalities, for example, we would have been drawn into the growing literature on the stratification of opportunities and provisions, and the strategies that differentially advantaged groups may employ to control and monopolise the more privileged sectors and, via them, similarly privileged positions in the wider society (Bowles and Gintis, 1976, Ch. 8; cf. pp. 130–1 above). At least until recently, as we saw in chapter 4, the ideology of equal opportunity has provided a widely accepted legitimation for the individualistic acquisition of formal qualifications within this unequal society—an acquisitiveness oriented to the preservation or improvement of credentials *relative* to those of others. Here the apparently unending expansion of demand for the life chances distributed through the social services is exposed as expressing not so much rising expectations of common standards of provision, but rather inherently unrealisable—because universal—demands for access to positions of privilege (see above, pp. 164–5; cf. Hirsch, 1977, esp. Ch. 3). Here then, still more strikingly than in the case of health care, the divergence is revealed between pursuit of self-interest and promotion of the general quality of a universalist service, and, hence, the political task that securing popular commitment to such promotion must entail (see above, pp. 173–4). At best, therefore, our limited focus has provided an exemplar for further studies and raised issues relevant to other chapters; at worst, however, it may encourage misleading and invalid generalisations.

Second, even within medical care, we have focused upon the public sector and largely ignored the private. The latter is, admittedly, used by only a small minority of the population (Parker, 1975, pp. 89–91). Yet the resources it attracts, its prospects for growth—particularly in the form of occupational fringe benefits—and its dissolution of a universal interest in improving the quality of public provision may be more significant. Titmuss and the other Social Democratic writers have been as vociferous as the neo-Marxists in their criticism (see Wilding, 1976, pp. 159–62). On the other hand, this choice of perhaps the most 'socialised' sector of social policy may, by the same token, have enabled us to examine most clearly how far life chance distribution can in principle be. extricated from the cash nexus historically dominant in our society—exposing most clearly, therefore, such new processes of inequality as tend to emerge in nominally universalist services (cf. Westergaard and Resler, 1976, pp. 128–9).

Third, we have neglected the social distribution of the burden of financing health care. This would have involved consideration of the national insurance and taxation systems, and the latter discussion would need to have included fiscal incentives to private health provision. We have, therefore, perhaps given insufficient attention to two of the three elements distinguished by Titmuss in his seminal essay on the social division of welfare—namely, occupational and fiscal welfare (on these, see Sinfield, 1978, and references therein). Had these findings then been used in a judgement on the distribution of the costs and benefits of health care, it would, of course, also have been necessary to take account of the longer life expectancy—and higher use of facilities for chronic illness— among the middle- and upper-income groups.

Returning then to the first of these limitations, it is an investigation of the need for, and the distribution of, benefits in cash that would have been an especially desirable addition, had space permitted. In recent decades the payment of direct taxation has extended to most of the population, at the same time as social security benefits have developed a concern with earnings-related benefits. There have in consequence been various political proposals for rationalisation or unification of the two systems (most notably the Conservatives' *Proposals for a Tax Credit System*—Treasury and DHSS, 1972), and several important recent studies of the net impact of the social security and taxation systems on those with different incomes and domestic responsibilities. These have exposed the non-progressive character of direct taxation, its increasing burden on the low paid and on those with families in particular and the lack of any redistribution among broad income categories via the two systems taken together (Kincaid, 1973, esp. Chs 5–7; Field *et al.*, 1977, esp. Chs 2, 4, 9). They tend, therefore, to challenge the confidence of political liberals that the state has, through these institutions, effected such redistribution to a significant degree. Yet the pattern of interests to which these systems give rise is hardly what the neo-Marxists would predict. Rather, as in our discussion of health care, common interests arise among those in common situations *vis-à-vis* such public bureaucracies. Hence, for example, the Child Poverty Action Group is currently seeking to establish a family—rather than a poverty—lobby by those with families, who, whatever their levels of income, have a common immediate interest in the expansion of universalist child benefits (Field, 1977; contrast Field, 1976). Here, then, as the Social Democrats argue, social rights may tend to generate areas of common interest—and, indeed, new lines of conflict—distinct from those defined by the market place, notwithstanding the apparent failure of such rights thus far to promote any marked income redistribution among classes. Nevertheless, the articulation of such interests involves political leadership and does not arise spontaneously; to this the Social Democrats (like their rivals) have perhaps given insufficient attention.

III DEPRIVATION IN THE WELFARE STATE

The second type of investigation appropriate to this chapter focuses not on some arm of social policy—for example, morbidity and health care—but rather on the overall life chances typically enjoyed by individuals variously situated in the society. More particularly, the classical and contemporary perspectives on industrial society and social policy explored in Part I alert us to the situation of the poor, who have been a perennial political concern. For example, it was on alleviation of their lot that the Beveridge Report on post-war reconstruction centred: it looked to the abolition of those apparently most gregarious of giants—Idleness, Want, Disease, Squalor and Ignorance.

Following in a long tradition of British empirical social science, there has been a rapid growth in the investigation of poverty over the last two decades. Some of this literature has attempted an overall assessment of the extent and distribution of poverty in contemporary Britain. It has tended to emphasise the financial or economic aspects and to take individuals or households as the units of its analysis (see, for example, Atkinson, 1969; Bull, 1972). We focus instead, however, upon the other main arm of this expanding literature—the study of local communities exhibiting long-term multiple deprivation. The studies we use may not immediately permit an assessment of the extent of such multiple deprivation in the society as a whole, but they do afford insight into its aetiology.

We recall, first, that for *neo-Marxist* writers the analysis and explanation of poverty must be firmly rooted in an understanding of the class situation of the poor, i.e. their position within the mode of industrial production. They are those who bear disproportionately the social costs of capitalist development. For they consist principally of an industrial reserve army ensuring adequate supplies of cheap unskilled labour as capitalist employment levels fluctuate, the technologically unemployed, as new techniques displace human skills, and such unemployables as the aged and handicapped, incapable of being rendered productive within capitalist enterprise. The continued dependence of housing allocation upon market power tends to result in the concentration of such poor in blighted zones of falling house values; political decisions over housing allocation, notably by the local authorities, have tended if anything to reinforce such zoning (Castells, 'Advanced Capitalism, Collective Consumption and Urban Contradiction' in Lindberg, 1975, esp. pp. 182–5). Attempts to redress the social ills of such areas through social policies will bear little fruit unless combined with an attack on capitalist property relations. Yet programmes under the auspices of the capitalist state by definition exclude such an attack.

Liberal writers have generally predicated their diagnoses of poverty upon a vision of society as a collection of atomised individuals—a vision that the market liberals see as threatened by the twentieth-century growth of collectivism but that the political liberals see as increasingly taking the form of a competitive meritocracy. Poverty is therefore seen as deriving either from the motivational—or even moral—inadequacies of the poor themselves, or else from incomplete realisation of the liberals' vision of the good society. More specifically, there has on the one hand been a variety of diagnoses and policy proposals focussing on some alleged 'culture of poverty' that inhibits the capacity of the poor to take up opportunities for full participation in the wider achieving society.[10] The prescription is remedial policies directed at the familial and community processes that foster and perpetuate such inhibitions. Alternatively, diagnosis and prescription may look to the peripheral malfunctioning of the wider society. Market liberals decry the welfare bureaucracies that sap incentives for self-help. Political liberals emphasise the need to equalise opportunities as between the poor and the non-poor—*inter alia,* through sustained efforts by local and national government to improve service delivery. The ultimate goal in each case is that the poor should be enabled individually to deploy their resources and to appropriate common opportunities within an open society. The optimistic liberal prognoses we saw in the previous section recur here. Benevolent 'treatment' of the poor together with improved efficiency in public services, involving only modest resource costs, are tending and will suffice to incorporate the poor into the mainstream of the improving wider society.

Tawney and T. H. Marshall, in his earlier essays, may have been overly optimistic as to the impact of the Welfare State upon poverty. Titmuss, however, is alert to the new—and not-so-new—intergroup struggles that determine life chance allocation, and he uses a broadly actionist perspective in exploring individuals' strategies and successes—or failures—in realising their life projects. The deprived then appear as those who have suffered persistent exclusion from resources and from power to realise their life projects. For example, they suffer disproportionately the 'social costs and social insecurities which are the product of a rapidly changing industrial–urban society'; social programmes intended to discriminate according to need are perennially in danger of stigmatising recipients, thereby reinforcing their exclusion and their inability to define themselves as full citizens (Titmuss, 1968, pp. 133–5, 158–9). The *Social Democratic* perspective is, therefore, distinguished from liberal views by its refusal to embrace a naive optimism as to any benign trend in our society towards the elimination of poverty, and in its emphasis upon a diagnosis in terms of differential power and advantage in inter-group struggles. It differs from the neo-Marxist accounts in wishing to distinguish the political, community and production milieux as potential arenas of such conflict, and in denying that it is the situation of the poor *vis-à-vis* the means of production that is invariably, necessarily and unambiguously dominant in the generation of deprivation.

Recent anti-poverty programmes have been predicated upon various of these theories and have incorporated a research commitment, with continuing diagnosis of deprivation and evaluation of different strategies for its extirpation. We have chosen to focus in this section upon the long-term multiple deprivation of local communities. It seems sensible, therefore, to concentrate upon the research findings of these projects in attempting an evaluation of the foregoing theories and of the role that social policies have played and can play in the elimination of deprivation. We focus on the findings of the Community Development Projects, which are located in areas of multiple deprivation and have been recently producing their final reports.

First, then, what do the findings of these action–research projects suggest in regard to the generation of deprivation? Their initial remit seems to have been implicitly predicated on a broad acceptance of the liberal diagnoses outlined above: the neighbourhood basis seems in part to have expressed official confidence that deprivation was a problem peripheral to the society as a whole. That problem, furthermore, was seen as deriving either from characteristics of the populations concerned, or else from technical malfunctioning of Welfare State agencies which were functioning satisfactorily as far as other sections of society were concerned. At the same time, some deliberate selection was attempted, to include a variety of areas for such action–research—ranging from isolated settlements in South Wales and Cumbria to inner-city neighbourhoods, and from contexts of prosperity such as Coventry to others of general decline (National CDP, 1974, paras 2.1, 3.3).

Yet the clearest conclusion to emerge from the national experiment is the inadequacy of this diagnosis. Typical have been the findings of the Coventry CDP. Hillfields, the area in which it was located, simply did not contain an abnormal share of 'inadequate' families. The most obvious problems of the area were ones of social circumstance rather than individual competence. Moreover, low incomes, poor housing and planning blight afflicted the mass of residents, and were similar in kind, if different in degree, to the problems of other inner-city areas (Coventry CDP, 1975a, para. 5.4). Nor could the assumption be maintained that it was the merely technical malfunctioning of public services that permitted the persistence of deprivation, and that improved communication would suffice to effect a significant change. For the technical and managerial skills of Coventry Corporation are second to none (1975b, Paper 7, paras 1.1–1.2).

Rather, the Inter-Project Report, drawn up approximately mid-way through the originally intended life of the national experiment, concludes that, while improved service coordination and communication might 'achieve some greater flexibility in the face to face delivery of services', for issues like redevelopment such strategies are by themselves largely futile, since 'there need to be basic changes of policy' (National CDP, 1974, para. 4.8; cf. paras 5.14–15).[11] Likewise, the 1975/6 Forward Plan for those projects still in operation rejects 'accounts [of area deprivation] ... based on social pathology', as also any hopes that 'improved coordination of existing social and welfare services can ... make [more than] ... a marginal impact' (National CDP, 1975, p. 1).

The CDP experiment points, therefore, to a diagnosis of deprivation that sees it as the precipitate of society-wide processes—a diagnosis that is, therefore, necessarily historical in orientation (National CDP, 1977, Ch. 1). Rapid urban–industrial change has widely varying consequences for different social groups: it tends to produce virtuous and vicious circles of advantage and disadvantage, with only those groups already relatively advantaged able to convert such advantages into the power or capacity to escape new forms of disadvantage. Thus some CDP neighbourhoods are reception areas for unskilled and semi-skilled newcomers to city regions enjoying rapid industrial growth. Yet these are groups likely to be badly organised, to include high proportions of non-whites exposed to racial discrimination, and to be especially vulnerable to redundancy in times of recession (National CDP, 1974, para. 3.14). Others are areas of population decline, with the skilled and the young among the first to depart, leaving behind those least able to arrest the general decline of the neighbourhood (para. 3.15; cf. National CDP, 1975, p. 2; Payne and Smith, 'The Context of the Twelve Areas' in Lees and Smith, 1975). In both cases, growing need is likely for public services to the dependent; but a shrinking rate base coupled with lack of political power for the residents affected instead typically promote a reduction in such services. Yet in general such causal chains are publicly neither anticipated nor recognised: deprivation and privilege appear instead as the rewards and penalties of individuals' traits and performances, or as the unfortunate but unavoidable by-product of the technical functioning of a developing urban–industrial society (National CDP, 1974, paras 3.16, 3.39).

Our attention is, therefore, directed to an analysis of much wider processes. Notwithstanding the variations among CDPs in the detailed issues faced and the specific strategies adopted, their reports suggest the foundations of a common diagnosis comprising perhaps three principal elements. It may be helpful to illustrate each of these strands by reference to one of the original projects, that in Coventry, which also claimed our attention in the previous chapter. Judging by the final reports that have appeared from other projects, there is little ground for major anxiety that the Coventry analysis will prove to have been markedly atypical. The Liverpool project, admittedly, differs in the inferences it draws for action, as we shall see in chapter 6, but in its historical diagnosis of deprivation it is broadly consonant with what follows (Topping and Smith, 1977, Ch. 3).[12]

(i) Many of the individual project reports have emphasised the fatefulness of investment and employment decisions by private industrial concerns whose organisation and policy-making are at a national—or even an international—level. Such decisions affect both the extent and the kind of employment and income opportunities—that is, the overall demand for labour and relative demand for different skills (National CDP, 1977, esp. Chs 1, 3). Several of the CDPs have examined the responsiveness of these decisions to regional policies; their findings suggest that such policies have only minimal impact in the face of market forces, and that they are insufficiently sensitive to small-scale variations in local needs (National CDP, 1977, Ch. 2).

In Coventry, dominated by the car industry, the post-war boom in domestic car production has passed its peak; further concentration of the industry nationally may put at risk the city's traditionally buoyant demand for labour. This is likely to hit the unskilled in particular, who over the past half-century have increased markedly in relation to skilled manual workers. It is these workers and their dependants who have come to form a major part of the population of Hillfields, the target area of the CDP, with its stock of cheaper and older housing. The neighbourhood, the CDP team argue, has come to serve as a 'reserve tank of labour' for the motor vehicle and associated industries in the city, with many of its employable residents readily available for unskilled work in times of boom but easily made redundant in times of slump. Its deprivation must, therefore, be seen as having as one of its major sources the changing fortunes—and the national and international reorganisation—of the motor industry (Coventry CDP, 1975a, paras 7.0–7.27; 1975b, Paper 6).[13]

This defines, therefore, a basic disjunction between the interests of industrial enterprise—in this case most notably the motor industry—and those of the city and, more particularly, the residents of such areas as Hillfields. An immediate corollary is a similar disjunction between residents' interests and the goals of local authority policy-makers, in so far as those goals, as we saw in chapter 4, are heavily moulded by industrial and commercial interests (see above, pp. 124–6). Instead, the CDP analysis distinguishes those sections of the city population who enjoy the benefits and bear the costs of industrial prosperity and expansion. It also exposes the costs, in terms of infrastructure and social services, imposed by industrial development on the local authority, and the dependence of local authority services' adequacy upon the demographic changes that investment and employment decisions by such nationally and internationally oriented industrial corporations induce (Coventry CDP, 1975b, Paper 7, paras 7.2–7.4).

(ii) A recurring theme in the reports has been the unanticipated tendencies of certain types of key decision in the public sector—both nationally and locally—to perpetuate and multiply this deprivation. Local authority decisions over land use, redevelopment and rehousing in these neighbourhoods are portrayed as typically promoting planning blight and exacerbating a competition over scarce inner-city land in which residents are least capable of securing their interests (cf. pp. 120–1, 123–5 above). Central and local government decisions over rents and rates have been the other principal area of public sector activity diagnosed as multiplying deprivation. Recent shifts in the burden of rates from industrial to domestic property have hit CDP residents particularly hard (National CDP, 1974, para. 5.11; cf. para. 5.30), as has the shift to 'fair rents' as a result of the 1972 Housing Finance Act.

Thus in the Coventry CDP, the fatefulness of public sector policies for the generation of deprivation is highlighted by the finding that if anything distinguished Hillfields from the rest of Coventry it was 'the lengthy assault of stop-go redevelopment'. (In chapter 4, we looked at these redevelopment programmes for Hillfields as a case study in the formulation and application of policy; here, in contrast, our interest is in their largely unanticipated consequences for residents.) 'Piecemeal and sporadic' action 'has set in motion a vicious spiral of planning blight, eroding certainty in the area and contributing to its physical, social and economic decline'. Industry and commerce have extended their share of Hillfields' valuable inner-city land, as also have public services oriented to the concerns of the wider city, e.g. the ring road. Likewise, the Hillfields experience is that shifts in rating and rents policies can unintentionally and 'at a stroke take more out of disadvantaged areas and . . . cities than the whole of the extra money put in through' the Urban Programme and similar forms of positive discrimination (Coventry CDP, 1975a, paras 5.4, 7.38, 7.40, 2.4, 7.33).

(iii) Alongside these economic and political processes of deprivation, there is a source more strictly 'social' in the sense of involving the social identities of individuals and neighbourhoods, for the deprived areas and their residents are typically the objects of stereotyping and stigmatisation by members of the wider society. This serves not only to underpin negative official definitions of such neighbourhoods and to discourage diagnosis in terms of wider societal processes, but also to promote changes in the social composition and amenities of such neighbourhoods that have the effect of a self-fulfilling prophecy (National CDP, 1974, para. 3.15). Hillfields in Coventry again offers a particularly clear illustration. Its persisting dilapidation has been conventionally attributed to the supposed internal pathology of the neighbourhood. Among official decision-makers, such labelling has hitherto served to reduce acceptance of official responsibility for the neighbourhood's physical environment and to legitimate minimal attention to residents' expressed preferences; it has ensured disproportionate attention from the police and the media; it has also accelerated the decline in property values (Benington, 1972, paras 3.12, 3.9).

Typical, then, of the conclusions offered by the CDPs in their analysis of deprivation is that of the Coventry team: 'as the root causes . . . operate largely outside democratic control, they cannot be dealt with by tinkering with technical procedures; they demand new kinds of political intervention which reach beyond existing jurisdiction, to claim greater local public control over the situation' (1975a, Concluding Propositions, para. 3.1). Whether as efforts in *action*–research the CDPs have promoted attempts at such enhanced control will be one of our concerns in the next chapter. These investigations therefore undermine any assumption—such as that common among liberals—that explanations of the generation and persistence of deprivation can be separated from more general accounts of inequality. First, the disadvantages prevalent in these deprived areas are different not in kind, but at most only in degree, from those of residents in other areas. The use of social indicators of area deprivation to guide programmes of positive discrimination has therefore only limited rational justification. Such justification requires that policy-makers recognise the diversity of areas in which various forms of need may be particularly high; such programmes must be situated within a universalist infrastructure, in recognition of the social and geographical universality of need (Hatch and Sherrott, 1973). Such indicators cannot, therefore, be taken as validly measuring the pathological traits of disadvantaged areas, as political liberals are wont to assume.

Still less can multiple need be taken as reliably indicated by low incomes, as market liberals would commonly avow (cf. pp. 163–4 above). Jordan points to similarities between the needs of the poor and of those with higher incomes. Social deviance and breakdown of social networks, taken by many recent writers including Seebohm as indicating 'social needs' (cf. p. 106 above), are high not only in areas of high unemployment and declining industry and population, but also in more prosperous immigration and reception areas, where populations are highly mobile (see, for example, Jordan, 1974, pp. 4, 12).[14] The causes and symptoms of social deprivation may differ, then, as between those conventionally labelled 'the poor' and the wider population; but in kind and even, perhaps, in degree, no such difference prevails, although there *are* likely to be differences in the resources they can call on to cope with such deprivation (see p. 111 above; cf. Packman, 1968)—and hence in the long-term cumulative consequences of the latter. (Cf. pp. 159–60 above on the class-related consequences of illness.)

Programmes of positive discrimination towards educationally deprived areas have been the other major national action–research innovation in recent anti-poverty measures (cf. p. 131 above). As with the CDPs, their initial remit betrays official commitment to a broadly liberal diagnosis of deprivation. Positive discrimination was meant, not merely to raise the quality of schools in such areas to the national average, but 'quite deliberately to make them better. The justification is that the homes and neighbourhoods from which many of their children come provide little support and stimulus for learning. The schools must provide a compensating environment' (quoted in Halsey, 1972a, p. 31). It is in the local institutions of home and community that the most deep-seated sources of educational under-achievement are assumed to lie.

The Halsey Report, however, as a result of the national action–research experiment, argues a very different diagnosis, which blends with that elaborated in our discussion of the CDPs. Educational under-achievement springs from the irrelevance of the curriculum to pupils' prospective adult destinations—particularly occupationally; from the apparent hopelessness of aspiring to any individual or collective future that is other than multiply disadvantaged; and from the mutual incomprehension and negative stereotyping of educators and parents—resulting in dissociation and incongruence between pupils' learning experiences at home and at school (Halsey, 1972a, pp. 11–12, 189–98, Chs 9–12). Effective measures for countering educational deprivation must, therefore, not only offer formal qualifications but also equip with the skills and competences relevant to likely adult destinations. Second, they must provide milieux that engender 'constructive discontent'—with collective criticism of the political decisions and non-decisions that govern those allocative processes of which this multiple deprivation is the fruit. Third, they must involve not compensatory but complementary and community education—with a partnership between teachers and parents who, while hitherto uncomprehending, are far from unconcerned about their children's education (Halsey, 1972a, pp. 117–18; cf. p. 163 above). In short, effective measures for countering educational deprivation must be predicated upon a diagnosis that acknowledges its rootedness in the prevailing relationships between education and the occupational, political and community milieux (cf. pp. 132–3 above). Again, it will be in chapter 6 that we investigate the directions of group formation and action that have accompanied such educational action–research.

Not, however, that this diagnosis has been uncritically accepted by the social scientific community. Indeed, officially sponsored research into the causes of deprivation has in some cases seemed reluctant even to acknowledge the CDP experiment and its findings.

Some of the DHSS Cycle of Deprivation studies, for example, initiated by the Conservative government in 1972, scarcely join battle with the CDP diagnosis.[15] We are thereby alerted to the inadequacies of any naive positivistic view of cumulative advance in the findings of social science, and to the sensitivity to the prevailing political climate of the assumptions employed in social scientific research, especially given the contemporary importance of governmental sponsorship.

Theoretical implications

If, however, the diagnoses of the CDPs *are* accepted, including their findings on the effectiveness of the main branches of social policy in alleviating deprivation, then significant implications follow for our evaluation of competing perspectives on social policy. We have already observed that the CDP and EPA programmes seem initially to have embraced a broadly *liberal* diagnosis of deprivation. The critique we have traced of this official remit therefore extends to liberal theories also. For example, these action–research projects have come to focus attention upon differential power and advantage as determinants of deprivation and to deny any 'automatic' benign trend (cf. p. 183 above).

Evaluation of the Social Democratic and neo-Marxist approaches—both being critiques of liberalism—in the light of the foregoing is rather more difficult. The Coventry CDP studies seem in important senses to vindicate the *neo-Marxist* case; indeed, the team there explicitly embrace such a stance (see above, p. 127). They seem to demonstrate, for example, that there is a fundamental identity of interests between the deprived and the working class, rooted in their common powerlessness *vis-à-vis* the means of production in a world of multinational corporations. Likewise, the Coventry studies in particular seem to demonstrate that the various factors contributing to deprivation are significantly moulded by industrial and commercial interests, and that it is therefore individuals' class situation that is the pre-eminent determinant of deprivation.

Yet our discussion suggests that in at least three respects the neo-Marxist approach is vulnerable. First, the deprivation of the CDP areas is typically reinforced and exacerbated by negative stereotyping by the wider society—stereotyping that is unjustified in terms of the social conditions actually obtaining, but that serves to legitimate irresponsible local authority policies and to promote blight and social decline. That is, social and political processes operate *selectively*—and at least partly independently of economic processes—with regard to certain areas, but not others, occupied by individuals in particularly weak class situations. Second, in the Coventry studies an overlap of interests is revealed between the residents of the CDP area and those of the wider city, given the trends in the multinationally organised motor industry (see above, pp. 185–6; cf. pp. 127–8), trends that have only accelerated since the team reported in March 1975. There are grounds for anticipating and building an alliance between the lumpenproletariat of such areas as Hillfields and the broad mass of the working class (see too Friedman, 1977, Ch. 16). Yet this constellation of interests seems to be contingent upon these particular employment and investment prospects; whether similar constellations will exist elsewhere must surely remain a matter for further empirical investigation. Third, the Coventry analysts look to 'new kinds of political intervention . . . to claim greater local public control' (cf. p. 187 above) over the sources of deprivation in general and over industrial and commercial decision-making in particular. They leave open, however, whether this requires socialisation of the means of production as a necessary condition for such reduction in the power of private property. In our discussion of policy development in the city, moreover, we argued the perennial fragility of the alliance between those exercising public and private power, and questioned thereby the cohesion and invulnerability of any capitalist 'ruling class' (see above, p. 128). To accept the CDP critique of liberal views does not, therefore, require that a distinctively Marxist position be embraced. It does, however, call for an analysis of deprivation (and of the associated patterns of interests) in terms of diverse forms of power exercised in political, community and production milieux—in line with the Social Democrats.

Nevertheless, *Social Democrats* such as Titmuss have often left such an exercise only superficially explored. They have instead been content to portray social needs as the precipitate not of such a continuing struggle but rather of technologically deterministic urban–industrial change (Sinfield, 1978, p. 134). They can tend in consequence to see statutory efforts to meet such needs as a legitimate responsibility of the state, compensating for costs imposed by society in general rather than by specific advantaged groups. The social rights they espouse are then—as the neo-Marxists would claim is more generally true—at most the collective reparation for depradations wrought by irresponsible minorities. The conditions under which this pattern of social responsibilities is accepted or challenged by citizens at large will be one of our concerns in the next chapter.

Second, the Social Democrats have at most suggested some of the constellations of interest that may develop between the deprived and members of the wider society; they have been slow to acknowledge, with Weber (see above, p. 35), the task of responsible political leadership that articulation of such common interests involves. We have, however, pointed to the variety of such possible constellations: the Child Poverty Action Group has tended to redefine the 'new corporate interest' in terms of a family lobby rather than a poverty lobby; the National Consumer Council is promoting a consumer lobby as the most promising vehicle for dealing with deprivation or 'consumer detriment' (Williams, 1977); finally, as we have seen in the present section, some writers espouse trade unions of organised workers as potentially the most willing and effective allies of the poor. Among these alternatives, competing political leaders cannot but make responsible but fateful choices, in terms of their potential for engaging effective action for social reform. To such engagement we turn in chapter 6.

IV CONCLUSION

The two empirical investigations in which we have engaged may seem somewhat unconnected. There are, however, important continuities and complementary conclusions. To start with, in both sections we found it necessary to explore how differences in power and advantage readily become generalised, with virtuous and vicious circles of privilege and deprivation at the extremes. We traced the economic, social and political powerlessness of CDP neighbourhoods and the cumulative deprivation this permits. We argued that the consequences of illness are commonly worse for the lower social classes and tend, when chronic, to promote downward mobility. At the same time, however, we have seen how the advantaged are most able to restrict the visibility of their privileges and of the processes whereby the costs of those privileges are imposed on others less powerful. As Sinfield has argued, 'inequality in the visibility of benefits is an important and integral part of the social division of welfare' (1978, p. 136).

In both of the preceding sections we have, moreover, seen how, notwithstanding the formal elimination of the cash nexus from the relationship between client and welfare professional in universalistic services, differences in power and resources continue to influence outcomes. Thus differences in knowledge of—and attitudes towards—health care and services seem important in explaining the significantly worse treatment received by the lower social classes and by such weak groups as the chronic sick and aged. The 'social distance' between medical professionals and lower-class patients also seems influential here. Likewise, in section III we saw that the educators in multiply deprived areas—in contrast to those elsewhere—have commonly disregarded as a resource of value the learning that their pupils undergo in home and neighbourhood, and have permitted the purposes and procedures of the educational process to be mysterious and incomprehensible to parents and pupils alike. That is, the exercise of professional power seems to have been significantly influenced by the resources that their clients are variously able to bring to bear, but in ways that none of our competing macro-theories emphasise. The enunciation of common social rights to be met by universalist services may then be a necessary but, *pace* the Social Democrats, is not a sufficient condition for the appropriation of these rights. To such issues of professional power, control and exclusion we return in the next chapter.

We have also explored the patterns of interest identity and conflict that the contemporary social division of welfare involves. In both sections we considered, for example, the impact of 'broad-grain' policies on different groups in the population. Preventive health measures may, we saw, benefit different social classes differentially, precluding any presumption that they are unambiguously in the common interest (see above, p. 173). In Coventry, public utilities may have benefited suburban commuters and the industry on which the city's prosperity until the 1960s was based; their benefits for Hillfields have been much less obvious (see above, p. 187; cf. pp. 124–5). More generally, we sought in section II to trace the lines of common and conflicting interest among the users of a universalist service; while in section III we considered the conflicts and harmonies of interest among the neighbourhoods of the deprived, the mass of the local working class and the regional population at large. Yet in none of these cases have we found the liberal or neo-Marxist portrayals of interests adequate—and even the Social Democratic account has proved too superficial. To all of these issues we return in the next chapter, examining the typical directions of action and group formation in relation to these patterns of interest.

Finally, we argued that attempts to implement the social right to medical care have tended to expose to political scrutiny those wider societal processes that vitiate its universal appropriation—not merely fiscal and occupational welfare benefits, but also the content of the work and residential activities of different social groups, with their unevenly distributed consequences for morbidity and other social needs. Likewise, the CDPs have pointed to an analysis of deprivation, not in terms of individual pathology or the technical demands of an urban–industrial society, but rather as the precipitate of socially unaccountable power. Thus the reproduction of the social division of welfare is revealed as in part dependent upon essentially political decisions, and therefore upon directions of political leadership. Furthermore, the very recognition of inequalities is in part a political process. For example, differential group outcomes and class gradients in health care may inform measures of positive discrimination; but they are not immediately visible to the advantaged or the disadvantaged. Finally, the pattern of interests flowing from the division of welfare is not, as we have just seen, self-evident, but rather requires articulation within a political arena if it is to issue in action.[16] It is through a process of selection by competing political leaders that we must expect these inequalities to become relevant to social action and social change, in a manner to be explored in the next chapter. Not that such action will necessarily express self-interest alone. Rather, we shall need to investigate the conditions under which political leadership can and does mobilise support for social policies from those whose self-interest is unaffected—or even adversely affected—by them. Yet this irreducibly *political* context and aspect of the social division of welfare is largely disregarded by liberal and neo-Marxist writers and has been inadequately explored by the Social Democrats.

NOTES

1. For a survey and methodological critique of the data published by central government, together with an evaluation of its usefulness and an extended bibliography, see Alderson, 'Central Government Routine Health Statistics' in Maunder (1974) Vol. 2. Cf. Culyer *et al.*, 'Health Indicators' in Shonfield and Shaw (1972).
2. She uses standardised mortality ratios, which indicate class gradients after allowing for the effect of different age structures; see (1975) pp. 73–4; cf. Halsey (1972b) Table 11.6.
3. A major obstacle to firm conclusions appears to be uncertainty over the adjustments that should be made in published data for the later years if occupations are to be classified on the same basis for the whole period. For example, Parker's adjustments for 1949/53 in standardised mortality ratios (1975, Table 5.1) give considerably lower values to the rates for Social Classes I and II than do the adjusted figures in Halsey (1972b) and Arie (1966). The latter's figures lead him to a markedly different conclusion from that of Parker: 'the overall gradient has become much less steep during this century (as indeed have the gradients for most individual diseases)' (1966, p. 310).
4. See Arie (1966) for evidence that in Scotland, at least, stillbirth rates in Social Classes I and V stand in a ratio of 2:5.
5. A somewhat different picture emerges if one considers not the proportion of a social class consulting, but rather the number of visits by those who consulted. On this basis, Rein (1969) finds higher consultation rates among the lower classes throughout the period after 1948.
6. That Halsey's study, published in 1972, has to rely upon information relating to the mid-1950s is indicative of the fragmented and unsatisfactory sources of data available in this field.
7. The proportion for the working class (58%) being more than twice that for the middle class (27%).
8. Among the market liberals, however, Lees (1976) accepts this criticism and sees the chronically sick as suitable subjects for special state concern. How in practice they are to be distinguished is left unclear.
9. This is touched on by Little and Westergaard (1964) esp. pp. 308–11, and Hope (1975) pp. 34–5. But in neither case do the authors go as far as we have in seeking to explicate the sociological assumptions informing the choice of measures of inequality.
10. Although these approaches display considerable variety, some differing significantly from the original use of the term 'culture of poverty' by such writers as Oscar Lewis.
11. However, the Report admits that *earlier* consultation over redevelopment may offer more hope of harmonious cooperation and agreement between residents and policy-makers (National CDP, 1974, para. 5.15).
12. In addition, however, the Liverpool project refuses to portray the local authority as the servant of local industrial and commercial interests: cf. pp. 124–7 above and p. 225 below.
13. See too a development of the Coventry studies: Friedman (1977) esp. Part 5.
14. A third major type of socially needy area is the council estate serving as a 'dumping ground' for the local authority's less 'deserving' tenants.
15. Thus in their review of research on deprivation, Rutter and Madge offer only a couple of pages of rather superficial comment on the CDP reports (1976, pp. 39–41).
16. This we also saw in the case of national superannuation and trade union interests (p. 91 above). Cf. Klein and Lewis (1976) pp. 92–3, 137. Cf. also the conclusion to Goldthorpe *et al.* (1978).

CHAPTER 6

Social Policy and Social Integration

One of the commonest and most generally accepted delusions is that every man can be qualified in some particular way—said to be kind, wicked, stupid, energetic, apathetic and so on. . . . And it is wrong. Human beings are like rivers: the water is one and the same in all of them but every river is narrow in some places, flows swifter in others; here it is broad, there still, or clear, or cold, or muddy or warm. It is the same with men. Every man bears within him the germs of every human quality, and now manifests one, now another. . . . [*Tolstoy* Resurrection *pp. 252–3*]

In truth, man is a polluted river. One must be a sea, to receive a polluted river and not be defiled.
Behold, I teach you the Superman: he is this sea. . . .
And this is the great noontide: it is when man stands at the middle of his course between animal and Superman and celebrates his journey to the evening as his highest hope: for it is the journey to a new morning. [*Nietzsche* Thus Spoke Zarathustra *pp. 42, 104*]

I INTRODUCTION

We turn now to the third issue around which debates over the significance of social policy in contemporary Western societies have centred: namely, its role in social integration. The 1834 Poor Law regime has provided the base-line for this debate, with present-day neo-Marxist and liberal writers, for example, either denying, deploring or ignoring any fundamental shift in the role of subsequent social policies. On the one hand, social policies have commonly been seen as most obviously concerned with the dependent, the poor, the deprived. What relationships do they engender between these categories and the wider society? No less importantly, however, social policies have also been acknowledged as having impli-cations for relationships among the citizenry as a whole—if only, as in the 1834 Poor Law, by reinforcing the work ethic through a deterrent regime. The competing visions of a harmonious commun-ity of free and enlightened citizens have then informed competing assessments of the social relationships among citizens in general that contemporary social policies promote.

Neo-Marxists have been concerned to argue that contemporary social policies have introduced no basic change in the mode of integration of our society. The disciplines of the cash nexus are not challenged; like the Poor Law of 1834, therefore, contemporary social policies are fundamentally an aid in the effective control of the labour force. Moreover, such policies render more plausible the claim by those in authority that exploitation has been mitigated and class conflict rendered obsolete. Fundamental social criticism is thereby deflected, the false consciousness of the working class is heightened and the revolutionary transformation of capitalist society into a truly humanised social order is postponed, perhaps indefinitely. Certainly no significant role is possible for social policies in the drive for fundamental social criticism and change.

Poverty may provide fertile soil for the stimulation of discontent.[1] Yet any fundamental transformation will require collective action that brings together the poor and the working class in a common conflict with capitalist social arrangements. Coercive and manipula-tive integration are, in contrast, the almost inevitable results of programmes that address themselves to the plight of the poor alone, particularly where they operate under state control. Thus, for example, Castells portrays American social programmes directed at areas of urban deprivation over the last fifteen years in terms of the capitalist response to the growing 'urban crisis', for the latter appears in social, as well as fiscal, terms. Such programmes were initially 'designed to improve social peace'; but so deep-rooted is the crisis that the programmes were themselves 'transformed into disruptive mechanisms', soon to be dismantled and replaced by 'massive repression', which proved, indeed, increasingly necessary as 'urban protest movements' increasingly 'defied . . . the legitimacy of traditional local authorities' (1976, pp. 13–14).

The *market liberals* postulate that a free market is a necessary condition for social harmony in an advanced industrial society, and that, but for a temporary safety-net of state-organised social services, the distribution of even the most fundamental life chances should be organised on market principles. Such a market system mediates a harmony of individual interests, promotes a sense of individual responsibility and realises individual freedom. These fruits cannot but evoke the consensus and approval of all rational citizens. Wide-ranging social policies organised on non-market principles must be expected to promote social discord, to undermine any expression of social responsibility and to involve state coercion. The *political liberals*, in contrast, have in general accepted the growth of modern social policies as a means of effecting the civic reintegration of the labour force. In a meritocratic and pluralistic society, such policies play a central role in rendering irrelevant, irrational and even meaningless the class antagonisms of early capitalism.

For liberal writers the causes of poverty reside either in the motivational inadequacies of the poor or in the peripheral malfunctioning of the open society. For the market liberals, such malfunctioning is, admittedly, becoming more than peripheral as welfare bureacracies extend their sway. Yet with a return to market disciplines, it will increasingly be the faults and inadequacies of minorities of individuals that account for persisting deprivation. Some of these inadequacies—for example, mental and physical handicap—will remain a legitimate concern of the state. Others, including the cultural handicap of those living in a culture of poverty, may require short-term remedial treatment by state agencies. Yet for many whose motivation for self-help and self-improvement is currently weakened by a prodigal state, the return of market disciplines will suffice to reverse the process of demoralisation. The exposure of all to the disciplines and freedom of the market will, moreover, evoke a no less universal acquiescence in, and approval of, societal arrangements.

Explanation of poverty in terms of individual cultural handicap is by no means confined to proponents of the market. The associated apathy and withdrawal from wider societal involvement represent a form of social mal-integration that political liberals regard as being in the interests neither of the individuals concerned nor of the wider society. Remedial treatment by state agencies is therefore legitimate for the elimination of this distinctive culture; its fruit will be a spontaneous social cohesion of free and enlightened citizens. Political liberals alternatively explain poverty in terms of marginal inefficiencies in the functioning of private and, more especially, public agencies of life chance distribution. Social unrest among the poor of a somewhat disorganised and destructive kind is then predictable; but social harmony can be restored through the essentially technical improvement of service delivery (cf. pp. 181–2 above).

Against the liberal views that social integration proceeds from the manifest rationality of a society organised in market or meritocratic terms, in which individual self-interest is in harmony with the common good, the *Social Democrats* deny that the pursuit of self-interest can, even in principle, be a sufficient condition for social integration in an advanced urban–industrial society. Social policies are evaluated in terms of their potential for evoking a commitment to the common interest. Against the neo-Marxist view that social integration, to which end social policies are means, is essentially coercive in contemporary Western societies, the Social Democrats argue that social policies may realise common interests as the basis of spontaneous and free solidarity.

Thus for Titmuss, the problem of stigmatisation must be central to any exploration of the social conflicts and integration that social policies may promote. Such stigmatisation concerns community membership and exclusion—essentially *moral* phenomena. The Poor Law functioned 'by operating punitive tests of discrimination; by strengthening conceptions of approved and disapproved dependencies; and by a damaging assault on the recipients of welfare in terms of their sense of self-respect and self-determination'. Its redistributive aim was therefore by means that were 'socially divisive'. Yet such a punitive administration undermined the developing preventive orientation: the effectiveness of the latter 'in a highly differentiated, unequal and class-saturated society' required that the services 'be delivered through socially approved channels . . . without loss of self-respect by the users and their families' (1968, pp. 190, 129; see too pp. 64–5 above).

For Titmuss, then, the exercise of social rights to universal services is to be understood as an expression of community membership—and therefore of moral obligations, rights and loyalties. The persistence of means-tested selectivity, in contrast, is likely to promote social divisions and losses of individual dignity paralleling those of the Poor Law. Yet given a concern over the gross inequalities and deprivations generated by our urban-industrial

society, the choice between means-tested selectivity and universality does not exhaust the stigmatising propensities of contemporary social policies. For, as a counter to such deprivations, we have in
the previous two chapters referred to new measures of positive
discrimination. However, these too will run the risk of inflicting 'a
sense of personal failure and individual fault', with its concomitant
threat to community integration. Titmuss concludes with his central
proposition on the preconditions for engaging in positive discrimination towards the most needy without stigmatisation:

> some structure of universalism is an essential pre-requisite . . .
> [for] it provides a general system of values and a sense of
> community; socially approved agencies . . .; it sees welfare, not as
> a burden, but as complementary and as an instrument of change
> and, finally, it allows positive discriminatory services to be pro-
> vided as rights for categories of people and for classes of need in
> terms of priority social areas and other impersonal classifications
> [1968, pp. 132–5; and see above, p. 188].

Let us, then, proceed by examining in turn selectivist, universalist
and positive discriminatory social policies and the forms of social
conflict and integration they engender. Throughout, our principal
interest is in the foregoing competing theories. Yet it will be neither
possible nor desirable to omit reference to a variety of questions
that have been raised but left unresolved in the previous empirical
chapters. Among these perhaps three stand out as particularly
noteworthy. First, we have touched on the role of political
leaders—their articulation of political choices and issues, their
institution of and responsibility for social policies, their mobilisation of political support. To what extent do such leaders thereby
have an active role in defining and evoking collective commitments
and hence in promoting social integration and transformation—or,
indeed, social conflict and disintegration? Second, a recurring
theme has been the mediating role of the social policy professional
in defining and ministering to the interests and needs of the
citizen—albeit within a context of politically specified priorities and
having due regard to citizens' preferences. In what sense is the
citizen thereby subject to disciplines and controls and what
rationale is offered for them? Finally, in what ways are citizens'
responses to social policies and their life projects within the wider
society affected and informed by the legitimacy they accord to such
professional and political activity? To what extent, that is, do

citizens accept politically articulated commitments and professionally mediated controls as binding in formulating and pursuing their life projects? These concerns will recur throughout this chapter; for all bear upon the competing arguments rehearsed above.

II SELECTIVITY AND STIGMA IN THE ACHIEVING SOCIETY

In previous chapters we have suggested that it is selective means-tested benefits, in cash and kind, that seem most obviously to perpetuate the relief functions of the 1834 regime. They provide the paradigm of the social provision advocated by market liberals and deplored by neo-Marxists. Moreover, like the 1834 relief, while they may be intended by their instigators as primarily redistributive towards the most needy, the pursuit of disciplinary and regulatory goals is also evident, as we shall see. We start, therefore, by examining the forms of social integration and conflict that such selective social policies may promote. Yet, as in earlier chapters, we must be selective, if only for reasons of space. The relief of 1834 focussed upon the destitution of the able-bodied adult male breadwinner (S. and B. Webb, 1963, Ch. 1); so also, therefore, shall we.

Means-testing is itself a form of rationing and hence control—for it involves the application of formal criteria to determine entitlement. In principle and by intent, such rationing is in terms of the financial resources that individuals in various circumstances require to meet basic human needs. Yet two further forms of rationing appear to operate—but in the form of deterrence to application. (They help to distinguish the means-tested benefits we are concerned with here from such selectivism as is embodied in proposals for a negative income tax.) First, secrecy and procedural complexities are often allowed to compound the general ill-informedness of claimants, so that the opportunity cost to the latter in terms of time and energy is high. Second, the manner in which officials deal with claimants in their face-to-face contacts typically reinforces the sense of stigmatisation that claimants may expect of their neighbours and fellow citizens (Jordan, 1974, pp. 68–9).[2]

To the extent that the administration of such means-tested benefits involves attempted control of beneficiaries, what are its intended ends and unanticipated consequences? Policy-makers seem typically to justify such disciplinary aims by reference to the promotion of individual responsibility and self-help through work. The wage-stop, for example, was long intended to eliminate any disincentive to re-enter the labour market (Atkinson, 1969, pp. 193–5; it was abolished in July 1975)—although many commentators have questioned whether such fears are well-grounded, given the intangible social sanctions and rewards that enjoin work (see, for example, Marsden and Duff, 1975), while others point out how a variety of means-tested benefits can combine to create just such a disincentive effect (see, for example, Bull, 1972, 'Postscript: The Poverty Trap'). Moreover, the administrators of policy may use various sanctions and strategies of occupational reclassification to channel claimants into low-paid work (Jordan, 1974, pp. 54–5; Stein, 1976). Additionally, however, Jordan argues that the stigmatisation is intended to deflect resentment of the subsidised by the lowest wage earners and hence to diffuse potential conflict. It serves, moreover, to deter them from seeking relief themselves, even if the alternative is degrading and debilitating work (1974, pp. 53, 133–4, 184). (On the other hand, the entitlement of strikers' families to supplementary benefits suggests that to see work enforcement as the overriding intent is a considerable over-simplification; but cf. Kincaid, 1973, pp. 226–9.)

Yet we have already hinted at some significantly different but unanticipated consequences of such a disciplinary regime. Unwillingness of the eligible to apply for benefits, except as a last resort, with consequently low rates of take-up, is by now well documented (see, for example, Bull, 1972, Chs 2–3; Lister, 1974). Second, such features of means-tested benefits as the wage-stop may promote family disintegration—and hence social need—thereby undermining the bread-winner's responsibility for his family that the measures are intended to encourage (cf. Jordan, 1974, pp. 128–9).

Over the past decade, partly perhaps in response to political pressure from welfare rights groups and the poverty lobby, there has been movement towards more automatic payment of benefits and some rationalisation of administrative arrangements. Yet the need remains for a local agency with the discretion and resources to deal with emergency and extraordinary financial needs, promptly and in the light of claimants' personal circumstances and crises. (Moves towards some form of negative income tax would probably tend to reinforce this need.) This task, Jordan argues, has devolved onto the personal social services. As a result they have found it increasingly difficult to exercise their distinctive professional skills, their clientele are predominantly low-income recipients, and they have unavoidably taken on the stigmatising and coercive character of a public assistance agency, to the detriment of any curative and preventive concern (1974, pp. 10–11, Ch. 7; cf. pp. 110–11 above).

It is this latter consequence that is particularly relevant here. For, Jordan argues, withholding of discretionary grants by the personal social services has typically become a sanction for controlling clients' social behaviour—involving a relationship very different from that of traditional case-work. Indeed, by virtue of their financial need alone, increasing numbers of clients have entered the purview of these disciplines, being imputed with socio-psychological inadequacies. Provision for their financial needs then becomes dependent upon their behaviour, and professional exper-tise serves not to identify an esoteric need (cf. pp. 104–5 above) but to mystify one that is mundane and prosaic (Jordan, 1974, Chs 6–8). The administration of means-tested benefits has thus come to involve not only the 1834 regime's stigmatising of claimants, but also its coercive moral re-education of the poor, who are seen as personally inadequate and in need of individual therapy (Handler, 1973, esp. Ch. 7).

What then, is the wider pattern of social integration and group formation that such measures promote and express? Jordan des-cribes the contemporary dependants of the state's means-tested benefits as 'the new claiming class'. Yet, in Weberian terms, the paupers he describes are a status group. For the process of pauper-isation involves the removal of individuals from the market (Gerth and Mills, 1948, p. 183), whether this process is fully realised, or only partially, as with recipients of Family Income Supplement (Jordan, 1974, pp. 56–7; 1973, p. 7–8). (The size of this sub-stratum, moreover, is determined, not by the numbers of the personally inadequate, but rather as an artefact of employment opportunities and pay, prices and scales of benefit—all determined in the wider society: Jordan, 1974, p. 49; cf. p. 188 above.) More specifically, they make up what Weber describes as a 'nega-tively privileged' status group (Gerth and Mills, 1948, pp. 189–90), suffering denigration and negative estimation by members of the wider society, who then see coercion of the pauper as necessary if he is to behave as they do. Such negative estimations, indeed, commonly dominate the self-images of claimants themselves (Jordan, 1973, p. 11; 1974, pp. 183, 56–7). This stratum, then, is significantly formed and identified through such social policies, which effect what Jordan terms the 'official deprivation' of the poor, who are publicly displayed as a 'dependent, passive and subsidised' stratum requiring paternalistic 'protection by virtue of [their] . . . moral, intellectual and industrial inferiority' (1974, p. 48).

Some have argued that such a stratum may become a threat to social and political order. This, they argue, is particularly likely in times of high unemployment, when large numbers are tending to be pauperised. It is then likely that the repressive aspects of social security provision will be relaxed, and that social insurance benefits as of right will be more politically acceptable to the powerful, as compared with means-tested benefits. In more prosperous times, a contraction of provisions is likely, with strategies of official coercion into the labour market. Piven and Cloward (1972), analysing the development of public welfare in the United States over the last half-century, provide a particularly clear example of such an account (cf. Jordan, 1974, Ch. 1). Yet it is an aspect of policy development that we cannot, for reasons of space, develop at all here. Nevertheless, later in this chapter we shall be considering various contemporary strategies of official control and transformation of communities of the poor, and the directions of group conflict that these strategies may themselves generate.

Theoretical implications

As already observed, such selective relief is the paradigm of social provision advocated by the *liberal*—particularly the market liberal. Yet our investigation suggests consequences for social integration and conflict at variance with the liberal prognoses. First, such writers typically portray these measures as particularly efficient, in terms of concentrating aid on the most 'needy', as measured by financial resources. They assume the 'rationality' of citizens in need: they will seek and accept such aid, as they self-interestedly maximise their extrinsic satisfactions (cf. p. 29 above). The hurdles of administrative complexity will assist in ensuring that it is indeed these most needy who are alone helped. Our immediate interest is less in such distributive aspects of social policy than in the relational. Yet our discussion has revealed that such distributive goals are typically undermined by potential claimants taking significantly different orientations. Low rates of take-up express in part their concern to remain members of the wider society of full citizens, rather than being identified as members of the pauper stratum. They are symptomatic of the proscription of certain sources of income for those laying claim to acceptance and honour, on whom an obligation is imposed, irrespective of the extrinsic benefits forgone.[3] The liberal analysis in terms of atomised hedonistic individualism is inadequate.

Second, liberal writers anticipate no necessary disharmony as the fruit of such selectivist measures. On the contrary, such measures, as distributive devices, ensure an adequate provision of life chances for all, but at minimum cost to the rest of the community. Any sense of grievance among either the needy or those bearing this cost is therefore minimised. Yet our investigation suggests, on the contrary, that these measures foster lines of perennial social conflict. For it is *par excellence* in the achieving society, where financial self-sufficiency is taken as a measure of individual dignity, that means-testing is socially divisive. To make individuals' achieved status—in this case as measured by financial means—the criterion of their treatment by the wider society is essentially corrosive of any collective obligation that this society may claim to exercise towards its members by virtue of their ascribed status as citizens.

Third, the liberals applaud the focus of these measures, not on needs universal to the population, but rather on individuals, selected according to their financial means. If Jordan's account is accepted, the agencies concerned with such a sub-group of the population tend typically to adopt a coercive policy towards it, attempting the moral re-education of the pauper—whether, for instance, by social case-work or by pressures to re-enter the enervating disciplines of the labour market. Yet we have questioned whether membership of this sub-group is attributable to any distinguishing individual pathology, suggesting, instead, that it is an artefact of opportunities and scales of benefit determined in the wider society. The liberals' preferred measures thus involve illiberal coercion of citizens indistinguishable in terms of individual traits from the remainder of the population. Moreover, this coercion may undermine the very family cohesion and bread-winner's responsibility with which liberals commonly profess to be concerned (see above, p. 50).

The social disciplines we have been discussing might seem a

particularly clear vindication of the *neo-Marxist* case. Jordan's account portrays claimants as paupers, similar in their social status and conditions to those of the 1834 regime—albeit with the elimination of 'indoor' relief. Thus their stigmatisation serves to discourage disaffection among the employed working class; and they are subject to the same attempted moral re-education. Yet while recognising this similarity, at least two questions must be posed in the light of the great extension of social policy over the last 150 years. First, do other branches of that extended social policy enforce similar modes of social integration and discipline? Second, do other programmes that focus upon 'the poor' enforce these same disciplines and attempt this same moral re-education for reincorporation into the mainstream of society? These two questions form the starting points for the next sections. Additionally, however, in arguing the need to see these paupers as a 'negatively privileged status group', we uphold and illustrate Weber's critique of orthodox Marxist interpretations of stratification, which rely upon categories of class alone, in regard to the paupers of 1834, no less than those of today. We put in question the conceptual clarity of any simple neo-Marxist claim that this 'official deprivation' of today's paupers is a paradigm of the state's treatment, in its other social policies, of the working class, whose situation is still fundamentally determined by immanent developments in the mode of production.

Our discussion has also demonstrated the relevance of the *Social Democrats'* concern with the processes of stigmatisation that dependence upon public agencies may engender. In accordance with their perspective, we have seen that such stigmatisation derives from the intrusion of considerations of personal achievement and failure into the provision of benefits. We, however, have gone beyond at least some of these writers in pointing to the wider distribution of power and advantage within which and in terms of which these processes must be seen as operating, and in looking at the modes of group formation that these measures promote.

Two brief comments must be added. First, it is not, of course, only the unskilled and low-paid who suffer interruptions of income. Yet for more privileged groups—and emphasising the social segregation to which we have already referred—there is an array of occupational and fiscal welfare provisions. Sinfield has taken up the task of mapping out these much less publicly visible and contentious supports, and of developing a sociological account of the social division of moral credibility that such stratified provision both expresses and reinforces (1976, esp. Ch. 4).

Second, means-tested benefits by no means exhaust those social measures whose provision depends on individuals' achieved status and thereby corrodes their ascribed status as citizens. For example, as we have seen in previous chapters, individualistic acquisition of formal educational qualifications has proceeded, albeit within a formally universalistic service, via exclusion on the basis of achieved status (see above, p. 178).[4] A graded hierarchy of educational status results and it is one that retains much of its inter-generational stability (Halsey, 1978, Ch. 6). Space prevents more extended discussion, however, of either of these points.

III UNIVERSALISM AND COMMUNITY IN THE RECIPROCATING SOCIETY

We turn now from the forms of social control, conflict and integration promoted by 'less eligible' selectivity to those fostered by universalism. It would seem wise to focus upon a branch of social policy that has been most removed from overt subordination to the market; we shall therefore take a case study from health care. It was, of course, to the latter that we devoted much of our discussion in chapter 5. There we concluded that the choice of summary measures of health inequalities cannot be made on wholly technical grounds, but involves value-judgements. We argued that these inequalities obtain their relevance for the sociologist by the way in which they constrain and become meaningful within actors' life projects, and that this is, indeed, clearly recognised in the classical perspectives surveyed in chapter 2. Here, then, our choice of health care has the added advantage of permitting further exploration of some of the typical implications of those health inequalities for group formation and action. Although this selection of the same area of social policy may, of course, equally hold the danger of under-rating the distinctive features of other branches of social policy and of over-confident extrapolation from our conclusions. Only at the end of the section do we speculate on the implications of universalism for such other branches.

Titmuss' study *The Gift Relationship* (1973) would seem highly relevant to our interest in the implications of social policies for social integration and conflict. It explores the dependence of the sick upon their fellow citizens, rather than upon medical professionals alone, for it is an investigation of the provision of blood for transfusion purposes. Titmuss is able thereby to explore the patterns of community formation and action that different modes of organising such medical care may foster. His account suggests that experience of universalist policies may mediate very different images of society from those evident in the previous section. Yet his study also serves as the vehicle for a polemical elaboration of the *Social Democratic* perspective on social policy to which he has been a major contributor; and our use of his findings must be accordingly circumspect.

Blood transfusion has assumed a continuously growing importance in medical services in recent decades: 'It has made possible the saving of life on a scale undreamt of several decades ago and for conditions which would have been considéred hopeless' (Titmuss, 1973, p. 33). There has been a rapid growth in the demand for blood and blood products, and 'in the foreseeable future, there appears to be no predictable limit to demand, . . . especially if account is taken of unmet needs for surgical and medical treatment and the great potentialities of demand in many areas of preventive medicine' (p. 47).

There are two critical characteristics of blood and of existing methods of collecting, storing and distributing it. First, it has a 21-day life when stored under refrigeration and despite the development of plasmapheresis techniques, outdating of blood can thus result in great wastage. Second, the presence of infection in donated blood—and, in particular, the problem of serum hepatitis—cannot be detected except by its effect on the recipient. This applies not only to whole blood, but also to plasma and certain blood products. These together imply that 'the attributes required of donors, if the needs of patients are to be properly met and if wastage is to be avoided, are consistency, regularity, responsibility and honesty. Dramatic, emotional and episodic responses to appeals for blood' addressed to donors whose honesty concerning their health is inadequate will foster wastage and the transmission of disease to recipients (1973, p. 27).

In the NHS, blood donorship is entirely voluntary: no penalties, financial or otherwise, are involved. Moreover, such donorship cannot be portrayed as narrowly self-interested: there are no 'tangible immediate rewards in monetary or non-monetary forms' and donors are not 'free to . . . decide on the specific destination of the gifts'. The latter choice is 'a moral and political decision for society as a whole' and the gift is thereby rendered anonymous. Yet such a delivery system appears to meet the criteria of effectiveness discussed above. Donors respond regularly and reliably to calls from the health service and 'this, together with the central coordination of a unified service, has meant that wastage has been minimal. Furthermore, the transmission of infection seems to have been particularly low by international standards, suggesting honesty of donors in respect of their medical histories. Finally, the NHS 'has never . . . been aware of a shortage or an impending shortage of potential donors' (1973, pp. 97, 272–3, 136). Those who already give are a broad cross-section of the society as a whole, rather than being self-selected in terms of some social or economic category; this confirms, for Titmuss, that there is no obvious constraint upon the long-term proportion of the population who may be recruited as donors, other than considerations of donors' own health (1973, pp. 141ff., 29–30).

What accounts, then, for this donating by such typical citizens? Titmuss, following the canons of *Verstehendesoziologie* (see above, pp. 68–70), enquires into the meaning that donors confer on their giving. The reasons uncovered by his survey include widespread feelings of altruism and reciprocity, 'suggesting a high sense of social responsibility towards the needs of other members of society'. At the same time, 'no donor type can be depicted in terms of complete, disinterested, spontaneous altruism. There must be some sense of obligation, approval and interest; some feeling of "inclusion" in society; some awareness of need and the purposes of the gift. What was seen by these donors as a good for strangers in the here-and-now could be . . . a good for themselves—indeterminately one day'. That is, they held confidently to a 'belief in the willingness of other men to act altruistically in the future, and to combine together to make a gift freely available should they have a need for it'. Titmuss concludes that this system of voluntary community donorship 'permits and encourages maximum truthfulness on the part of donors', minimising the risk of transmitted infection, and involves a sense of social obligation that secures a willing and reliable response to calls for blood, minimising waste (1973, pp. 266, 268–9, 163).

Yet, Titmuss argues, the trust and social obligation among citizens expressed by such voluntary donation is dependent upon the NHS principle of treating according to medical need without charge to the patient. Hence, for example, what the supplier has donated the NHS may not sell, but 'must respect the donor's intentions and ... use it for the purpose for which it was intended' (Heath, 1976, p. 153). The intrusion of the cash nexus would render the altruism of one's fellow citizens as blood donors an insufficient condition for receipt of effective medical treatment, and would, moreover, tend to corrode that altruism, by defining medical care as the object of an individual contract rather than a community obligation. Or, equivalently, citizens' experience of the NHS mediates an image of society as a community of citizens with mutual obligations and rights, despite their anonymity; it is in terms of this image that they orient their actions.

In further support of this thesis, Titmuss ventures a comparison with blood collection within the largely commercial health care system of the United States. There, the contribution of the voluntary donor has fallen markedly in recent decades. Most blood is supplied either for cash or in return for past or potential future demands for blood by the donor or his relatives (1973, Ch. 6). This delivery system, however, suffers major defects. First, such incentives to suppliers seem incapable of securing an adjustment of supplies to the short-term changes in demand within any locality. In consequence, hoarding and wastage by hospitals are common. Second, they encourage the 'deliberate concealment of personal information' about the medical histories of 'donors'; these are recruited disproportionately from among 'the poor, the unskilled, the unemployed, Negroes and other low income groups', who are particularly likely to supply low-quality and infected blood. This has probably been a major contributing factor in the rapidly rising numbers of reported cases of serum hepatitis. Yet the deleterious effects of such induced concealment are not confined to the recipient of the blood; the supplier himself has his health put at risk by too frequent bleeding. Finally, there have been perennial shortages of supply, with 'a failure of recruitment ... campaigns to obtain sufficient donors to meet demands' (1973, pp. 87, 134–5, 163–74, 56).

The commercialisation of health care thus mediates an image of society very different from that traced above for the British NHS. Individuals perceive and respond to those in need of blood in terms of the cash nexus and the individualistic contract of the market place. Titmuss postulates that those who might nevertheless wish to give freely and voluntarily, without recompense, to strangers in need, are discouraged from so doing: first by the risk, however minimal, of suffering medical harm for which they might themselves have to pay; and, second, by the dependence of their own future medical treatment upon their individual resources, which must therefore not be squandered through ill-advised generosity. It is, instead, those most in need of cash who are disproportionately recruited; with 'a new class . . . emerging . . . of high blood yielders', whose poverty is compounded by the deterioration of their health (1973, p. 135).

A comparison with the analysis in the previous section then suggests certain still more fundamental conclusions as to the implications of social policies for social integration and community formation. In both sections, we have discussed relationships of dependence between the needy and members of the wider society, albeit a relationship that is mediated by social policy professionals. We have seen how different social policies may evoke varied responses from those non-needy, upon whose discretionary actions provision for the needy is heavily dependent. We have explored the patterns of group formation and exclusion that different social policies may express and promote among the anonymous strangers of a mass urban–industrial society.

The NHS mediates a transfer of blood donations—a circulation of gifts that Titmuss likens to those documented for simple societies by Mauss (1970). Or, equivalently, its principles of treatment not only involve a collective obligation towards the sick, but also give public recognition and symbolic expression to the circulation of citizens among the roles of the healthy, the sick and the relatives of the sick. For those principles formally involve a treatment of the sick on criteria of medical need alone, and the provision of health care resources according to the abilities of the healthy to contribute. Such circulation is in turn acknowledged by citizens, who recognise their obligation to contribute when healthy, at least to the extent of freely providing blood. Mutual dependence, rather than the pursuit of independence, is the basis of mutual regard (cf. p. 50 above).

In contrast, the provision of means-tested benefits tends to promote an image of two distinct categories of human being: those who are independent and competent and those who 'do not share the same human feelings that move the rest of the population to behave decently' (Jordan, 1974, p. 183), and who therefore need to be controlled and disciplined for their own good, as well as that of society as a whole. Such social policies thus give symbolic expression to the supposedly minimal movement of individuals between the roles of the needy and the independent. This gulf is in turn acknowledged by citizens of the wider society, who respond in social stigmatisation of the dependent and in political support for social policies that, being focussed upon the multiple pathology of that well-defined category, will deny the universality of need as the basis for inclusion of the dependent in the community of full citizens.

Elsewhere, Titmuss argues that similar social division typically results when a substantial private sector exists alongside the public: whether in pensions, health, education or housing (Wilding, 1976, esp. pp. 159–60). The public sector tends to become—by default or even intent—that of lower quality; the universal obligations of common treatment are corroded by the self-regard of the cash nexus. While we have been unable to explore this here, our discussion of such dual health delivery systems in the previous chapter was broadly consonant with this conclusion (see above, esp. pp. 163–4).

Theoretical implications

How damaging, then, are the conclusions of this apologia of Social Democracy for liberal and neo-Marxist approaches?

Liberals

For Titmuss himself, it is liberal writers who are the prime target for criticism. First, the liberal tradition asserts that the untrammelled pursuit of self-interest by atomised individuals can be made the sufficient basis of social solidarity—whether by extending the realm of the market place or, for the political liberals, by promoting a meritocratic equality of opportunity. Titmuss, however, is pointing to social obligation, duty and altruism as a socially necessary—but logically distinct—orientation of social action. He seems additionally to assert that this is a mode of action towards which individuals are readily aroused, for they are enabled thereby to affirm commitments to collective, as distinct from narrowly self-interested, goals.[5]

His liberal opponents—and, more particularly, market liberals using the perspectives of neo-classical economics—seem to interpret Titmuss here as believing in altruism as a trait or urge of abstract individuals. They reply that this can readily be subsumed under their paradigm of self-interested 'economisers'—abstractly conceived individuals engaged in the maximisation under constraints of their utilities or satisfactions (Culyer, 'Quids without Quos: A Praxeological Approach' in Institute of Economic Affairs, 1973). Yet Titmuss is committed to a conception of man as insociate, with concerns and interests rooted in his social experience, rather than to the reification of these concerns as pre-social 'traits' in a fixed preference array. In this particular case, it is the experience of NHS treatment according to medical need that brings individuals to see themselves as having obligations toward the anonymous sick. Such obligation, as an orientation of meaningful action, must then be recognised as logically distinct from immediate self-interest: its pursuit is by definition unconditional on personal marginal opportunity cost. Its empirical relevance, as a category of sociological explanation, is evidenced in the meanings that Titmuss' respondents give to their actions, providing we embrace a commitment to *Verstehendesoziologie*. The differences between such liberals and Titmuss therefore spring, at least in part, from their contrasting philosophical anthropologies; to this extent they are irresolvable by appeal to empirical evidence alone.

Alternatively, such liberal writers question whether philanthropy and self-interest are in any necessary conflict or tension as social bonds, as policy-makers seek to ensure that citizen cooperation upon which their measures are dependent. Thus, in this particular example, pecuniary incentives may support moral obligation in motivating donors (Cooper and Culyer, 1968). Yet as far as Britain is concerned, Titmuss' account questions the need to offer such extrinsic incentives. He posits an analogue of Gresham's Law, with the intrusion of the cash nexus tending to erode and hence displace the social bond of altruistic obligation that currently serves the NHS well. For the USA, he traces the reduction of purely voluntary donation under the progressive commercialisation of health care. These liberals also argue that commercial organisations need not fear that their subsequent sale of blood will of itself reduce voluntary donation. Partly under the influence of Titmuss' study, there is some movement in the USA towards increasing reliance upon voluntary donors, while retaining the cash nexus, albeit in modified form, as the principle of health treatment (Surgenor, 1973). Should these attempts prove successful, in terms of maintaining and increasing the supply of pure blood, Titmuss' thesis would be seriously undermined. For he sees voluntary donation in Britain as being effectively evoked by the universalism of the NHS and its provision of treatment free to the patient. Policy-maker and citizen cooperate in discharging a collective moral obligation towards the dependent: donors' free provision of blood out of a sense of individual moral obligation cannot be expected when the society's health care provisions are not equally free to the patient.

Finally, if appeals to self-interest and to moral obligation are indeed mutually exclusive as means of social discipline, liberal critics of Titmuss affirm the superiority of the former. More specifically, pecuniary rewards can more effectively ensure a sufficient, regular and pure supply of blood, given safeguards on those accepted as suppliers and on its quality. It is the alleged scarcity of blood that is central to this argument. Such writers first deny that Titmuss has adduced any empirical evidence that shortages have been less in Britain than in the USA (Cooper and Culyer, 'The Economics of Giving and Selling Blood' in IEA, 1973). Yet Titmuss does in fact show that the NHS has not needed to increase the relatively low frequency of donations, as would presumably have happened if shortages had been recurrent, and has been able continuously to expand its panel of regular donors (1973, pp. 49–53). Second, these liberals apply the general theorem of neo-classical economics that individuals' supply of goods or services can be increased only by increasing the rate at which such supply is rewarded relative to other possible behaviour. Yet here, again, we encounter the very different philosophical anthropologies of Titmuss and his critics; we must choose between the abstract formalisations of neo-classical economics and the *Verstehendesoziologie* of Titmuss. Third, they look to improved techniques for detecting and eliminating infected blood (Salsbury, 'Medical Evidence' in IEA, 1973), or else to the selection of suppliers from social categories likely to be uninfected. Such a policy may, indeed, be optimal in the absence of an extrication of health care as a whole from the market: it may, that is, be a fine example of the neo-classic's 'second-best' (the classic statement is by Lipsey and Lancaster, 1956). Yet these extra techniques must themselves surely involve increased costs—unnecessary if there are in fact no obvious limits to the voluntary supplies that a national health service can evoke. Finally, these liberals see litigation as securing in the last resort compensation for transmitted infection (Ireland, 'The Legal Framework of the Market for Blood' in IEA, 1973). Yet they offer no counter-evidence to Titmuss' finding that 'it is still virtually impossible in most cases to establish a causal relationship, and to connect the infection . . . to the blood-transfusion or the blood product' (1973, p. 161)—preventing any legal redress.

With Titmuss, then, our conclusion must be that such market disciplines are in general necessarily less effective and more costly of resources than are those of moral obligation. Moreover, such pecuniary disciplines, while introducing the 'freedom' of the market place, close off certain other rights and freedoms that Titmuss deems important—including the 'right to give' (1973, Ch. 14; cf. p. 29 above) and thereby to create and express social relationships other than those of the market. What is more, they seem more likely to support and consolidate the lines of inequality and potential social conflict associated with individuals' differential class situations in the wider society. Liberals, recognising the varying quality of blood in a commercial system, have recommended its labelling and pricing according to the social category of its supplier, even though the broad consequences would presumably be well-defined class gradients in the quality of blood transfused. Indeed, the liberal proposal to select as suppliers only those from social groups and classes with low infection rates tends to create two categories of citizen, and may be as stigmatising of the excluded as the measures discussed in the previous section.

Neo-Marxists

The foregoing case study seems vividly to express the Marxian portrait of distribution in a communist society: 'From each according to his ability, to each according to his need'. Not only is this the formal principle for securing and distributing resources that underpins the NHS; rather, as in the Marxian prognosis, alongside this distributive principle is a pattern of social relationships fundamentally different from those among the strangers of 'civil society'. For, as we have seen, citizens' perceptions of the formal principles governing the NHS evoke their cooperation with, their moral commitment towards, and their trust of, their fellow citizens. Such a social policy seems, then, to involve patterns of group discipline and obligation that transcend the divisions and conflicts of the market society.

Yet such patterns are rooted, not in the development of the social relations of production but rather in those of social policy 'consumption' and participation. Titmuss' study might be taking as illustrating and vindicating Marx's thesis that 'it is men's social being that determines their consciousness' (Preface to *A Contribution to the Critique of Political Economy* in Marx, 1975), provided that, *contra* contemporary neo-Marxists, this 'social being' is not seen as predominantly and exclusively located in the production milieu. Or we might present our conclusion in Weberian terms, continuing the critique of Marxist approaches to stratification that Weber was himself developing: the community of citizens engendered by such a universalist social policy is a form of status group, the members sharing access to a common patrimony. It is in their acknowledgement of the latter that citizens' responses to such a policy are rooted (cf. pp. 64–5 above). Such a pattern of status group formation is then to be contrasted with the creation of a 'negatively privileged' status group through selectivist policies. But in neither case are analyses in terms of orthodox Marxist categories of class satisfactory.

Neo-Marxist writers might, of course, take Titmuss' study as supporting their own pessimism over the capacity of the capitalist state, through use of social policies, to deflect attention and criticism from the inequalities in power and privilege that obtain in contemporary society. After all, did not our discussion in the previous chapter reveal the continuing class gradients in health; and are not these gradients at least as serious in respect of other life chances? The Titmuss study merely shows how formal equality of access can mask gross inequalities of outcome, and how citizens' loyalties and obligations can be kept inconsistent with their true class interests. Yet if this analysis is to be faithful to that of Marx, these writers would need also to indicate what processes of immanent development are at work in the mode of production, tending to promote conditions in which the illusions of welfare capitalism are demystified. In chapter 3 we pointed to the paucity of such fully fledged neo-Marxist accounts (see above, esp. pp. 47–8). In the next two sections, in contrast, we shall suggest a 'logic' according to which such demystification may indeed occur in contemporary society; yet it will be fundamentally different from that which a neo-Marxist might embrace.

Social Democrats

Particularly when taken in conjunction with the previous section, therefore, this study displays some of the insights and strengths of the Social Democratic case. It reveals the novel forms of social integration that universalist social policies may create. It also serves to justify these writers' distinction between the civil and social rights of citizenship. In the case of selective benefits, individuals' personal achievements and failures—typically seen as deriving from their exercise of civil rights—are made a condition of access; there are no common social rights to particular unconditional outcomes. In contrast, such achieved status is formally eliminated from NHS treatment. The contrasting responses of stigmatisation and altruism reveal, moreover, the relevance of this distinction to actors themselves and to the 'images of society' they embrace.

Nevertheless, the study also has certain important limitations, which suggest that we must be circumspect in accepting Titmuss' extrapolation of the capacity of universalist policies to evoke moral commitment among citizens (see above, pp. 64–5), however much we may accept his judgement that in our contemporary complex urban–industrial society such moral integration is the only alternative to authoritarian repression or accelerating social conflict (1973, p. 224).

First, universalist social policies may indeed tend to engender altruistic obligations among citizens. In criticising liberal writers, we supported Titmuss' implicit distinction between moral obligation and immediate self-interest as possible orientations of meaningful action, the former being unconditional on personal marginal opportunity cost. Yet this cost is low in the case of donating blood; the *strength* of the obligation has, therefore, hardly been tested (cf. Collard, 1978, pp. 142–3). We cannot, therefore, infer from Titmuss' study that universalist social policies in general will eliminate citizens' concern with the personal opportunity cost that such measures involve, and hence with the levels of provision they offer. Second, Titmuss has chosen to study a need and service that may appear to the typical citizen as particularly 'objective' and of unproblematic definition. Moreover, as citizens circulate between the ranks of the sick and the healthy, they may be especially aware of the potential universality of this need. This is then likely to be seen as particularly deserving of treatment, without regard to the ability of the 'consumers' to reciprocate. *Ceteris paribus*, therefore, the problems may be minimised of gaining society's commitment to this common goal: treatment according to need. Generally, however, the definition of the needs that should properly be a community concern may be politically more contentious—as we shall see in the next two sections. The sociologist will need to attend more explicitly to the role of political leadership in articulating collective goals and mobilising collective support. Third, Titmuss has selected an area where professional claims to esoteric knowledge and public trustworthiness would seem particularly well-developed and secure. The gift relationship is mediated by professionals who, rightly or wrongly, are confidently expected to be objective in their judgements and capable of controlling consumer abuse of the service. Elsewhere, however, those who dispense discretionary benefits in cash, kind and services may lack this professional aura. Again, therefore, in generalising from Titmuss' account of a universalist social policy, it will surely be necessary to attend to the varying social definitions of the professionals through whom services and hence community obligations are mediated.

The financial benefits discussed in the previous section—or more particularly, discretionary emergency awards—then appear as likely to be particularly recondite to public acceptance as a social right. For financial need is typically deemed indicative of individual incompetence, even without reinforcement of these definitions by means-testing agencies, except where an individual's work record or family responsibilities are taken as criteria for benefits. The level of provision for such needs—and the costs they involve for the wider community—are hardly less politically contentious than they were 150 years ago. The inability of the supplementary benefits official to claim esoteric knowledge may mean that the wider community perceives his discretion as more open to 'abuse' by claimants; the personnel of the personal social services may be seen as little more reliable. Rigorous means-testing and the quasi-coercive 'treatment' of recipients then seem to be preconditions for the political acceptability of these benefits. It must remain a matter for speculation whether the 'multiplier' effect posited by Titmuss, with the experience of altruistic giving in one area of social policy influencing citizens' orientation to other areas (Collard, 1978, Ch. 14), can and will serve to modify this persisting social definition of such financial benefits.

In chapter 4 we encountered other areas of social policy where a universalist orientation is intended to promote a gift relationship between the independent and the dependent, by giving public expression to the circulation of citizens among these roles (see also R. H. S. Crossman, 'The Role of the Volunteer in the Modern Social Service' in Halsey, 1976). First, the Seebohm reforms looked to the break-down of the 'distinction between the givers and takers of social services and the stigma which being a client has often involved (see above, p. 105); the new department would, like Titmuss' NHS, mobilise mutual aid and reciprocal service in recognition and meeting of common needs. The mutual aid fostered by community development is the concern of our next section. Second, the Halsey and Russell Reports look in community and recurrent education to 'teaching and learning roles for all social positions' (Halsey, 1972a, p. 189); the obligations and rights developed through the first official endeavours in such education—however halting and limited these may be—will be our concern in section V. Third, moves towards pay-as-you-go pensions involve the assumption that the working population is willing to pay the higher contributions dictated by politically chosen levels of pensions in payment—in recognition of an inter-generational moral obligation. Indeed, the Crossman and Castle schemes anticipate that such a commitment will also permit the crediting of various unemployed categories with generous notional contributions (As in the donation of blood, the purpose to which the increased contribution is put is clearly specified and the intentions of the contributor cannot be disregarded, DHSS, 1969, para. 52, cf. p. 210 above). Whether the Castle scheme results in such novel inter-generational obligations must remain a matter for future empirical investigation. Yet the high rate of contracting-out (Redden *et al.*, 1977) surely bodes ill for the generation of such universalistic commitments. It makes more likely, perhaps, the inter-generational solidarity within particular industries or occupations familiar in such countries as France (Lynes, 1967, esp. Ch. 6), and the social divisions that seem commonly to accompany major private sectors in welfare.

We have touched on the possible 'multiplier' effect of such universalistic social policies on the dominant social definition of discretionary and emergency financial benefits. Yet the Social Democrats argue a more general thesis on the multiplicative or catalytic effect of such policies: their morally reintegrative effects extend into all spheres of societal life. To what extent, for example, does the experience of universalistic social policies tend to promote articulation and popular recognition of the social right to self-developing work? At the same time, to what extent does this same experience tend to promote—not least among the propertied—the universal recognition and reliable discharge of a social obligation to work, no less effective than market inducements and disciplines in securing participation in the division of labour? In short, to what extent is the mode of social integration mediated by the division of labour moulded by—or even dependent upon—that mediated by the social division of welfare? Again, these are questions that, while susceptible in principle to empirical investigation, must remain incompletely unanswered here, although we reflect upon them further in our final chapter.

IV COMMUNITY DEVELOPMENT AND THE INCORPORATION OF THE DEPRIVED

Positive discrimination towards communities suffering multiple deprivation has been accorded growing attention in debates over social policy during the last fifteen years. In this section we focus upon the recent programme of Community Development Projects, to which we also referred in the previous two chapters. In chapter 4, they were briefly of interest in suggesting how politically acceptable would be the implementation of Seebohm's proposals for widescale community development. In chapter 5, their research orientation was of principal interest, as we weighed alternative diagnoses of deprivation. Here they are of interest as *action*–research projects: projects committed to involvement of, and consultation with, the poor themselves.

During the 1960s and 1970s, a vast literature has been spawned on community action, community work and community development (see, for example, Calouste Gulbenkian Foundation, 1968).[6] We cannot even sketch its outlines. Yet, strictly speaking, much of this literature is not relevant to some of the key questions to which we need here to address ourselves: we are concerned with the implications for social relations among citizens of the social policies of statutory agencies and this defines certain questions that do not arise—or arise only in a much weaker form—in the case of non-statutory efforts. Indeed, in selecting the CDPs as our starting point for the investigation of the impact of the state's social policies, we are taking a sub-class of those statutory efforts that has certain distinctive features and poses still more specific questions. For CDP, as one of the recent national action–research projects, involves certain specific strategies, modes of legitimation and governmental commitments; and highlights the problematic relationships among social policy development, life chance distribution and citizen response, which have been the themes of our three chapters of empirical investigation into the contemporary Welfare State.

Our concern, then, is with the ways in which the common experience of poverty and of measures directed at its elimination may affect citizens' definition of their individual and group interests and may evoke responses of concurrence in, or conflict with, wider societal arrangements—although the actors of interest include not only the poor themselves, but also the non-poor. This suggests three stages for our analysis: (i) we must investigate the ways in which the various actors involved typically define their situations and their interests and goals; (ii) what are the processes of group formation and action that flow from these definitions of the situation? (iii) what are the typical outcomes of such actions by the various individuals and groups concerned? How successful are they in the pursuit of their respective life projects, what accounts for these outcomes, and what are actors' typical responses to success or failure?

(i) The experience of the CDPs reveals how problematic is any definition of the interests and rights of the various actors involved in social policy. Initially, the political and professional sponsors of the CDPs seem to have taken for granted that they and the residents of the target areas shared a common interest—the elimination of the neighbourhood's deprivation by the technically most effective means, among which the prevailing wisdom was coming to emphasise 'community resources' of mutual aid and voluntary effort, as the necessary complement to the resources of statutory agencies, if these were not to be poured into a 'bottomless pit' (see above, pp. 105–6). Yet the attempted mobilisation of such resources, involving as it did a commitment to early consultation with, and participation by, the poor themselves, served to alert the CDP teams to fundamental divergences between the official and the resident definitions of the 'problem' and of their respective interests.

More specifically, from the start residents typically saw their deprivation as neither generated within the neighbourhoods themselves (Coventry CDP, 1975b, Paper 2, paras 2.11–2.13), nor amenable to significant reduction through improved communication and personal social services. Rather, as the Coventry team report, 'they saw the problem as their powerlessness to influence the decisions which affected their lives, their homes and their area'—particularly official policy in regard to such issues as housing, redevelopment and welfare rights (1975b, Paper 1, paras 3.3, 4.2). Being a problem of powerlessness, moreover, as much as one of disadvantage, they saw it in political rather than technical terms. The learning experience of involvement with an action–research programme such as the CDPs served merely to extend and confirm this perception: with, on the one hand, a growing appreciation of the consequences for their neighbourhood of decisions and non-decisions over public and private resource allocation; and, on the other, the reluctance of local professional and political power-holders to respond significantly to this critique of wider policy-making. In short, in so far as their perception developed during the period of the projects, it seems typically to have approximated increasingly to that of the CDP teams, which we sketched in chapters 4 and 5 (see esp. pp. 123–6, 184–7). (Although, since we are relying fairly uncritically upon the CDP reports themselves, it is unclear how far the CDP teams adopted a 'directive' as distinct from a 'non-directive' role in this learning process; even though they typically claim simply to have catalysed the articulation of issues and interests already identified by residents.)

(ii) Consider the typical patterns of group formation and action fostered by the CDPs. For the professional and political sponsors of these projects, expectations as to such patterns seem to have been somewhat inchoate and contradictory. For on the one hand, the initial rationales for the national experiment involve an expectation of, and a concern for, the development of mutual aid and the strengthening of community disciplines over its deviant and delinquent members. Yet on the other hand, these neighbourhoods seem often to have been perceived in highly negative terms, as irredeemable blackspots whose elimination as communities could not but be in the interests as much of the residents as of the wider society (see, for example, Coventry CDP, 1975b, Paper 1, para. 2.2; Paper 2, paras 2.6–2.10).[7] From the latter standpoint, it is the destruction of 'pathological' neighbourhoods—at least as the home of a deviant sub-class—and the incorporation of their members into the wider communities of their cities that is the anticipated and desired consequence of the catalytic activity of the CDP.

Yet the *actual* directions of individual and group action engendered by the CDPs follow neither of these prognoses and prescriptions; instead they expose their common limitations. (Although, as with the definition of residents' interests, the catalytic role of the CDP teams rendered such group action essentially mediated by professionals.)[8] Among these developing forms of community action, welfare rights movements have been common. They are, moreover, of particular interest here, given our analysis in section II of the predominant mode of integration effected and expressed by means-tested benefits. The CDPs have found the financial poverty of their neighbourhoods' residents to be in no small measure the result of low take-up of means-tested benefits: through fear of stigmatisation, lack of knowledge and unwillingness to see such benefits as more than a last resort. In terms, therefore, of both the original official CDP remit and residents' own perception of their condition, the ineffectiveness of income maintenance schemes has been a central concern for the projects: they have typically sought to promote awareness of entitlements and readiness to claim (National CDP, 1974, para. 5.9). Thus, for example, in Batley a major attempt was made to experiment with programmes of education and publicity as means of improving the take-up of benefits (Lees and Smith, 1975, Ch. 11). In Hillfields, Coventry, a CDP information centre offering advice over entitlements has increasingly involved resident control and generated collective action, developed an advocacy and legal advice service, and crystallised demands for a simplification and rationalisation of administrative procedures (Lees and Smith, 1975, Ch. 10; Coventry CDP, 1975b, Paper 3, para. 5). Such welfare rights movements, both derivative and constitutive of solidaristic collectivism (cf. Goldthorpe and Lockwood, 1963) among residents, may differ little from those sponsored by voluntary bodies and neighbourhood organisations—save, perhaps, in the sophistication of the expertise made available. What is distinctive here is the legitimation of the projects' attempts to foster such movements—grounded as it is in their initial, officially sponsored concern with the persistence of area deprivation and their diagnosis of that deprivation, as it emerged in the course of their action–research.

In section II we were also discussing means-tested benefits. Here, however, individuals' life projects differ significantly in several systematically interrelated ways. First, the goals pursued seem to be less the avoidance of the direst destitution than the appropriation of all benefits to which there is a formal entitlement. Second, instead of the general lack of information among such claimants being compounded by administrative procedures, we find collective demands for simplification of the latter coupled with publicising of benefits and regulations. Third, instead of expectations of stigmatisation by neighbours being reinforced by the manner in which officials exercise their discretion and sanctions, confidence in a collective affirmation of claimants' rights promotes collective criticism of the moral regulation implicit in much official practice. Community action engendered by the CDP thereby involves appropriation of those life chance outcomes and affirmation of the dignity that official policy formally enunciates as the right of each full citizen. To compare this discussion with section II is to display the capacity of other social policies to transform claimants' orientations to means-tested benefits; while to compare it with our discussion of *The Gift Relationship* is to expose how inequalities of power and advantage may obtain a significance for patterns of community membership and action that the earlier discussion could ignore. Such comparisons will provoke further reflections later.

The quality of other social and public services in these neighbourhoods has become of similar concern to such developing communities. The meaningfulness of formal equality of access has been challenged in the light of gross inequalities of outcome—in the personal social services and educational provision, for example (Coventry CDP, 1975b, Papers 4 and 5). Moreover, in the light of our earlier discussion of health care, it is of interest that health care provision has become no less an object of community criticism (Topping and Smith, 1977, pp. 101–2). Yet the most common and intense concern of much developing community action seems to have been issues of housing and redevelopment, which, as we saw in chapter 5, have been central to the persistence of deprivation of many of the CDP areas—or, at least, of those in inner-city areas. In Coventry, for example, neighbourhood groups have campaigned for particular streets to be declared General Improvement Areas, for a reversal to the intrusion of industry into residential areas and for the development of tenants' housing cooperatives. The CDPs themselves have provided essential technical skills and information, together with advice on tactics (Benington, 'Gosford Green Residents' Association' in Leonard, 1975).[9]

There are even hints in the CDP reports of community action directed at challenging and controlling much wider distributive processes: notably the private and public investment decisions that, we saw in chapter 5, have been prime factors in the generation and persistence of deprivation in these neighbourhoods. Yet these are no more than hints—for perhaps three reasons. First, such challenges as have developed have not, perhaps, been least among the factors contributing to premature winding-down of the national experiment (see above, pp. 112–13). Second, the time-scale of the projects has hardly been sufficient to see and report upon the development of action with such a wider orientation. Finally, the CDP reports, if not their experiences, have often given only secondary attention to community action; in such cases, the lack of detailed histories is nowhere greater than in respect of *community* challenges to these wider allocative and distributive processes. Instead, many reports focus upon the diagnosis of deprivation and upon clarification of the political context of life chance distribution—with the CDP personnel acting more as tribunes for their neighbourhoods than as facilitators of community action.[10]

This third point is perhaps least true of the Liverpool project, which eschewed this change of emphasis while still accepting that the deprivation of its neighbourhood arose 'from outside the area, the result of wider social and economic developments' (Topping and Smith, 1977, p. 25). It sought to promote community organisation and dialogue with the local authority, as the continuing impetus to improvement of local services (Ch. 4). Challenges to the imposition on this particular neighbourhood of the costs of wider urban–industrial change could most effectively be mounted through organised community pressure on the local authority, for decisions by the latter were all-pervasive. Yet 'the local authority was not cast, as it is in the demonology of some projects, as a force that must ultimately serve the interests of dominant groups in society' (p. 29). An impressive array of community groups was established, reversing the break-down of traditional local organisation occasioned by population movements and economic decline.

Some of the later project reports discuss the formation of alliances between residents in neighbourhood communities and workers in trade union and shop-floor groupings. This was indeed, an explicit and major aim in North Tyneside, where the project team became an informational and research resource as much for organised labour as for the deprived of their target area (North Tyneside CDP, 1978b, Part 2; 1978c, pp. 12–16). (On the other hand, the reports do not dispel the fear that, rather than cementing an alliance between residents of deprived areas and workplace groupings, the Tyneside project merely switched its focus and principal clientele from the former to the latter; 1978b, p. 186.) Studies of claimants unions and welfare rights movements suggest that such alliances with shop-floor groupings may indeed develop through a constellation of interests—albeit in the face of hostility from official trade unions. Jordan, for example, traces such a development in a situation of threatened redundancy as a result of employment plans made at a national level. Yet he also points to the conflict of interests between such alliances of paupers and prospective paupers and other workers in well-paid and secure employment (Jordan, 1973, pp. 4–5, Ch. 3).

In this discussion of group formation and action, we have admittedly hardly distinguished between the two types of area that, we saw in chapter 5, have been most common in the CDP programme: the reception areas of inner cities, accommodating high proportions of migrants, and areas of general industrial, social and population decline (see above, p. 184). In the former, to speak of a single existing community that requires 'development' and resuscitation has much less historical basis than in the latter. Distinctively different directions of group formation and action must be expected, in what typically are ethnically plural neighbourhoods, where the demographic pattern may broadly comprise young non-white families and middle-aged or elderly long-established whites. While available CDP material gives insufficient basis for exploring these differences, other studies of community action in ethnically plural neighbourhoods make clear the distinctive lines of potential conflict (see, for example, Rex and Moore, 1967, esp. Ch. 9; Adenay, 1971, pp. 15–20—both dealing with the Sparkbrook area of Birmingham). Not, however, that community action within CDPs has otherwise been invariably productive of community integration and solidarity in the face of more distant holders of private and public power (Lees and Smith, 1975, pp. 74–5).

Let us reflect, then, upon those official expectations of group formation and action with which this stage of our discussion began. These, we saw, were rooted in two not wholly consistent perspectives on the existing forms of community: the first portrayed it as being in a state of disrepair, requiring 'urban first-aid' if it were to be a milieu of effective social control and mutual aid; the second, as an irredeemable black-spot. The foregoing account lends some credence to the former view. The CDPs did promote community integration and collective purpose; in those neighbourhoods that are inner-city reception areas, this was to some extent a creation *ex nihilo*. Yet in thus speaking of collective purpose some criticism is involved of the official assumptions—for that purpose, as we have seen, has typically been one of transforming the situation of powerlessness and invisibility that these neighbourhoods have previously suffered.[11] What the CDPs seem to have provided has been not so much an officially sponsored therapeutic device for the resuscitation of atrophying communities, but far more an instrument with which the residents of such communities have sought publically to articulate a critique of official policy. Such strengthened community solidarity as has developed has been as productive of demands for wider change as of control over its members.

On the second view, a CDP such as that in Coventry was seen officially as 'removing Hillfields from the public conscience', precluding 'the possibility of any long-term programme to help the present community to develop its indigenous life and culture' (Benington, 1972, para. 3.12; cf. Coventry CDP, 1975b, Paper 2, paras 2.6–2.10). Indeed, the very notion of a 'deprived' community can, for official policy-makers, serve to justify neglect of the valuable and distinctive elements in that life (Benington, 'Strategies for Change at the Local Level' in Jones and Mayo, 1974, pp. 263–4). Yet the community action we have traced has commonly rejected the redemption that official programmes have ostensibly offered residents as individuals—exposing, instead, the orientation of these programmes to very different interests (see above, pp. 123–6; but cf. the Liverpool reservations, p. 225 above). Rather, such action has typically involved residents' affirmation of the dignity of their neighbourhood life and their right as citizens collectively to participate in choices over its future.

(iii) What have typically been the outcomes of these patterns of group formation and action? In some projects, local groups gained 'small but valuable changes' (Coventry CDP, 1975a, para. 7.51). In Liverpool, after community organisations had been built up to apply long-term pressure on public policy-makers, 'it was far less likely ... that any department would have lightly embarked on proposals unacceptable to residents, as they had often blithely done at the start' (Topping and Smith, 1977, p. 120). More generally, however, the reports indicate failure to achieve substantial change—if this be judged in terms of the elimination of deprivation in the neighbourhoods concerned or the modification of wider social policies in the light of this action–research experiment. Withdrawal of local and central government support has been common, and, if the accounts offered by the CDP personnel themselves are accepted, has been the direct response to the CDP diagnosis of deprivation we traced in chapter 5 and to the community action recounted above. Yet if this *has* been the general outcome, we must go on to enquire into citizens' further responses to such imposed constraints upon change. Not least, in what ways and to what extent has the withdrawal of commitment by the original sponsor affected the legitimacy of the latter in the eyes of the population?

Few, if any, local authorities granted their CDPs freer reign than did Coventry. This has been a major reason for the extensiveness of the project's action–research programme, which we have traced in this and preceding chapters. In contrast, few projects seem to have encountered more early local authority opposition than did the one in Southwark. The perception by local residents of both the project and the local authority suggests what may be the typical implications for a local authority's legitimacy in the eyes of its constituents, when it withdraws sponsorship from such a project.

In the Southwark CDP area, as in so many, one of the key concerns identified by residents was redevelopment and planning blight (for a description of this neighbourhood, see Hatch *et al.*, 1977, Chs 6–7). The local authority's initial commitment to the CDP—one of the first to be established—was in part just one element in a new commitment to consultation with residents over planning decisions, encouraged by the Skeffington Report of 1969. The CDP personnel were to service the consultative meetings over a draft plan, preparing the residents for active participation and making them aware of 'the nature, range and implications of possible solutions', so that they might exercise rational choice (Rossetti, 1974, p. 4; cf. Hatch *et al.*, 1977, pp. 176–96). Such consultation was initially to be between the residents of individual neighbourhoods and planning officials; subsequently, basic political and policy issues would be settled through meetings with elected members.

Yet from the earliest of these encounters, resentment and conflict surfaced between residents and policy-makers; a long history of effective disenfranchisement, with available electoral choices limited to a paternalistic Labour Party and the Conservatives, had enforced non-participation, fatalism and resentment. Residents' hostility was only compounded when consultation revealed the lack of any coherent rationale in those earlier redevelopment programmes that had blighted the area and put in doubt the technical legitimacy and competence of the policy-makers' decisions (Rossetti, 1974, pp. 13–16). As a result, consultation was quickly shelved by the elected members, notwithstanding the difficulties of legitimating such a reversal of earlier public commitments. The CDP, as the advocate and catalyst of participation, wholly forfeited its local authority support—from councillors if not from officials. (Although this change in the local authority's policy was also importantly affected by shifts in the balance of power among the political blocs within it—shifts having no direct relation to the CDP experience of interest here—Rossetti, 1974, pp. 6–12; Rossetti, 'Politics and Participation' in Curno *et al.*, 1978.) Among residents, disillusionment and resentment grew apace; the CDP team, in contrast, received increasing endorsement in its critique of official procrastination. They tended, indeed, to become 'the uninvited and unelected local representatives . . . [but] with full support of local people'. Neighbourhood groups formed defensive associations; they drew on the CDP team's expertise in developing a more informed understanding of local needs and government policies and resorted to the media as a means of voicing their grievances (Rossetti, 1974, pp. 19, 5–6).

That this account of citizen responses may be not untypical is suggested by the second of Dennis' studies of planning in Sunderland, which, while not an account of a CDP, *is* concerned with citizen responses to publicly sponsored programmes dealing with deprivation. In chapter 4 we traced Dennis' own critique of the professional judgements reached by planners. In *Public Participation and Planners' Blight* (1972), he traces a process of disillusionment among residents of a redevelopment area, very similar to the account by Rossetti, with a loss of official legitimacy in the eyes of those residents, who resorted to the press, their MP and alternative forms of local political organisation. The principal difference seems to have been that while in Southwark it was the elected members whose strategy attracted such hostility, in Sunderland the professional planners were to the fore.

As for the project teams, there has evidently been a clarification of the practical tensions among the goals of retaining legitimacy in the eyes of government, of the residents of their areas and also, perhaps, of the social scientific community with its canons of rigorous research. Many have sought to promote new programmes of community development, which, owing less allegiance to official sponsors, may more single-mindedly be rooted in legitimation by residents—as well, perhaps, as by trade unions. While, therefore, the CDPs have as a result of their activities suffered a loss of governmental legitimation, it is perhaps no less valid to suggest that for local residents the CDPs have served vicariously to articulate their refusal to accord legitimacy to governmental processes and policies.[12] At the same time, such wider programmes seem increasingly to emphasise the interdependence of community development and community education. We shall, therefore, in the next section, turn to some of these links—taking as our starting point, however, discussion of educational programmes aimed at areas of deprivation. We shall then be able to bring together the findings and conclusions of both types of programme relevant to our interest in social integration and conflict.

Yet we shall also be in a position to confront, albeit only tentatively, certain wider questions that flow out of the preceding discussion. We have already noted the hints in some CDP reports of a developing community concern with wider processes of resource allocation in the private and public sectors. To what extent, then, has the winding-down of these projects been perceived by citizens as deriving from a refusal by the powerful in those sectors to submit themselves to greater social control and accountability; and to what extent is one consequence the undermining of the legitimacy of the wider socio-economic order, at least in the eyes of these citizens?

V COMMUNITY EDUCATION AND THE TRANSFORMATION OF SOCIETY

In chapter 4, we saw how positive discrimination towards educationally deprived areas has been justified as a necessary condition for the realisation of a substantive equality of opportunity. Along with the national CDP experiment, an action–research programme in four English and one Scottish educational priority areas (EPAs) has formed the principal British imitation of the American anti-poverty programmes of the 1960s. In chapter 5, we referred to their research findings on deprivation—albeit more briefly than our account of the CDPs (see above, pp. 131–2, 188–9). Here too, if only for reasons of space, we restrict our discussion of the group formation and action they provoked to issues of particular relevance to the preceding section.

The official remit underlying the EPA programme displays significant similarities with that for the CDPs. In chapter 5 we traced the negative view of home and local community that commonly underpins the notion of 'compensatory' education; children are to be rescued from deprived and stultifying backgrounds and enabled to compete on equal terms within the wider society. Yet as with the CDP brief, alongside this negative portrayal of pathological communities is a somewhat contradictory view: namely, one of communities in a state of disrepair, demoralised and unable to control their deviant members or to support their children motivationally. The EPA programme aimed, for example, not only at raising children's educational performance, but also at improving teacher morale, involving parents in their children's education and increasing residents' sense of responsibility for their neighbourhoods (Halsey, 1972a, p. 57).

Yet no less than in the CDPs, there seems to have been a significant divergence between official expectations and actual directions of group formation and action engendered by the EPA action–research projects. Or, more precisely and generally, the EPA experience points to the need for a very different relationship between school and community if lasting success is to be achieved in terms of the programme's various goals. Reflecting on this experience, the Halsey Report argues for 'educationally informed families' and 'socially informed schools'. This means, *inter alia*, that 'schools must . . . understand the families and environments in which the children live. . . . Only if education in the schools is relevant to the children's direct experiences will it engage their attention and interest'. Yet such a curriculum would be relevant not only to 'the child's own experience but also . . . to the community in which he lives and . . . [would] promote a sense of community spirit and responsibility'. Here, then, Halsey concludes, 'the child-centredness of the progressive educator and the social precepts of the community educator meet'. Such a notion of a community-based syllabus involves the 'critical and constructive understanding of the environment'. This understanding is, moreover, one in which parents share through the home–school links integral to community education. This is likely to receive further emphasis through the promotion of adult education schemes, with local educational institutions becoming 'deeply involved in the whole variety of the problems facing such communities'. This tends, then, 'to obliterate the boundary between school and community, to turn the community into a school and the school into a community' (Halsey, 1972a, pp. 117–18, 142–4, 159, 189).

This shift from the initial prescription and prognosis of the relationship between such deprived communities and positively discriminating educational institutions therefore runs parallel to that in the previous section (see esp. pp. 222–7 above). The community curriculum and the cooperative partnership it involves between parents and teachers attribute worth to the child and his community experience (Halsey, 1972a, p. 144); no longer is that experience represented as wholly negative. The participation of parents—and residents more generally—promotes community responsibility and discipline over its members; yet it also means that they share in critical collective enquiry into their social environment, not least into the generation of the deprivation they suffer.

Indeed, many of those involved in the EPA action–research programmes have gone on to argue—and often to investigate practically—the complementarity of such community education and community development of the form discussed in the previous section. Thus as Midwinter argues, writing out of experience of the Liverpool EPA, if the community education discussed above is not to be frustrated and trivialised, it must be allowed to issue in collective regeneration of the neighbourhood concerned—albeit via action directed at changing wider distributive and allocative agencies. On the other hand, if community development and action are not to be inchoate and lacking coherent purpose, they require informed understanding and evaluation of their world by community members—albeit an understanding that focusses centrally on the wider processes rendering that world one of disadvantage and powerlessness (Midwinter, 1972, pp. 23–5, Ch. 8). *Inter alia*, 'community education is that element in community development

which most lucidly emphasises the growth in skills of community management' (Midwinter, 'A Note on Community Education' in Lees and Smith, 1975, p. 120). Yet many of the CDP
personnel have become no less convinced of this essential
interrelationship—pursuing not only community education for
children but also a variety of adult education programmes (National
CDP, 1974, paras 5.18–5.21). One corollary is that the latter come
to have a clientele far wider and a format more community-oriented
than has traditionally been the case—realising thereby important
features of the proposals for adult education advanced in the
Russell Report (National CDP, 1974, para. 6.14; Lovett,1975, esp.
pp. 45–53 and Chs 7–8). Our discussion of recurrent education in
chapter 4 was not, therefore, entirely futuristic.

The likely fruit, then, of such joint community education and
development is a coherent critique by the community of the multiple deprivation it suffers. Among the causes of the latter, we
argued in chapter 5, are wider processes of resource allocation in
both public and private sectors that are productive and expressive of
gross and unprincipled inequalities of power and advantage across
the society as a whole. It follows that this developing critique carries
the likelihood that the wider socio-economic order will lose its
legitimacy in the eyes of such communities—even though such
legitimacy as it has hitherto enjoyed may have involved no more
than fatalistic acceptance, coupled with low expectations of individual or collective improvement (cf. Runciman, 1966). Not least,
our account suggests that such criticism and withdrawal of legitimation may extend to work and market situations in production and
occupational milieux. In the North Tyneside CDP, for example,
strong demands for industrial democracy were catalysed (North
Tyneside CDP, 1978b, Part 2, Ch. 4). Nevertheless, further empirical investigation would here be highly desirable.

Goldthorpe, we may observe, has interpreted the disorder of
contemporary industrial relations as expressing the lack of legitimacy enjoyed by the wider unequal society; indeed, he argues that it
is not in the political sphere but in the economic that the most
far-reaching implications of that inequality occur ('Social Inequality and Social Integration in Modern Britain' in Wedderburn, 1974,
p. 222). We, however, are pointing, not to an endemic *anomie*
expressing the absence of any widespread commitment to the
prevailing distribution of life chances, but rather to 'constructive

discontent', expressing commitment to some *alternative* mode of distributing power, advantage and opportunities. Moreover, our approach differs from Goldthorpe's principally in exploring the potential for radical criticism of the economic and occupational order that is rooted in actors' experience of social policy initiatives.[13] In a complete investigation, however, it would be necessary to investigate the conditions for, and consequences of, alliances between neighbourhood and workplace groupings (cf. p. 226 above).

The foregoing invites one final comment. These action–research projects have focussed upon 'the deprived'—typically seen by the political sponsors as qualitatively apart from the mainstream of society and their fellow citizens. The findings of the projects suggest, however, that such communities are distinctive principally in the extent to which they bear the social costs of change in our urban–industrial society; or, equivalently, in their powerlessness to avoid those costs. As we saw in the previous chapter, the disadvantage and needs prevalent within them do not differ in kind from those common in the wider society; positive discrimination cannot be justified as distinct in its rationale from universalism (see above, p. 188). The projects' experience has likewise highlighted the redistribution of effective social, economic and political power that will be required if deprivation is to be reduced and even eliminated. Yet this would necessarily be a redistribution not only towards these most powerless of communities, but rather across society as a whole. That is, these projects have offered a critique not only of the exclusion of 'the deprived', but more generally, although to a lesser degree, of the restricted realisation of all citizens' civil, political and social rights.

These projects were initially portrayed as pilot schemes or laboratories, establishing guidelines for subsequent more grandiose efforts to help deprived communities. In practice, the findings have been largely disregarded by their political sponsors. Yet if the argument of the foregoing paragraph is valid, the processes of loss of legitimacy that withdrawal of political sponsorship has engendered may be used cautiously as the basis for generalisations about the political society at large. That is, we may think of these projects as having served as 'laboratories' offering insights into typical citizen responses in the wider society to situations of greater or lesser powerlessness, greater or lesser disillusionment with failed political promises. Thus, for example, we have found the apathy and fatalism of the poor to be, not pathological individual traits, or even the fruits of disadvantage as such, but rather expressions of non-commitment to a socio-political order that grants them little say in decisions affecting their lives. If we may then generalise such a finding, doubt is cast on those political liberals, for example, who see some apathy as a necessary precondition for the stability of mass democracies (see Pateman, 1970), and who hail low or only moderate levels of political participation as symptoms of a growing recognition that the issues confronting contemporary society are of an increasingly technical kind, safely and properly to be left in the hands of the technically expert.

Theoretical implications

Political liberals

There seem to be close resemblances between political liberalism and the rationales typically provided by the personnel of the welfare bureaucracies for their actions. For example, such professionals have commonly assumed an identity between their definition of the 'problem' of deprivation and that held by the poor themselves. This 'problem', moreover, has been seen in largely depoliticised terms and no potential conflict of interest between client and professional acknowledged. Likewise, official definitions of deprivation have characterised it as epiphenomenal to society. The goals of anti-deprivation programmes have then included the rescuing of the victims of socially and educationally debilitating milieux and their incorporation into the wider society. To this extent, our account of how the CDP and EPA experiences have undermined this professional rationale may be taken as a critique of the political liberal perspective too. The latter's value-ladenness is then also apparent.

Within the liberal tradition there is little place for collective action, particularly of a solidaristic kind. Social policies concerned with the incorporation of the poor will, these political liberals anticipate, erode such self-protective collectivism as the poor often display, with its associated hostility towards members of the wider society. Yet the empirical studies we have used point to significantly different conclusions: residents of deprived neighbourhoods articulate demands, not for individual escape and upward mobility, but for collective improvement and power. (Although this may have been less true for the ethnically plural neighbourhoods than for stable but declining working-class areas; generalisations about the implications of social policies for such group formation and action must not lead one to overlook the diverse local historical contexts in which that action develops—National CDP, 1974, para. 3.21.)[14] Here, then, is the promotion through social policies of life projects very different from the atomised individualism that the liberal expects in the emerging open society. Other political liberals admittedly see the good society not as a collection of atomised individuals but as a bargaining process among competing interest groups. Such liberals might then see community development, for example, as a means of ensuring that certain ill-organised groups are enabled more effectively to compete within that bargaining process (National CDP, 1974, para. 4.2; cf. p. 108 above). Yet their assumption is that the 'rules' that govern bargaining and the channels of negotiation may and will be taken for granted by all (Benington, 'The Flaw in the Pluralist Heaven' in Lees and Smith, 1975, p. 182). In our empirically oriented discussion, however, such therapeutic community organisation has resulted in purposive community action aimed at changes in those very rules.

Third, political liberals seem confident that the general trend of social policy developments will be towards the removal of the last remaining barriers to the open—indeed, the good—society, and, at the cognitive level, towards making clearer to citizens the rationale of that society. Committed participation in, and support for, the liberal society will thus be the response of an enlightened and rational citizenry (cf. pp. 29–30 above). We have, however, seen how officially sponsored programmes of community development (although central to the Seebohm reorganisation proposals and justified on a wide variety of other grounds—see above, pp. 105–6, 111–12) have failed to eliminate deprivation and disadvantage, and have exposed the lack of *any* rationale to wider distributive processes—save, as Goldthorpe argues, 'the principle of "to them that have shall more be given"' (in Wedderburn, 1974, p. 224). For the deprivation of the CDP neighbourhoods is revealed as merely part of a wider process of life chance distribution where power and advantage are the principal determinants of outcomes in a situation pre-eminently conflictual (cf. pp. 183–7 above). It is, moreover, exposed as the fruit, not of technically or 'functionally' necessary processes, but rather of essentially political decisions and non-decisions. These social policy innovations seem, therefore, more likely to corrode than to promote the legitimacy enjoyed by the wider socio-economic order in the eyes of its citizens.

Market liberals

As was evident when we summarised the competing expectations of citizens' responses to deprivation and its treatment, the views of the market and political liberals substantially overlap. For while they may differ in their portrait of the liberal society into which the poor are to be incorporated, they agree in defining deprivation as epiphenomenal, and in citing individual pathology or the inefficiency and unanticipated consequences of welfare bureaucracies as the principal causes of its persistence. In respect of the market liberals, we therefore add just two points. First, we have traced the emergence of forms of community and of social relationship very different from those of the market place, yet conferring—or at least grasping for—greater autonomy and freedom of the individual. These forms of social relationship, moreover, far from undermining individual responsibility—particularly that of the bread-winner (see above, p. 50)[15]—seem generally to corrode apathy and to promote mutual aid. Second, we have admittedly traced forms of coercion and loss of freedom that overweening public bureaucracies may enforce. Yet in some cases at least, this seems to have proceeded from their subordination to the interests, or their use of the techniques, of private business (see above, pp. 124–6). Reversal of this movement along the 'road to serfdom' seems feasible therefore, not by an extension of market disciplines in the administration of relief, but rather through a political commitment, by the society as a whole, to the extension of democracy that is integral to the CDP and EPA recommendations.

Neo-Marxists

Turning to the neo-Marxists, it is difficult to accept that the social policy innovations we have discussed are necessarily coercive or obfuscating in both their intent and their effect. It is admittedly true that some of the official rationales for instituting these anti-poverty programmes display a concern, not to resuscitate and support, but rather to control and even destroy 'pathological' communities. Those involved with the EPA projects seem aware of the dangers of allowing 'community education' to equip the deprived to do no more than accommodate themselves to their life-long fate (Midwinter, 'Curriculum and the EPA Community School' in Hooper,

1971, p. 489), producing what Bowles and Gintis term the 'correspondence' between their goals and aptitudes on the one hand and the functionaries demanded by local industry on the other (1976, Chs 4–5). Moreover, the experience of all these projects reveals the constraining and controlling power of the wider fabric of pre-existing social policies: the lack of consultation in redevelopment, official secrecy over welfare benefit entitlements and the irrelevance of a conventional education that does not develop even the competence to cope with an adult destination of multiple disadvantage. It is also true that, especially in the earlier phases of the projects we have examined, the official preference for improved 'communication' and 'dialogue' tended to divert 'attention . . . from . . . fundamental issues since the sort of dialogue situations acceptable to those in authority focus on immediate symptoms rather than underlying causes'. At this stage, 'it was all too easy for CDP to become institutionalised as "the private conscience of the Corporation"', providing an instant humanitarian commentary at every stage of decision-making, but impotent to influence the actual outcome on the ground' (Coventry CDP, 1975a, paras 5.5, 6.2).

Yet we have also traced emerging demands for radical change, not only in prevailing social policies but also in the wider socio-economic order; these, while catalysed by project personnel, seem to have come from the poor themselves. The projects may have been limited in both their numbers and their duration; their critiques have been anything but limited. Moreover, instead of the individuation of failure and of horizons that, neo-Marxists affirm, is a precondition for the continuing legitimation of capitalism and is both the intent and achievement of social and educational policies (Bowles and Gintis, 1976, Ch. 4), these are *collective* critiques. They have been predicated on a developing diagnosis of deprivation as, *inter alia*, the by-product of public and private sector resource allocation and as by no means confined to sub-categories of the population conveniently labelled 'the poor'. Such demands and their associated critique, moreover, have been the *typical* outcomes of the officially sponsored programmes we have examined.

Furthermore, for the Marxist tradition the distinction between the objective and the subjectively perceived interests of a class obtains its historical significance and practical relevance from the demonstration of some objective process at work, tending to dispel illusions. Here, too, we have traced a process of disillusionment and enlightenment among residents of these neighbourhoods, involving the withdrawal of legitimation from wider distributive processes in a grossly unequal society. It is, we have suggested, a process typical of such programmes; yet it is rooted, not in the immanent economic development of the capitalist mode of production, but rather in the search for political legitimation of public intervention. As such, it cannot be reduced to an explanation in orthodox Marxist class terms, even though it may spill over, as earlier suggested, into working-class critiques of capital accumulation (see above, pp. 191, 233); rather, it is a process centring in the relationships among policy-makers, welfare professionals and citizens. Equally, however, it can hardly be disregarded by the neo-Marxist who is interested in 'necessary' processes at work in contemporary society and promoting a withdrawal of legitimation from the dominant socio-economic order.

Second, the patterns and directions of group formation and action we have traced are not rooted exclusively in the work and market components of individuals' class situations. Rather, they are rooted in a common experience of disadvantage and powerlessness—*vis-à-vis* the labour market, the political system and other communities—and we have found little justification for seeing such multiple sources of deprivation as reducible to any one. Moreover, the community formation and mobilisation in question are the fruit, not of developments in work and market situations *à la* Marx, but rather of the catalytic activity of social policy agencies—the offspring of political initiatives. We have pointed to the need for further empirical investigation of possible links between community and workplace groupings; yet in line with the Social Democrats, our account discourages confidence in the unproblematic priority of such workplace groupings as the agent of social criticism and transformation.

Third, the limited success of these projects may seem strong evidence favouring the neo-Marxist case: there is a cohesive capitalist elite that either adapts social policy innovations to benefit itself or, where they are incapable of being adapted, suffocates them. The state apparatus, while enjoying a 'relative autonomy' from the various sections of the dominant class, employs this autonomy in the long-term collective interest of the class. The sorry fate of these projects, whose findings have hardly been treated as pilot projects for subsequent larger-scale efforts, is precisely what the neo-Marxist might predict. However, our empirical investigations at least suggest an alternative conclusion. In the Coventry studies, for example, the processes of criticism and withdrawal of legitimation catalysed by the action–research project have exposed fundamental conflicts of interest between, on the one hand, private industrial capital with its national or even international organisation and, on the other, local welfare professionals and politicians (see above, pp. 127–8). Such projects seem essentially corrosive, therefore, not only of the legitimacy of our grossly unequal social order, but also of what may be a perennially fragile constellation of interests among the various elite groups, locally if not nationally.

Social Democrats

These two sections have displayed the relevance of the *Social Democrats'* concern with moral obligation and community membership. The CDP and EPA action–research has exposed the political and moral choices and commitments that confront the wider society in its relationship to the deprived. For their diagnoses reveal that effective alleviation of this deprivation requires changes in resource allocation and political control going far wider than those initially anticipated by the political sponsors. Likewise, their findings are at least consistent with Titmuss' argument that for positive discrimination to be non-stigmatising it must be situated within an infrastructure of universalist services (cf. p. 200 above). For the action–research has demonstrated that the problems of these deprived areas are not different in kind from the deprivations more widely distributed within urban–industrial society; it has thus revealed that positive discrimination is other than a simple unilateral transfer from the non-poor to the deprived.

What changes, however, have resulted within the perceptions of the deprived neighbourhoods held by members of the wider society? To what extent, for example, were such perceptions affected by the revelation that these neighbourhoods are deprived because they bear disproportionately the costs of socio-economic change and that their deprivations and vulnerability are greater in degree but not different in kind from those to which the wider community is also vulnerable? That is, did these revelations engender recognition of a common condition and hence a sense of mutual obligation paralleling the one we found in our discussion of the gift relationship? The adequacy of the Social Democratic approach to social policy and social integration is heavily dependent on these considerations.

Unfortunately, the available project reports barely touch on these questions; we must, therefore, limit ourselves to brief informed speculation. Recall the three conditions that, we argued when criticising *The Gift Relationship*, determine how easily moral solidarity may be created between the independent and the dependent (see above, pp. 217–18). The opportunity cost to the wider society of heeding the findings of these anti-deprivation projects may well be perceived as high; communal responsibility for the deprived is a politically contentious goal, especially where their situation is one to which others are apparently invulnerable; and the CDP and EPA professionals have a fragile political legitimacy. That is, here are social policies that fulfil the conditions for maximising the problems of politically mobilising citizens' moral commitment.

Of course, variations must be anticipated among different areas—depending, for example, on the moral credibility of the deprived, on the general level of deprivation in the wider area, including the level of unemployment, and on local traditions of collective action and mutual aid. We may take two illustrations. The North Tyneside CDP was dealing with working-class poor in socially stable neighbourhoods that are suffering general decline (1978b, Part 1) but that also enjoy long traditions of working-class solidarity, albeit not militant (1978a; 1978c, pp. 81–3). In these conditions, the project was to some extent able to develop wider community action on behalf of the poor, for example in the form of a broad-based housing campaign (1978c, pp. 47–58); it accounted for its failure to achieve more in terms of long-standing working-class fatalism rooted in apparent powerlessness (1978c, p. 81). In contrast, Piven and Cloward (1972), in their study of American welfare policy, take as their principal focus Negro migrants to the northern cities, suffering a rate of unemployment markedly different from their hosts and entering areas with long-entrenched ethnic and religious communities (which, along with organised economic interests, monopolise patronage through public policies). Not surprisingly, therefore, Piven and Cloward find little mutual sympathy evoked between these poor and non-poor by the programmes of the 1960s: the gift relationship is poisoned. They tend, however, to overlook this specific context, and too readily to extrapolate their findings into the general view that welfare will be expanded only in so far as this is necessary to manage the poor. So, too, Jordan is perhaps unduly eager to argue that the state will typically face a backlash from the non-deprived and hostility to any significant redistribution of power and advantage (1974, pp. 153–4). Nevertheless, here is an area that the Social Democrats tend, if not to neglect, perhaps to over-simplify: the task of political leadership in articulating collective goals and mobilising collective support, that is, in creating a vehicle of social reform. At the same time, however, their liberal and neo-Marxist critics—the latter perhaps including the authors just mentioned—seem equally guilty of such over-simplification.

VI CONCLUSION

Towards the end of our introductory section, we suggested that three issues thrown up by previous chapters would necessarily be touched on here—issues to which none of the competing macro-theories we are evaluating does justice. These were the role of political leadership, the mediation of welfare professionals and the legitimacy of such politicians, professionals and the wider socio-economic order in the eyes of citizens.

(i) In the present chapter we have seen how the articulation of interests and needs has necessarily involved political leadership (cf. pp. 35–6, 194 above). So too, the directions of group formation and action have depended crucially upon political leadership and mobilisation—whether exercised through formal representative processes or informally. In section III this line of analysis was, admittedly, conspicuous by its paucity, but this merely exposed the limits on unqualified extrapolation from Titmuss' account of the gift relationship. In sections IV and V, this active role of political leadership has been more evident and the studies used have revealed considerable variety in the strategies pursued. In section IV, for example, we touched on the importance of wider party affiliation in overruling local politicians' concern with their own wards, although we have not provided any systematic explanation of their choice of goals (see above, p. 229).[16] We have hinted—but no more—at how informal political leadership may develop, for example within the CDPs (see above, pp. 229–30). While, therefore, we have justified our affirmations in earlier chapters that citizen responses to policy development are irreducibly dependent upon patterns of political leadership, in a relatively 'open' situation (see above, p. 144), we have only begun an explanation of how that leadership is typically exercised. Nevertheless, we *have* explored in some depth the extent to which—and the conditions under which—political leaders seek to retain and even enhance their legitimacy in the eyes of those affected by their social policy decisions (questions that were posed at several major points in earlier chapters—see above, pp. 128–9, 136–7).

(ii) The perennial and ubiquitous mediation of welfare professionals has been no less apparent, displaying a significant contrast with the modes of group formation and action of classical perspectives. Yet in our discussions, two very different—indeed, antithetical—roles for such professionals have been implicitly distinguished. On the one hand, the welfare professional may exploit the aura of his expertise and position to define needs and priorities with little reference to consumer preferences or even to overt political debate. This has been common among planners, for example, if the case studies of Sunderland and Coventry in chapter 4 are at all typical. In section IV of this chapter, we traced challenges to such professional definitions of the 'true' interests of residents. Likewise, in section V we saw the challenges mobilised by the EPA action–research projects to conventional professional definitions of what is educational deprivation and what constitutes a proper educational curriculum (see too, pp. 189, 193 above). Earlier, in section II, we sketched Jordan's account of how financial needs presented to the personal social services have been professionally redefined as indicating socio-psychological individual pathology. These were all, to varying degrees, instances of coercion by bureaucratised welfare professionals, imposing uniform categorisations of stereotyped 'need' upon the consumers, and justifying this in terms of their publicly authenticated credentials.

Yet such coercion has not been evident in all the professional action discussed. The medical professionals of the NHS were seen in section III to mediate bonds of moral obligation among the anonymous citizens of a mass society (although this seems principally to derive from the political context of treatment according to health need, within which both professional and citizen are acting). The professionals of the CDPs and EPA projects have commonly afforded expertise to their communities: they have served as a resource for action, as well as a catalyst. We have traced some of the self-creative and self-assertive collective activity in which such communities have been enabled thereby to engage. Moreover, we have seen that the goal of rendering such communities self-supporting can no longer be that of the original official brief, where it denotes the elimination of individual and social pathology through appropriate professional therapy from outside. Rather, the self-supporting community is necessarily engaged in a critique of the wider society, although such critique and action are inchoate without this professional servicing (see, for example, Midwinter, 1972, pp. 161–2; National CDP, 1974, paras 4.10, 5.25; Coventry CDP, 1975a, paras 7.50–7.51). We have, moreover, argued against seeing this analysis as being applicable only to deprived communities.

Discussion of this catalytic and enabling role of the welfare professional then encourages us to reconsider those whom we have characterised as 'coercive', to explore the wider groups who may be enforcing their interests through such professionals. Dennis finds such exploration unnecessary: it is their own interests that are served by the overweaning professional planners. Benington, however, sees the Coventry officials as allied to—as well as constrained by—local industrial and commercial interests. Within the present chapter, we have sought to relate the degree and patterns of such coercive activity to the political and moral commitments that members of the wider society recognise towards the dependent, and the duties they may wish to impose upon them (see above, pp. 201–4, 211–12).

(iii) Citizens' responses to social policies have proved importantly dependent upon the legitimacy they ascribe to such political leadership and professional mediation. Here, moreover, we are referring as much to the responses of the independent as of the dependent. First, for example, we saw in section II how selectivism in cash benefits both reinforces, and for the wider society is legitimated in terms of, public affirmation of the value of individualistic achievement and visible expression of the gulf between providers and the incompetent. The welfare rights movements traced in section IV involved the latter in overt challenges to such denigration, and to the legitimacy of the punitive regime it enforces. Second, in section III we saw how altruistic blood donation within the NHS expressed citizens' affirmation of the legitimacy of a universalist health service that gives public recognition and expression to the circulation of citizens between dependent and discretionary roles. (Although we noted that this legitimation of a preventive, freely accessible service might be facilitated by certain peculiarities of the NHS, and need not, moreover, be inconsistent with local communities' development of challenges to the differential *outcomes* within that service—see above, p. 224). Third, we have traced the discrediting of positively discriminating policies predicated upon the epiphenomenal genesis of deprivation. We have seen how, in the hands of deprived communities, the associated projects may promote a critical transformation of the wider social order. Yet we have also had to note their frequently sorry fates: their loss of legitimacy in the eyes of the powerful and the intensified loss of legitimacy of those original sponsors in the eyes of the deprived (cf. Piven and Cloward, 1972, p. 273). Not, however, that such loss of legitimacy necessarily evokes any overt threats to social order. Rather, the lack of available economic and political weight and of collective organisation may make apathetic and sullen compliance appear the only realistic responses (Coventry CDP, 1975a, para. 5.4 (iii)); the costs to the wider society of refusing a gift relationship are largely hidden.

These responses thus range from acquiescence in, or compliance with, the reproduction and reinforcement of the prevailing pattern of social relations—a compliance by the dependent that is sullen and apathetic and an acquiescence by the independent that is pre-eminently self-regarding—to collective criticism of that pattern and the articulation—and even, in germ, the creation—of an alternative. The former commonly obtains in the case of means-tested selectivism—although it is challenged by welfare rights movements—and in the case of positive discrimination denied expansion into a programme of wider social transformation. It involves the social definition of a gulf between the dependent and the independent, with lines of moral obligation and responsibility defined in terms of that gulf. The latter response, in contrast, obtains in the gift relationship of universalism, and in positive discrimination allowed thus to expand in creative critique. It involves affirmation of a shared dignity, transcending the social divisions of power, advantage and capacity but requiring collective commitment to their abolition.

NOTES

1. Although there is considerable variation in Marxist views of the poor. For Marcuse's hopes for this sub-stratum, see p. 47 above; contrast Marx's own view of their reactionary tendencies (Giddens, 1973, p. 37).
2. Cf. Dearlove, 'The Control of Change and the Regulation of Community Action' in Jones and Mayo (1974) pp. 23–4, for detailed references to a wide literature.
3. Cf. Weber's discussions of the proscription of certain forms of occupation for the mass of citizens, typical in many societies (e.g. see Gerth and Mills, 1948, pp. 188–9).
4. For Titmuss' fears of such division, see Reisman (1977) p. 86.
5. His perspective on man and society thus closely parallels that of Durkheim (see, for example, 1961, esp. Chs 4–7). Weber is no less concerned to affirm this logical distinction between self-interested and dutiful action—which at least approximates to his distinction between *zweckrational* and *wertrational* action. Both classical writers are here heavily influenced by Kant; and both, like Titmuss, are *inter alia* concerned to criticise the liberal view of the self-interested abstract individual. Collard's recent exploration of altruism and economic action has demonstrated that conventional modes of economic analysis need by no means be wedded to liberal prescriptions. Instead, he broadly supports Titmuss' argument, not least in regard to the contagion of altruistic action on the one hand, self-interested misanthropy on the other. Here, Collard concludes with the Social Democratic writers, 'the role of politicians as entrepreneurs . . . is vital, for the universalisation of benevolent impulses has to be articulated as policy' (1978, p. 180).
6. Among the most interesting of recent individual projects in Britain are Jacobs (1976) and Baine (1975).
7. A similar confusion within the American literature on the supposed 'culture of poverty' is highlighted in Valentine (1968).
8. The dilemmas thereby posed for CDP team members over the degree to which they should seek to influence the direction of residents' actions and group formation are frequently evident in their reports: e.g. see Lees and Smith (1975) pp. 73–4.
9. For discussion of the similar concerns of the Tynemouth CDP residents, see Lees and Smith (1975) Ch. 8.
10. This is especially true of the Coventry studies, on which we have especially relied (but see Benington in Leonard, 1975, for some of the most recent developments).
11. Cf. the contrast between 'traditional' community development and community action drawn by the National CDP (1974) paras 4.7, 4.11ff.
12. The *locus classicus* for discussion of these various bases of legitimation and the practical difficulties that arise in seeking their retention is Marris and Rein (1974). Rein (1974).
13. Goldthorpe, admittedly, explores the potential growth of articulated criticism; yet he confines his attention to the economic and industrial spheres and to criticism that is simply an exacerbation of the anomie prevailing therein: see Goldthorpe in Wedderburn (1974) pp. 228ff.
14. In some community action and development, moreover, local authorities have been able to remove the informal leaders of the poor by offering them opportunities for individual escape and self-advancement: see, for example, Jacobs (1976) p. 111. Some of the CDP reports—and our account—may have tended to idealise the solidarism and lack of self-interestedness created or reinforced among the deprived as a result of such community action.
15. Contrast the effects of means-tested benefits (pp. 202, 205 above).
16. For the beginnings of such an account, by one of the writers on whom we have drawn, see Dennis, 'Community Action, Quasi-Community Action and Anti-Community Action' in Leonard (1975).

CHAPTER 7

Conclusion

Politics is a strong and slow boring of hard boards. It takes both passion and perspective. Certainly all historical experience confirms the truth that man would not have attained the possible unless time and again he had reached out for the impossible. But to do that a man must be a leader, and not only a leader but a hero as well, in a very sober sense of the word. And even those who are neither leaders nor heroes must arm themselves with that steadfastness of heart which can brave even the crumbling of all hopes. This is necessary right now, or else men will not be able to attain even that which is possible today. [Max Weber, 'Politics as a Vocation' in H. H. Gerth and C. W. Mills (eds) From Max Weber, *p. 128*]

I INTRODUCTION

Our concern has been to investigate the significance of social policy in advanced Western societies—in societies, that is, that have historically been organised in capitalist market terms. This investigation has admittedly been far from exhaustive. There has been only fleeting reference to any country other than Britain. Even here, the space devoted to any of the areas of empirical enquiry in Part II could have been multiplied many-fold; and had the number of such areas chosen been greater, it would doubtless have permitted firmer conclusions. Nevertheless, the care with which we have indicated the criteria for selecting material of relevance should have justified the focus upon highly specific and well-defined areas of investigation; the broad conclusions presented in previous chapters are likewise justified in terms of the empirical evidence offered. We have, moreover, if only at times by implication, indicated how a more extended treatment would, in principle, proceed.

247

In addition, however, it might be claimed that in our initial exposition of the neo-Marxist, liberal and Social Democratic arguments, set out in chapter 3, insufficient cognisance was taken of the range and diversity within each school. We have, perhaps, selected those writers whose arguments are especially vulnerable, and failed to recognise that there are other contemporary exponents of the Marxist and liberal traditions in particular to whom our criticisms —both methodological and empirical—do not apply. Whatever the merits of such rejoinders, however, we would claim that the sets of arguments expounded in chapter 3 and investigated empirically in Part II do represent typical perspectives adopted by these writers; and that, while we may indeed not have come to grips with other of their arguments or representatives, the debate over social policy has in at least some key respects been advanced. Not the least of the merits that a work in the social sciences may possess is the clarification of those issues around which subsequent debate must centre, and the reorientation of the terrain upon which opposing intellectual forces must henceforth do battle.

It might, lastly, be argued that, acknowledging some force to these criticisms, the form of the present work cannot be justified, given its limited length. In the first place, we have considered three areas of empirical investigation, the subjects of chapters 4, 5 and 6 respectively; more detailed investigation of one area only would have permitted more extended and detailed evaluation of the opposing arguments relating to that area. Second, we have sought to compare neo-Marxist, liberal and Social Democratic perspectives on social policy; a comparison of just two of these would have permitted a more refined and therefore more sympathetic consideration of the variations within each of the schools of thought chosen. However, against the latter criticism it may be pointed out that liberal and Marxist perspectives have to a significant extent been forged through mutual criticism (at the time of their classical formulation as well as in their contemporary versions) and that the Social Democratic approach to social policy can hardly be appreciated except in terms of an implicit critique of the parameters of the liberal–Marxist debate. Such interrelationships were evident in chapters 2 and 3. They serve to justify our attempt to isolate some, at least, of the fundamental issues in these continuing debates and mutual criticisms, and to make these issues the concern of our empirical discussion. Likewise, while chapters 4–6 were indeed concerned with three different areas of interest, it will have been evident that the arguments examined and the conclusions reached have been interrelated and interdependent in fundamental ways, requiring, therefore, that they be investigated jointly. These continuities will also be evident in the next section, as we recall some of our principal findings.

II SOCIAL POLICY, STRATIFICATION AND POLITICAL ORDER

It is the legacy of the 1834 Poor Law that has provided the starting point for debates over the role of social policy in our society. Social measures appear there as punitive and as a mere adjunct to the wider market society: subservient and reactive to its distributive principles, dynamics of change and mode of social integration. Against this, an increasingly preventive orientation has been evident in major branches of the social policies we have investigated, concerned with the anticipation and arresting of circumstances generating deprivation.[1] Even so, being concerned with the diswelfares generated by the wider society, prevention too is in a sense merely reactive. However, the social policy developments we have considered go beyond incorporation of the deprived and do not always take mere prevention of socially generated diswelfares as their primary orientation. Rather the 'needs' with which they deal are continuously experienced by the whole population and must be defined, not in terms of the relative deprivation and exclusion of minorities, but rather in terms of the collective self-realisation of the citizenry as a whole (see, for example, pp. 104–5 above).

Here social policy exhibits an emerging promotive concern and must be seen as unavoidably involved in nothing less than active transformation or reproduction of the stratification and political order of our society (see p. 143 above).[2] Hence, while our main exploration has been of the statutory social services, we have pointed to the need for the student and practitioner to be alert to wider elements of such reproduction—including the distribution of advantage and the exercise of power in urban and industrial milieux. So, too, promotion of social rights within such industrial milieux and the likely consequences for occupational hierarchies of reward and authority have recently been examined by some investigators; although again we have had to limit ourselves to the barest suggestions (see above, pp. 89, 220; Goldthorpe in Hirsch and Goldthorpe, 1978, esp. pp. 203ff.).

Nevertheless, the interrelations of social policy and social stratification were the recurring concerns of Part II, focussing our attention on the strengths and weaknesses of the competing schools of thought we have chosen to study. First, encouragement to private welfare schemes tends to reinforce and reproduce the prevailing map of inequality and the associated lines of social conflict (see above, pp. 212, 215). The other directions of social policy development we have investigated, however, involve distributional and/or relational modifications in—if not radical challenges to—the stratification system. Means-tested selectivity tends to create a negatively privileged status group of paupers: the new serfs of the liberal state. Universalism may not of itself challenge and reduce class gradients in deprivation, unless extended into positive discrimination (see above, pp. 171–2); yet it does counter the immiseration of the public sector that a dual system promotes and before which the lower classes are particularly vulnerable (see above, pp. 111, 167). It creates new lines of interest identity and conflict, and hence of potential group formation and action aimed at redistribution, albeit not necessarily between classes (see above, pp. 174, 179–80). It also seems to be a necessary—if not a sufficient—condition for the political mobilisation of bonds of mutual obligation between the advantaged and disadvantaged, upon which the acceptability of such redistribution in part depends. The consequences of positive discrimination for stratification are no simpler, since they are heavily dependent on the associated patterns of group formation and action by the advantaged as well as the disadvantaged (see above, pp. 244–5).

Thus the implications of social policy for social stratification are in general importantly dependent upon—and involve—such patterns of group formation and action. Yet we have also seen how such social action is itself moulded by the political strategies of social policy-makers. For example, the pursuit of universalist and positive discriminatory policies tends to expose the obstacles imposed upon their success by wider socio-economic arrangements, to corrode the popular legitimacy of the latter, and to promote popular articulation of alternative modes of distributing such wider power, advantage and opportunities (see above, pp. 93–4, 127–8, 187,

233–4, 236–7). (Not least, instead of relieving industry of all social responsibility outside the employment contract, as the Poor Law had done—see above, p. 11—it results in calls for the greater social accountability of such industry—see above, p. 187; cf. p. 161.) On the other hand, *failure* to pursue such policies tends, especially where popular support for them has initially been cultivated and expectations raised, to corrode the legitimacy of the political leaders concerned—or even, indeed, of the political order as such (see above, p. 245). (This latter conclusion was, admittedly, derived principally from study of social policies in deprived neighbourhoods; yet we argued that cautious generalisation of the results was permissible—see above, pp. 234–5.) Implementation of selectivist policies, in contrast, tends to threaten the legitimacy of neither the political nor the socio-economic orders in the eyes of the independent, but to evoke sullen compliance, rather than willing commitment, from the dependent (see above, p. 245). Yet maintenance of such wider legitimacy seems to involve recurrent efforts at, for example, priority treatment for the 'pathological' neighbourhoods of the deprived—treatment, however, that has typically enabled the resentment of the latter to be transformed into overt challenge and protest.

At the same time, both the choice and justification of social policy strategies and the popular evaluation and acceptance of them tend perennially to be obscured and vitiated by the necessary mediation of bureaucratised welfare professionals, themselves in considerable measure the creation of social policies. They may, moreover, ally themselves with established powerful groups in jointly subverting the social measures implemented. Yet the continuation of such joint action cannot be taken for granted; still less is this new serfdom systemically or technically 'necessary' (see above, p. 236).

III SOCIAL SCIENCE AND POLITICAL PRACTICE

Our investigation of recent British social policies has lent most support to the *Social Democratic* writers. It has, first, displayed the significance of their distinction between the exercise of civil and social rights and its importance when analysing the implications of social policy for social action and stratification. Second, it has vindicated their concern with the diversity of values that can inform social policies, with the search for political legitimacy and popular support as a goal of social policy-makers, and with the critical politicisation of wider societal arrangements that the attempt to implement social policies and social rights typically involves. Finally, it has justified their contention that different policies may promote sharply contrasting modes of social control and integration—recognising with them, however (and *contra* the political liberals), that the development of social policy must also involve perennial value conflict over the ends of policy. (Although such value conflict and political struggle need not result in overt social conflict; indeed, it is a principal thesis of the Social Democrats that the collective experience of universal social rights will evoke the moral commitment and disregard of pure self-interest that realisation of the collectively chosen future requires and entails.)

Moreover, we have vindicated the Social Democrats' insistence on investigating social policy within an essentially historical framework—in contrast to the dominant tendencies of many liberal and neo-Marxist writers. In chapter 4, for example, we saw that social policy development typically involves a process of learning-by-doing (see above, p. 142). In chapter 5, it was necessary to explain inequalities in personal health care in terms of the historical expectations, aspirations and endowments with which individuals come to the attention of the health services. Likewise, our investigation of multiply deprived neighbourhoods pointed to a diagnosis of this deprivation as the precipitate—the *historical* precipitate—of society-wide processes, including certain social policies. In chapter 6, sections II and III, the patterns of social integration and control were part of an evolving historical dialectic between conditions of access imposed on welfare institutions and the active responses of citizens. In the subsequent two sections, we traced a process, catalysed and mediated by social policy agencies, of developing action, group formation and critical challenge to the wider social, economic and political arrangements—very often ending in a loss of popular faith in the willingness of the powerful to honour political commitments. (Although what consequences this loss of faith might hold for societal functioning was a matter for separate empirical investigation.)

As part of this historical investigation, we have traced how the definition and enrichment of social rights—whether taken by the political instigators as ends or as mere means to such goals as economic growth, social control or military preparedness— typically change citizens' expectations and demands and their capacities to translate these into action. So that the withdrawal or dismantling of some policy and its associated rights cannot be thought of *simply* as restoring the *status quo ante*. Equally, the failure of policy-makers to engage in positive action to deal with the wider societal arrangements exposed as obstacles to the realisation of declared social rights cannot be thought of as leaving unchanged citizens' perceptions of—and actions towards—those arrange- ments. Hence is justified the interest of the Social Democrats in social rights as mediating a dialectic between 'legislation from above and active citizenship from below' (Terrill, 1974, p. 261).

The foregoing then prompts recall of some of the major weaknes- ses, both conceptual and methodological, identified in the liberal and neo-Marxist writers. *Liberals* commonly portray society as in principle capable of—if not actually tending towards—an equilib- rium. This we have repeatedly found lacking in verisimilitude; it betrays their ahistorical bias. It also testifies to their unreadiness to admit any conflictual notion of power (see above, pp. 84, 101, 122, 165, 169, 172).[3] Second, they portray society as composed of atomised pre-social, and therefore ahistorical, individuals; yet we have, again, found this frequently meaningless (see above, pp. 109, 135, 141–2, 235–6). Likewise in their policy recommendations, liberal writers commonly delineate as historically invariant some absolute level of needs (see above, pp. 84, 164–5, 176–7); it is man the pre-social animal, rather than the insociate human, who is the prime—or even the sole—proper concern of the state. Third, in so far as (political) liberals focus not on individuals but on legitimate interest groups as the parties in a bargaining process, 'legitimacy' is taken as unproblematic because ahistorical: the processes whereby legitimacy is secured or denied are left unexamined (see above, pp. 108, 168–9, 236).

Rather than rehearsing at length our further substantive criti- cisms of these writers, let us recall a few of the illiberal conse- quences of social policies informed by liberal principles. Reliance on the individualistic contract tends, we argued in chapter 4, not to guarantee the real value of pensions, but rather to render it depen- dent upon rates of inflation; while reliance on private supplementation tends to allow the balance of power between employed and employer to override considerations of equity (see above, pp. 84–5). Private health insurance, we saw in chapter 5, tends to make the accidents of chronic disablement more significant than the individual's responsible foresight in determining the treatment he receives (see above, p. 164). In chapter 6, finally, we saw how means-testing tends to promote the illiberal coercion of beneficiaries and to undermine discharge of their domestic responsibilities—to create, indeed, a new serfdom (see above, pp. 205, 237; cf. p. 50).

The *neo-Marxists* broadly retain the classical Marxist account of developing inequalities and even immiseration, and of the progressive or eventual loss of legitimacy of the dominant capitalist order. In chapter 3, however, we found their accounts of this historical process inchoate (see esp. pp. 47–8 above); while in Part II we traced a significantly different development. First, we saw new processes of immiseration, arising out of political decisions over the degree of universalism in social provisions: see, for example, the consequences for the chronically sick of abandoning universalism and for the CDP neighbourhoods of failing to locate poverty programmes within a universalist infrastructure (see above, p. 167 and chapter 5, section III). To these the lower social classes are likely to be especially—but not uniquely—vulnerable; but these are irreducibly political processes. Second, the 'logic' of demystification of the wider socio-economic order traced in chapter 6 involved political leaders and citizens in jointly developing an immanent practical critique of the wider society. It was not possible to portray these processes in terms of the overall legitimacy of an integrated socio-political system, nor, again, to see these political processes as derivative of economic. Yet the demystification and loss of legitimacy we traced were far from epiphenomenal.

Some of the latter conclusions proceeded, admittedly, from an investigation of social policies, not among the working class or the population at large, but rather in neighbourhoods of the publicly recognised deprived. What remained unclear was, therefore, the more general lines of common interest and alliance that might develop among these various groupings—although these lines were, we argued in chapter 5, likely to be importantly dependent upon common situations *vis-à-vis* social policy agencies, as distinct from the mode of industrial production. Also uninvestigated were the alternative strategies that might be open to other groups than the deprived seeking to articulate their withdrawal of legitimation from social policy-makers.

Here, then, is the development of an immanent practical critique of wider societal arrangements; yet it is irreducibly centred in social policy developments, rather than in the process of capital accumulation. It involves the break-down of the insulation of economy and polity upon which, neo-Marxists commonly argue, the stability of capitalist society depends. It similarly involves what Giddens, writing in neo-Marxist vein, terms 'revolutionary consciousness', as distinct from mere resentment at the prevailing order; for it includes the emerging articulation of a fundamentally alternative social order (1973, pp. 114, 116). Superior power may still allow the advantaged to resist this critique. Yet with social policies serving decreasingly to legitimate the dominant order and to rationalise and regulate the contemporary relationship of wage labour to capital, overt repression becomes the only alternative for the propertied and increasing social disorganisation its likely consequence. Systemic stability and the mere adjustment of social policies to the requirements of capital accumulation are not available options.

If, however, we have found the *Social Democratic* position on balance the most satisfactory, both methodologically and empirically, we have also exposed some weakness and gaps in the existing accounts by its proponents; although these often seem to date from—and express—the euphoria of the immediate post-war period and are less imputable to more recent writings (see above, pp. 39, 65–6).

(i) To start with, they have perhaps overestimated the readiness of policy-makers to draw on social scientific analysis in choosing the means most adequate to their social goals,[4] and their capacity and willingness, in a relatively 'open' situation, to aim at major societal transformation. Thus, where social scientific analysis has pointed to changes in social measures as the necessary means of achieving proclaimed objectives, powerful vested interests have often been able to impede or modify them—even where the policy research has initially enjoyed strong political sponsorship (see above, pp. 90–1 and our discussion of the CDP research). So too, we have criticised certain policy-makers' attempts to portray their activities as enjoying a coherent rationale, as judged by the canons of social science;

instead we have pointed to the ways in which these activities are moulded and deprived of their substantive rationality by other self-interested groups (see above, pp. 96, 110–11, 123ff.). Second, we have indicated some differences in the social goals of Labour and Conservative administrations, with the former apparently more ready to challenge the values of acquisitive individualism (see, for example, chapter 4, section II); yet modification or even retreat from such challenge have been not uncommon in the face of vested interests. We have hardly ventured any *explanation* of these limitations upon the will or ability of Labour political leaders to choose and pursue social goals distinct from those of their political rivals. We have, however, argued that the constellations of interest between such political leaders and particular advantaged groups in the wider society must be seen as perennially contingent. In short, then, these writers may have tended to take for granted the reliability of Social Democratic politicians in progressively enlarging social rights and in modifying civil rights as required for this enlargement (see above, pp. 142–3).

(ii) There is a certain naivity over the accountability and beneficence of bureaucratised welfare professionals, taking for granted their promotion of citizens' interests. We have, however, exposed their susceptibility to manipulation by more advantaged sectors of the population—whether middle-class patients obtaining privileged treatment within the NHS or industrial and commercial elites gaining privileged access to planning and redevelopment policy-making. We have traced the variety of coercive and catalytic roles in which these professionals may engage and the circumstances in which they may mystify and disregard citizens' needs and interests, rather than clarifying and meeting them. We have pointed to some of their strategies for legitimating these various activities. In short, we have developed a critique of professional judgement, grounded in an understanding of the wider distribution of power and advantage within which such professionals act—and of which, indeed, they form an important part. Again, this weakness seems in part to express the Fabian influence on the Social Democratic tradition, with its confidence in the dispassionate and professional public servant as the protector of the citizen against the vicissitudes of the market society and as the mediator of his political rights.

(iii) There is perhaps an over-optimism as to the capacity of policy-makers to evoke widespread commitment to shared social goals, whose pursuit will involve all in some sacrifice of narrow and immediate self-interests (see above, pp. 173–5, 217–18, 240–2). The preventive and promotive policies we have explored may in some circumstances evoke fraternal participation in social provision for the dependent. Yet they seem also to evoke and encourage strategies of self-interested manipulation and monopolisation by the more advantaged and powerful. The political task is not confined, therefore, to a choice among alternative societal futures, but also includes the continuing mobilisation of support and collective commitment to that chosen future and the *moral* order it embodies. It is the feasibility of such mobilisation that cannot be taken for granted. Indeed, the unprincipled nature of the wider distribution of power and advantage in our society arguably renders this political task impossible, unless the social policies being advanced are openly and explicitly linked to the wider reconstruction of society as a moral order (cf. Goldthorpe, 'Social Inequality and Social Integration in Modern Britain' in Wedderburn, 1974). Although whether failure produces—in both the political and the economic realms—overt social conflict or merely fatalistic apathy and sullen compliance is likely to depend upon the power and resources of the most disaffected and their opportunities for collective organisation and action (see above, pp. 226, 234–5, 245).

One aspect of this optimism merits more specific note. The Social Democratic writers commonly suggest that collective commitment to shared goals may be achieved, providing that the privileges of the few are not so much removed in a 'levelling-down' as extended to become universal rights. Sufficiently high-quality collective provision will attract support and use even by the middle and upper classes.[5] Admittedly, the progressive translation of privileges into universal social rights is likely to promote escalation of statutory social budgets; yet the appropriation of social rights also may be expected to generate an increased willingness by all sectors of society to contribute to those budgets and to supplement statutory resources with voluntary effort, as a social duty of citizenship (see above, p. 65). Against these hopes, two points may be made (see esp. pp. 217–18, 240–2 above). First, our evidence, such as it is, hardly suggests that this progressive cultivation of altruism will be politically easy. Second, these writers perhaps neglect the extent to which privileges may be desired—and their extension resisted—precisely because they *are* privileges, symbolising the life style and granting access to the monopolised opportunities of powerful strata.[6] (A corollary is that they have been insufficiently concerned to identify which social actors have both the will and the capacity to act as an effective vehicle of social reform—see above, pp. 95, 143, 176, 242. Equally, they have inadequately spelled out the patterns of social control and regulation that the advantaged may seek to impose on the dependent—see above, esp. pp. 242–5; cf. Sinfield, 1978, p. 138).

This points, therefore, to the likelihood—or at least the strong possibility—of a political future starkly different from the social democratic commonwealth for which these writers hope, although Titmuss, at least, is well aware of its availability, warning of a moral 'vacuum likely to be filled by hostility and social conflict' (1973, p. 224). This blends, indeed, with the prognoses offered in two recent but more general analyses of the social integration of our Western urban–industrial societies. Hirsch contemplates our 'depleting moral legacy': he restates Durkheim's thesis that the 'non-contractual element of the contract' and shared social purposes cannot be created—but are, rather, eroded—by self-interested market activity. Like Titmuss, he points to the moral 'vacuum in social organisation [whereby] the market system . . . may sabotage its own foundations' (1977, p. 143). So too, Fox points to the economic and industrial costs that a 'low trust' society, lacking shared moral purposes, must bear; he warns that 'once the low-trust framework exists it tends to . . . enlarge rather than minimise the area of conflict'. He searches for 'the social forces which [can] set limits to the expression of low-trust behaviours', and argues that these can result only from 'a radical reconstruction [of social institutions] which seeks to rally major sections of society behind shared purposes of social justice' (1974, pp. 318–19, 358; cf. pp. 36–7 above). Here, then, is a society in which the fragile legitimacy of our contemporary Welfare State has been further eroded: the political order is characterised by widespread apathy or overt social conflict, together with authoritarian attempts to impose social order (Goldthorpe in Wedderburn, 1974, p. 233). Yet our analysis implies that such a future will not have come inevitably, but to some degree will rather have been the fruit of decisions by political leaders and , indeed, by the citizenry at large that centre in their lack of commitment to a promotive social policy as the basis for that social reconstruction for which these writers search and plead.

Finally and more specifically then, what form do such decisions over these alternative futures currently take? In the present situation of recession and public expenditure cuts, combined with renewed agitation across the advanced Western world over levels of personal taxation, the Social Democrats' hopes of translating privileges into universal social rights are rendered increasingly difficult. Indeed, what has for several decades been taken as perhaps the most well-established universalist social right—that to employment—has increasingly been translated into a privilege of the more powerful (Sinfield, 1977). At the same time, in Britain at least, the social policy debate has tended to shift from positive discrimination for the underprivileged towards issues of educational and family policy, for example, having more of a universalist—and self-interested—appeal. (As we saw in chapter 5, this shift has been acknowledged in the changed strategies adopted by pressure groups for the poor such as the Child Poverty Action Group—see above, p. 180). Together these developments seem to signify the erosion of altruism and moral solidarity in the face of shared adversity—an erosion that political leaders and those groups wielding power in the wider society (including the trade unions) have promoted, whether by intent or neglect. Yet it is an erosion that is likely to escalate, as Fox and Hirsch emphasise, with costs imposed more widely in society.

To this extent, such political leaders and powerful social groups have refused to embrace the 'ethic of responsibility' to which Weber summoned the Social Democrats and other political actors of his day (see above, pp. 35–6). To issue a similar summons remains the task of the sociologist today. He may, with Barrington Moore, fear that in a society such as the United States this is unlikely to be heeded and that 'the obstacles [to] ... some democratic and humane socialism ... are staggering' (1972, p. 192). Yet in respect of Britain at least, he may equally point to traditions of mutual aid among both working and middle classes (Halsey, 1978, pp. 162–3) and to the experience of altruism generated by universalist social policies as sources of authoritative values, which responsible political leadership can cultivate in opposition to those of acquisitive individualism. As Halsey can therefore conclude, 'adversity itself is now sufficient to give social response to political initiative' (1978, p. 168).

NOTES

1. See, for example, the preventive concern of Seebohm (esp. pp. 104–5 above) and Cullingworth's redefinition of the proper concern of local housing authorities (p. 117 above).
2. Indeed, this provides a definition of *social* policy in terms of some specific and distinguishing object. It is nothing less general or less fundamental than the state's policy *vis-à-vis* social stratification, i.e. the wider distribution of power and advantage—whether this be a policy of reinforcing and upholding the prevailing distribution, or actively challenging it (cf. the rather unsatisfactory attempts at a general definition summarised by Titmuss, 1974, Ch. 2).
3. The neo-classical economists have been an important influence on the market liberals in particular; note, therefore, the parallel controversy among economists over such notions of equilibrium: see Hahn (1973).
4. Herein they to some extent follow their Fabian forebears' reliance upon rational persuasion of elite groups as the path to social transformation: see Wilding (1976) p. 150.
5. See Crossman and his advisers' hopes that national superannuation would attract the voluntary entry of many at present in generous private schemes (p. 87 above), and our discussion of common health interests (pp. 173–5 above).
6. Cf. Hirsch's analysis of 'positional goods' that enjoy an inherent social scarcity (1977); and p. 178 above.

Bibliography

BRITISH GOVERNMENT PUBLICATIONS

DEPARTMENT OF EDUCATION AND SCIENCE (1967) *Children and Their Primary Schools* A Report of the Central Advisory Council for Education (Plowden Report) London, HMSO

DEPARTMENT OF EDUCATION AND SCIENCE (1972) *Educational Priority* (Halsey Report) London, HMSO

DEPARTMENT OF EDUCATION AND SCIENCE (1973) *Adult Education: A Plan for Development* (Russell Report) London, HMSO

DEPARTMENT OF ENVIRONMENT (1977) *Housing Policy—A Consultative Document* Cmnd 6845, London, HMSO

DEPARTMENT OF HEALTH AND SOCIAL SECURITY (1970) *The Future Structure of the National Health Service* (The Second Green Paper) London, HMSO London, HMSO

DEPARTMENT OF HEALTH AND SOCIAL SECURITY (1970) *The Future Structure of the National Health Service* (The Second Green Paper) London HMSO

DEPARTMENT OF HEALTH AND SOCIAL SECURITY (1971a) *Strategy for Pensions: The Future Development of State and Occupational Provision* Cmnd 4755, London, HMSO

DEPARTMENT OF HEALTH AND SOCIAL SECURITY (1971b) *National Health Service Reorganisation: Consultative Document* London, HMSO

DEPARTMENT OF HEALTH AND SOCIAL SECURITY (1972) *Management Arrangements for the Reorganised NHS* London, HMSO

DEPARTMENT OF HEALTH AND SOCIAL SECURITY (1974a) *Better Pensions—Fully Protected Against Inflation: Proposals for a New Pensions Scheme* Cmnd 5713, London, HMSO

DEPARTMENT OF HEALTH AND SOCIAL SECURITY (1974b) *Democracy in the NHS* London, HMSO

GOVERNMENT ACTUARY (1972) *Occupational Pension Schemes 1971: Fourth Survey by the Government Actuary* London, HMSO

MINISTRY OF HOUSING AND LOCAL GOVERNMENT (1969) *Council Housing: Purposes, Procedures and Priorities* (Cullingworth Report) London, HMSO

PRIME MINISTER'S OFFICE (1976) *Occupational Pension Schemes: The Role of Members in the Running of Schemes* Cmnd 6514, London, HMSO

Report of the Committee on Higher Education (1963) (Robbins Report) Appendix One, Cmnd 2154–I, London, HMSO

Report of the Committee on Local Authority and Allied Personal Social Services (1968) (Seebohm Report) Cmnd 3703, London, HMSO

Social Insurance and Allied Services (1942) (Beveridge Report) Cmd. 6404, London, HMSO

TREASURY AND DEPARTMENT OF HEALTH AND SOCIAL SECURITY (1972) *Proposals for a Tax-Credit System* Cmnd 5116, London, HMSO

OTHER PUBLICATIONS

ABEL-SMITH, B. (1971) 'The Politics of Health' *New Society* 29 July, pp. 190–2
ABEL-SMITH, B. (1976) *Value for Money in Health Services* London, Heinemann
ABEL-SMITH, B. and TITMUSS, R. M. (1956) *The Costs of the National Health Service in England and Wales* Cambridge University Press
ADENAY, M. (1971) *Community Action: Four examples* London, Runnymede Trust
ALFORD, R. R. (1975) *Health Care Politics: Ideological and Interest Group Barriers to Reform* University of Chicago Press
ANDERSON, P. and BLACKBURN, R. (eds) (1965) *Towards Socialism* London, Fontana
ARIE, T. (1966) 'Class and Disease' *New Society* 27 January, pp. 8–12
ARIE, T. (1975) 'Community Medicine' *New Society* 5 June, pp. 584–6
ARONOVITCH, B. (1974) *Give It Time* London, Andre Deutsch
ATKINSON, A. B. (1969) *Poverty in Britain and the Reform of Social Security* Cambridge University Press
ATKINSON, A. B. (1970) 'National Superannuation: redistribution and value for money' *Bulletin of the Oxford University Institute of Statistics* Vol. 32, No. 3, pp. 171–85
AVINERI, S. (1968) *The Social and Political Thought of Karl Marx* Cambridge University Press

BAINE, S. (1975) *Community Action and Local Government* (Occasional Papers in Social Administration, No. 59) London, Bell
BALOGH, T. and STREETEN, P. P. (1963) 'The Coefficient of Ignorance' *Bulletin of the Oxford University Institute of Statistics* Vol. 25, No. 2, pp. 97–107
BARAN, P. and SWEEZY, P. M. (1968) *Monopoly Capital* Harmondsworth, Penguin
BANKS, O (1955) *Parity and Prestige in English Secondary Education* London, Routledge and Kegan Paul
BEETHAM, D. (1974) *Max Weber and the Theory of Modern Politics* London, Allen and Unwin
BELL, D. (1974) *The Coming of Post-Industrial Society* London, Heinemann
BELL, D. (1976) *The Cultural Contradictions of Capitalism* London, Heinemann
BELL, D. (1978) 'A Report on England—The Future That Never Was: Part 1' *The Public Interest* No. 51, pp. 35–73
BENINGTON, J. (1972) *Coventry Community Development Project Background and Progress* (CDP Occasional Paper No. 1) London, Home Office (Urban Deprivation Unit)
BERLANT, J. L. (1975) *Profession and Monopoly: A Study of Medicine in the United States and Great Britain* University of California Press
BEVERIDGE, W. H. (1942) *Social Insurance and Allied Services* Cmd 6404, London, HMSO
BLACKBURN, R. (ed.) (1972) *Ideology in Social Science* London, Fontana
BLACKBURN, R. and COCKBURN, A. (1967) *The Incompatibles* Harmondsworth, Penguin
BLAU, P. M. and DUNCAN, O. D. (1967) *The American Occupational Structure* New York, John Wiley
BLAUG, M. (ed.) (1968) *Economics of Education I* Harmondsworth, Penguin
BOWLES, S. and GINTIS, H. (1976) *Schooling in Capitalist America: Educational Reform and the Contradictions of Economic Life* London, Routledge and Kegan Paul
BREBNER, J. B., (1948) 'Laissez Faire and State Intervention in 19th Century Britain' *Journal of Economic History* Supplement VIII, pp. 59–73

BREMNER, M. (1968) *Dependency and the Family* London, Institute of Economic Affairs

BRUCE, M. (1961) *The Coming of the Welfare State* London, Batsford

BULL, D. (ed.) (1972) *Family Poverty* London, Duckworth

BURN, W. L. (1964) *The Age of Equipoise* London, Allen and Unwin

BUTLER, J. R. and KNIGHT R. (1974) 'General Practice Manpower and Health Service Reorganisation' *Journal of Social Policy* Vol. 3, Part 3, pp. 235–51

CALOUSTE GULBENKIAN FOUNDATION (1968) *Community Work and Social Change: A Report on Training* London, Longman

CANTOR, M. (1976) 'Killing the Voice of Community Development in the National Arena' *Health and Social Services Journal* Vol. 86, No. 4506, 4 September, pp. 1584–5

CARSTAIRS, V. *et al.* (1966) 'Distribution of Hospital Patients by Social Class' *Health Bulletin* Vol. 24, No. 3

CARTWRIGHT, A. (1964) *Human Relations and Hospital Care* London, Routledge and Kegan Paul

CASTELLS, M. (1976) 'The Wild City' *Kapitalistate: Working Papers on the Capitalist State* (Frankfurt), Nos 4–5, pp. 2–30

CASTLES, S. and KOSACK, G. (1973) *Immigrant Workers and Class Structure in Western Europe* London, Oxford University Press

'CDPS writ larger' *New Society* 17 July 1975, p. 122

CHESTER, T. E. (1973) 'Health Service Reorganised' *Westminster Bank Review* November, pp. 41–54

CLARKE, S. and GINSBERG, N. (1976) 'The Political Economy of Housing' *Kapitalistate: Working Papers on the Capitalist State* Nos 4–5, pp. 66–99

COLLARD, D. (1978) *Altruism and Economy: A Study in Non-Selfish Economics* London, Martin Robertson

COLLETTI, L. (1972) *From Rousseau to Lenin* London, New Left Books

COOPER, M. (ed.) (1973) *Social Policy* Oxford, Blackwell

COOPER, M. H. (1975) *Rationing Health Care* London, Croom Helm

COOPER, M. H. and CULYER, A. J. (1968) *The Price of Blood* London, Institute of Economic Affairs

COVENTRY CDP (1975A) *Final Report Part 1: Coventry and Hillfields: Prosperity and the Persistence of Inequality* London, Home Office

COVENTRY CDP (1975b) *Final Report Part 2: Background Working Papers* London, Home Office

CRIPPS, T. F. and TARLING, R. J. (1973) *Growth in Advanced Capitalist Economies*, Cambridge University Press

CROSSMAN, R. H. S. (1972a) *The Politics of Pensions* Liverpool University Press

CROSSMAN, R. H. S. (1972b) *A Politician's View of Health Service Planning* University of Glasgow

CROSSMAN, R. H. S. (1977) *The Diaries of a Cabinet Minister Vol 3: Secretary of State for Social Services 1968–70* London, Hamish Hamilton and Jonathan Cape

CULLINGWORTH, J. B. (1965) *English Housing Trends* (Occasional Papers in Social Administration, No. 13) London, Bell

CULLINGWORTH, J. B. (1966) *Housing and Local Government in England and Wales* London, Allen and Unwin

CULLINGWORTH, J. B. (1969) *Council Housing: Purposes, Procedures and Priorities* London, HMSO

CURNO, P., JONES, D. and MAYO, M. (eds) (1978) *Political Issues and Community Work* London, Routledge and Kegan Paul

DEANE, P. and COLE, W. A. (1962) *British Economic Growth, 1688–1959* Cambridge University Press

DAWE, A. (1970) 'The Two Sociologies' *British Journal of Sociology* Vol. 21, pp. 207–18

DENISON, E. F. (1967) *Why Growth Rates Differ* Washington, DC, Brookings Institution

DENNIS, N. (1970) *People and Planning* London, Faber

DENNIS, N. (1972) *Public Participation and Planners' Blight* London, Faber

DENNIS, N. (1978) 'Housing Policy Areas: Criteria and Indicators in Principle and Practice' *Transactions, Institute of British Geographers* New Series, Vol. 3, No. 1, pp. 2–22

DONNISON, D. V. (1971) 'Taking Your Choice in Welfare' *New Society* 14 January, pp. 61–2

DURKHEIM, E. (1933) *The Division of Labor in Society* New York, Free Press

DURKHEIM, E. (1951) *Suicide* New York, Free Press

DURKHEIM, E. (1961) *Moral Education* New York, Free Press

ECKSTEIN, H. (1958) *The English Health Services* London, Oxford University Press

EDELMAN, M. (1964) *The Symbolic Uses of Politics* Urbana, University of Illinois Press

EDWARDS, J. (1975) 'Social Indicators, Urban Deprivation and Positive Discrimination' *Journal of Social Policy* Vol. 4, Part 3, pp. 275–87

ENGELS, F. (1969) *The Condition of the Working Class in England* London, Panther

FELDSTEIN, M. S. (1967) *Economic Analysis for Health Service Efficiency* Amsterdam, North Holland

FIELD, F. (1976) *The New Corporate Interest* (Poverty Pamphlet 23) London, Child Poverty Action Group

FIELD, F. (1977) 'The Need for a Family Lobby' *Poverty* No. 38, pp. 3–7

FIELD, F., MEACHER, M. and POND, C. (1977) *To Him That Hath: A Study of Poverty and Taxation* Harmondsworth, Penguin

FOX, A. (1974) *Beyond Contract: Work, Power and Trust Relations* London, Faber

FRIEDMAN, A. (1977) *Industry and Labour: Class Struggle at Work and Monopoly Capitalism* London, Macmillan

FRIEDMAN, M. (1962) *Capitalism and Freedom* University of Chicago Press

GALBRAITH, J. K. (1962) *The Affluent Society* Harmondsworth, Penguin

GALBRAITH, J. K. (1967) *The New Industrial State* Harmondsworth, Penguin

GEORGE, V. and WILDING, P. (1976) *Ideology and Social Welfare* London, Routledge and Kegan Paul

GERTH, H. H. and MILLS, C. W. (1948) *From Max Weber: Essays in Sociology* London, Routledge and Kegan Paul

GIDDENS, A. (1970) 'Marx, Weber and the Development of Capitalism' *Sociology* Vol. 4, pp. 289–310

GIDDENS, A. (1972) *Politics and Sociology in the Thought of Max Weber* London, Macmillan

GIDDENS, A. (1973) *The Class Structure of the Advanced Societies* London, Hutchinson

GILL, D. G. (1974) 'The British National Health Service: Professional Determinants of Administrative Structure' *International Journal of Health Services* Vol. 1, No. 4, pp. 342–53

GLAZER, N. (1975) *Affirmative Discrimination: Ethnic Inequality and Public Policy* New York, Basic Books

GLYN, A. and SUTCLIFFE, B. (1972) *British Capitalism, Workers and the Profits Squeeze* Harmondsworth, Penguin

GOLDTHORPE, J. H. (1964) 'The Development of Social Policy in England 1800–1914' *Transactions of the Fifth World Congress of Sociology (1962)* pp. 41–56, London, International Sociological Association

GOLDTHORPE, J. H. (1971) 'Theories of Industrial Society: Reflections on the recrudescence of historicism and the future of futurology' *European Journal of Sociology* Vol. 12, No. 2, pp. 263–88

GOLDTHORPE, J. H. (1972) 'Class, Status and Party in Modern Britain: Some Recent Interpretations, Marxist and *Marxisant' European Journal of Sociology* Vol. 13, No. 2, pp. 342–72

GOLDTHORPE, J. H. and BEVAN, P. (1977) 'The Study of Social Stratification in Great Britain, 1945–75' *Social Science Information* Vol. 16, Nos 3/4, pp. 279–334

GOLDTHORPE, J. H. and LOCKWOOD, D. (1963) 'Affluence and the British Class Structure' *Sociological Review* Vol. 11, No. 2, pp. 133–63

GOLDTHORPE, J. H., LOCKWOOD, D., BECHHOFER, F. and PLATT, J. (1969) *The Affluent Worker in the Class Structure* Cambridge University Press

GOLDTHORPE, J. H., PAYNE, C. and LLEWELLYN, C. (1978) 'Trends in Class Mobility' *Sociology* Vol. 12, No. 3, pp. 441–68

GOUGH, I. (1975a) Review of J. O'Conner (1973) *Bulletin of the Conference of Socialist Economists* June, pp. B.R. 3–7

GOUGH, I. (1975b) 'State Expenditure in Advanced Capitalism' *New Left Review* No. 92, pp. 53–92

GOUGH, I. R. (1970) 'Poverty and Health—A Review Article' *Social and Economic Administration* Vol. 4, No. 3, pp. 211–23

GOULDNER, A. W. (1971) *The Coming Crisis of Western Sociology* London, Heinemann

HABERMAS, J. (1976) *Legitimation Crisis* London, Heinemann

HAHN, F. H. (1973) *On the Notion of Equilibrium in Economics* Cambridge University Press

HAHN, F. H. and MATTHEWS, R. C. O. (1965) 'the Theory of Economic Growth: A Survey' in American Economic Association/Royal Economic Society *Surveys of Economic Theory Vol. 2: Growth and Development* London, Macmillan

HALEVY, E. (1972) *The Growth of Philosophic Radicalism* London, Faber

HALL P. (1976) *Reforming the Welfare: The Politics of Change in the Personal Social Services* London, Heinemann

HALL, P., LAND, H., PARKER, R. and WEBB, A. (1975) *Change, Choice and Conflict in Social Policy* London, Heinemann

HALSEY, A. H. (ed.) (1972a) *Educational Priority* London, HMSO

HALSEY, A. H. (ed.) (1972b) *Trends in British Society since 1900* London, Macmillan

HALSEY, A. H. (ed.) (1976) *Traditions of Social Policy* Oxford, Basil Blackwell

HALSEY, A. H. (1978) *Change in British Society* Oxford University Press

HALSEY, A. H. and FLOUD, J. (1957) 'Intelligence Tests, Social Class and Selection for Secondary Schools' *British Journal of Sociology* Vol. 8, pp. 33–9

HALSEY, A. H., HEATH, A. F. and RIDGE, J. M. (1979) *Origins and Destinations* Oxford University Press

HANDLER, J. F. (1973) *The Coercive Social Worker* Chicago, Rand McNally

HARRIS, N. (1972) *Competition and the Corporate Society: British Conservatives, the State and Industry, 1945–1964* London, Methuen

HARRIS, R. and SELDON, A. (1971) *Choice in Welfare 1970* London, Institute of Economic Affairs

HARTWELL, R. M. (1971) *The Industrial Revolution and Economic Growth* London, Methuen

HATCH, S., FOX, E. and LEGG, C. (1977) *Research and Reform: Southwark CDP 1969–72* London, Home Office (Urban Deprivation Unit)

HATCH, S. and SHERROT, R. (1973) 'Positive Discrimination and the Distribution of Deprivations' *Policy and Politics* Vol. 1, No. 3, pp. 223–40

HAYEK, F. (1944) *The Road to Serfdom* London, Routledge and Kegan Paul

HEATH, A. (1976) *Rational Choice and Social Exchange* Cambridge University Press

HECLO, H. (1974) *Modern Social Politics in Britain and Sweden* New Haven, Conn., Yale University Press

HELLER, R. (1978) *Restructuring the Health Service* London, Croom Helm

HICKS, J. R. (1966) *After the Boom* (Institute of Economic Affairs Occasional Paper, No. 11), London

HIRSCH, F. (1977) *Social Limits to Growth* London, Routledge and Kegan Paul

HIRSCH, F. and GOLDTHORPE, J. H. (1978) *The Political Economy of Inflation* London, Martin Robertson

HOBSBAWM, E. J. (1964) *Labouring Men: Studies in the History of Labour* London, Weidenfeld and Nicolson

HOBSBAWM, E. J. (1969) *Industry and Empire* Harmondsworth, Penguin

HOLMES, C. (1975) 'Housing: Public Money and Private Space' *New Society* 13 February, pp. 384–6

HOOPER, R. (ed.) (1971) *Curriculum: Context, Design and Development* Edinburgh, Oliver and Boyd

HOPE, K. (1975) 'Trends in the Openness of British Society' (Paper presented to SSRC Conference on Social Mobility, Aberdeen, September)

'Housing Finance Act, 1972: A Guide' *New Society* 28 December 1972, pp. 734–7

HOWLETT, A. and ASHLEY, J. (1972) 'Selective Care' *New Society* 2 November, pp. 270–1

INSTITUTE OF ECONOMIC AFFAIRS (1973) *The Economics of Charity* London

INSTITUTE FOR HUMANE STUDIES (1971) *Towards Liberty: Essays in Honor of Ludwig von Mises* Vol. II, Menlo Park, California

JACOBS, S. (1976) *The Right to a Decent House* London, Routledge and Kegan Paul

JANOWITZ, M. (1976) *Social Control of the Welfare State* New York, Elsevier

JENCKS, C. *et al.* (1975) *Inequality: A Reassessment of the Effect of Family and Schooling in America* Harmondsworth, Penguin

JEWKES, J. and S. (1961) *The Genesis of the British National Health Service* Oxford, Basil Blackwell

JONES, D. and MAYO, M. (eds) (1974) *Community Work One* London, Routledge and Kegan Paul

JONES, D. and MAYO, M. (eds) (1975) *Community Work Two* London, Routledge and Kegan Paul

JONES, K. (ed.) (1973) *Year Book of Social Policy in Britain, 1972* London, Routledge and Kegan Paul

JORDAN, B. (1973) *Paupers* London, Routledge and Kegan Paul

JORDAN, B. (1974) *Poor Parents* London, Routledge and Kegan Paul

KAHN, R. and POSNER, M. (1977) 'Inflation, Unemployment and Growth', *National Westminster Bank Quarterly Review* November, pp. 28–37

KALDOR, N. (1955–6) 'Alternative Theories of Distribution' *Review of Economic Studies* Vol. 23, pp. 83–100, reprinted in B. J. McCormick and E. Owen Smith (eds), 1968, *The Labour Market*, Harmondsworth, Penguin

KALDOR, N. (1961) 'Capital Accumulation and Economic Growth' in F. A. Lute and D. C. Hague (eds), *The Theory of Capital,* London and New York, International Economic Association

KALDOR, N. (1966) *Causes of the Slow Rate of Economic Growth of the United Kingdom* Cambridge University Press

KALDOR, N. (1968) 'Productivity and Growth in Manufacturing Industry: A Reply' *Economica* Vol. 35, pp. 385–91

KALDOR, N. (1975) 'Economic Growth and the Verdoorn Law—A Comment on Mr. Rowthorn's Article' *Economic Journal* Vol. 85, pp. 891–6

KALDOR, N. and MIRRLEES, J. A. (1962) 'A New Model of Economic Growth' *Review of Economic Studies* Vol. 29, No. 3, pp. 174–92

KARABEL, J. and HALSEY, A. H. (eds) (1977) *Power and Ideology in Education* New York, Oxford University Press

KERR, C. *et al.* (1964) *Industrialism and Industrial Man* London, Oxford University Press

KINCAID, J. C. (1973) *Poverty and Equality in Britain* Harmondsworth, Penguin

KLEIN, R. (1972) 'The Politics of PPB' *Political Quarterly* Vol. 43, No. 3, pp. 270–81

KLEIN, R. (1974) 'Policy-Making in the National Health Service' *Political Studies* Vol. 22, No. 1, pp. 1–14

KLEIN, R. (1977) 'The Corporate State, the Health Service and the Professions' *New Universities Quarterly* Vol. 31, No. 2, pp. 161–80

KLEIN, R. and LEWIS, J. (1976) *The Politics of Consumer Representation: A Study of Community Health Councils* London, Centre for Studies in Social Policy

KOGAN, M. (1975) *Educational Policy-Making: A Study of Interest Groups and Parliament* London, Allen and Unwin

KOGAN, M. and TERRY, J. (1971) *The Organisation of a Social Services Department* London, Bookstall Publications

LACLAU, E. (1975) 'The Specificity of the Political: the Poulantzas–Miliband Debate' *Economy and Society* Vol. 4, No. 1, pp. 87–110

LEES, D. (1976) 'Economics and Non-Economics of Health Services' *Three Banks Review* No. 110, pp. 3–20

LEES, R. and SMITH, G. (eds) (1975) *Action–Research in Community Development* London, Routledge and Kegan Paul

Legal Action Group Bulletin September 1975, pp. 211–16

LEONARD, P. (ed.) (1975) *The Sociology of Community Action* (Sociological Review Monograph No. 21), University of Keele

LINDBERG, L. *et al.* (eds) (1975) *Stress and Contradiction in Modern Capitalism: Public Policy and the Theory of the State* Lexington, Mass., Lexington Books

LIPSET, S. M. (1964) 'The Changing Class Structure and Contemporary European Politics' *Daedalus* Winter, pp. 271–303

LIPSEY, R. G. and LANCASTER, R. K. (1956) 'The General Theory of Second Best' *Review of Economic Studies* Vol. 24, No. 63, pp. 11–32

LISTER, R. (1974) *Take-Up of Means-Tested Benefits* London, Child Poverty Action Group

LITTLE, A. and WESTERGAARD, J. (1964) 'The Trend of Class Differentials in Educational Opportunity in England and Wales' *British Journal of Sociology* Vol. 15, No. 4, pp. 301–16

LOCKWOOD, D. (1958) *The Blackcoated Worker* London, Allen and Unwin

LOCKWOOD, D. (1974) 'For T. H. Marshall' *Sociology* Vol. 8, No. 3, pp. 363–7

LOGAN, W. P. D. and CUSHION, A. A. (1958–62) *Morbidity Statistics from General Practice* London, HMSO

LOVETT, T. (1975) *Adult Education, Community Development and the Working Class* London, Ward Lock

LOWI, T. J. (1969) *The End of Liberalism: Ideology, Policy and the Crisis of Public Authority* New York, W. W. Norton
LUKES, S. M. (1973a) *Emile Durkheim: His Life and Work* London, Allen Lane
LUKES, S. M. (1973b) *Individualism* Oxford, Basil Blackwell
LYNES, T. (1967) *French Pensions* (Occasional Papers in Social Administration, No. 21) London, Bell
LYNES, T. (1969) *Labour's Pension Plan* London, Fabian Society

MACPHERSON, C. B. (1962) *The Political Theory of Possessive Individualism* London, Oxford University Press
MARCUSE, H. (1968) *One Dimensional Man* London, Sphere
MARRIS, P. and REIN, M. (1974) *Dilemmas of Social Reform* Harmondsworth, Penguin
MARSDEN, D. and DUFF, E. (1975) *Workless: Some Unemployed Men and their Families* Harmondsworth, Penguin
MARSHALL, T. H. (1965) *Class, Citizenship and Social Development* New York, Doubleday Anchor
MARSHALL, T. H. (1975) *Social Policy* London, Hutchinson
MARX, K. (1970a) *Economic and Philosophic Manuscripts of 1844* London, Lawrence and Wishart
MARX, K. (1970b) *Capital* Vol. 1 London, Lawrence and Wishart
MARX, K. (1975) *Early Writings* Harmondsworth, Penguin
MAUNDER, W. F. (ed.) (1974) *Reviews of United Kingdom Statistical Sources* London, Heinemann
MAUSS, M. (1970) *The Gift* London, Routledge and Kegan Paul
MIDWINTER, E. (1972) *Priority Education* Harmondsworth, Penguin
MILIBAND, R. (1969) *The State in Capitalist Society* London, Weidenfeld and Nicolson
MILL, J. S. (1848) *Principles of Political Economy* 2 vols, London, Parker
MILLS, C. W. (1963) *The Marxists* Harmondsworth, Penguin
MISHRA, R. (1977) *Society and Social Policy* London, Macmillan
MOORE, B. (1972) *Reflections on the Causes of Human Misery and upon Certain Proposals to Eliminate Them* London, Allen Lane
MORRIS, J. N. (1964) *Uses of Epidemiology* Edinburgh, Livingstone

NATIONAL COMMUNITY DEVELOPMENT PROJECT (1974) *Inter-Project Report* London, Home Office (Urban Deprivation Unit)
NATIONAL COMMUNITY DEVELOPMENT PROJECT (1975) *Forward Plan 1975/76* London, Home Office (Urban Deprivation Unit)
NATIONAL COMMUNITY DEVELOPMENT PROJECT (1977) *The Costs of Industrial Change* London, Home Office (Urban Deprivation Unit)
NEVITT, A. A. (1966) *Housing, Taxation and Subsidies* London, Nelson
NICHOLS, T. (1970) *Ownership, Control and Ideology: An Inquiry into Certain Aspects of Modern Business Ideology* London, Allen and Unwin
NISKANEN, W. A. (1973) *Bureaucracy: Servant or Master?* London, Institute of Economic Affairs
NORTH TYNESIDE CDP (1978a) *North Shields: Working Class Politics and Housing, 1900–1977* London, Home Office
NORTH TYNESIDE CDP (1978b) *North Shields: Living with Industrial Change* London, Home Office
NORTH TYNESIDE CDP (1978c) *North Shields: Organising for Change in a Working Class Area* London, Home Office

O'CONNOR, J. (1973) *The Fiscal Crisis of the State* New York, St. Martin's Press
OFFE, C. (1974) 'Structural Problems of the Capitalist State' in K. Beyme (ed.) *German Political Studies* Vol. 1, pp. 31–57
ORGANISATION FOR ECONOMIC COOPERATION AND DEVELOPMENT (1971) *Educational Policies for the 1970s* Paris

PACKMAN, J. (1968) *Child Care: Needs and Numbers* London, Allen and Unwin
PARKER, J. (1965) *Local Health and Welfare Services* London, Allen and Unwin
PARKER, J. (1975) *Social Policy and Citizenship* London, Macmillan
PARKIN, F. (1971) *Class Inequality and Political Order* London, MacGibbon and Kee
PASINETTI, L. L. (1965) 'A New Theoretical Approach to the Problems of Economic Growth', Pontificiae Academiae Scientiarum *Scripta Varia* pp. 571–696, Amsterdam, North Holland
PATEMAN, C. (1970) *Participation and Democratic Theory* Cambridge University Press
PEEL, J. D. Y. (1971) *Herbert Spencer: The Evolution of a Sociologist* London, Heinemann
PERKIN, H. (1969) *The Origins of Modern English Society, 1780–1880* London, Routledge and Kegan Paul
'PERSPECTIVES ON INEQUALITY', *Harvard Educational Review* Vol. 43, No. 1, pp. 37–164
PIGOU, A. C. (ed.) (1925) *Memorials of Alfred Marshall* London, Macmillan
PINKER, R. (1971) *Social Theory and Social Policy* London, Heinemann
PIVEN, F. F. and CLOWARD, R. A. (1972) *Regulating the Poor: The Functions of Public Welfare* London, Tavistock
PLOWDEN (1967) *Children and their Primary Schools* A Report of the Central Advisory Council for Education, London, HMSO

REDDEN, R. *et al.* (1977) 'In or Out: Not such a clear choice as it looks' *The Guardian* 5 September, p. 13
REICH, C. A. (1964) 'The New Property' *Yale Law Journal* Vol. 73, No. 5, pp. 733–87
REIN, M. (1969) 'Social Class and the Health Service' *New Society* 20 November, pp. 807–10
REIN, M. (1970) *Social Policy: Issues of Choice and Change* New York, Random House
REISMAN, D. (1977) *Richard Titmuss: Welfare and Society* London, Heinemann
REX, J. (1970) *Race Relations in Sociological Theory* London, Weidenfeld and Nicolson
REX, J. and MOORE, R. (1967) *Race, Community and Conflict* London, Oxford University Press
RIMLINGER, G. V. (1971) *Welfare Policy and Industrialisation in Europe, America and Russia* New York, John Wiley
ROBERTS, D. (1960) *Victorian Origins of the British Welfare State* New Haven, Conn., Yale University Press
ROBBINS (1963) *Report of the Committee on Higher Education* Appendix One, Cmnd 2154–I, London, HMSO
ROSSETTI, F. (1974) 'A Case Study of Participation in Planning' (mimeo) Association of Community Workers/Royal Town Planning Institute Joint Working Party, Workshop on Planning and Community Work, 22 June
ROWTHORN, R. E. (1975) 'What Remains of Kaldor's Law?' *Economic Journal* Vol. 85, pp. 10–19

RUBINSTEIN, D. and STONEMAN, C. (eds) (1972) *Education for Democracy* Harmondsworth, Penguin
RUNCIMAN, W. G. (1966) *Relative Deprivation and Social Justice* London, Routledge and Kegan Paul
RUSSELL (1973) *Adult Education: A Plan for Development* London, HMSO
RUTTER, M. and MADGE, N. (1976) *Cycles of Disadvantage* London, Heinemann

SAUL, S. B. (1969) *The Myth of the Great Depression, 1873–1896* London, Macmillan
SCHROYER, T. (1973) *The Critique of Domination* New York, George Braziller
SEEBOHM (1968) *Report of the Committee on Local Authority and Allied Personal Social Services* Cmnd 3703, London, HMSO
SELF, P. (1975) *Econocrats and the Policy Process: The Politics and Philosophy of Cost-Benefit Analysis* London, Macmillan
SHONFIELD, A. (1969) *Modern Capitalism* London, Oxford University Press
SHONFIELD, A. and SHAW, S. (eds) (1972) *Social Indicators and Social Policy* London, Heinemann
SINFIELD, A. (1976) 'Transmitted Deprivation and the Social Division of Welfare' prepared for the Department of Health and Social Security and Social Science Research Council Working Party on Transmitted Deprivation
SINFIELD, A. (1977) 'The Social Meaning of Unemployment' in K. Jones (ed.) *The Year Book of Social Policy in Britain 1976* London, Routledge and Kegan Paul
SINFIELD, A. (1978) 'Analyses in the Social Division of Welfare' *Journal of Social Policy* Vol. 7, Part 2, pp. 129–56
SMELSER, N. (ed.) (1973) *Sociology* New York, John Wiley
SMITH, G. A. N. and LITTLE, A. (1971) *Strategies of Compensation: A Review of Educational Projects for the Disadvantaged in the U.S.* Paris, Organisation for Economic Cooperation and Development
SMITH, M. E. H. (1975) 'Housing Management in the Future: Problems and Opportunities' *Housing Monthly* January, pp. 2–8
SPECHT, H. (1976) *The Community Development Project* London, National Institute for Social Work
SPENCER, K. (1973) 'The Housing Finance Act' *Social and Economic Administration* Vol. 7, No. 1, pp. 3–19
SRAFFA, P. (ed.) (1951–55) *Works of David Ricardo* Cambridge University Press
STEIN, B. (1976) *Work and Welfare in Britain and the USA* New York, Halsted
STIMSON, G. V. (1976) 'General Practitioners, "Trouble" and Types of Patients' in M. Stacey (ed.) *The Sociology of the NHS* (Sociological Review Monograph 22) University of Keele
SURGENOR, D. M. (1973) 'Human Blood and the Renewal of Altruism: Titmuss in Retrospect' *International Journal of Health Services* Vol. 2, No. 3, pp. 443–53

TAWNEY, R. H. (1938) *Religion and the Rise of Capitalism* Harmondsworth, Penguin
TAWNEY, R. H. (1964) *Equality* London, Allen and Unwin
TERRILL, R. (1974) *R. H. Tawney and his Times* London, Andre Deutsch
TITMUSS, R. M. (1950) *Problems of Social Policy* London, Longmans
TITMUSS, R. M. (1962) *Income Distribution and Social Change* London, Allen and Unwin
TITMUSS, R. M. (1963) *Essays on 'the Welfare State'* London, Allen and Unwin
TITMUSS, R. M. (1968) *Commitment to Welfare* London, Allen and Unwin
TITMUSS, R. M. (1973) *The Gift Relationship* Harmondsworth, Penguin
TITMUSS, R. M. (1974) *Social Policy: An Introduction* London, Allen and Unwin

TOPPING, P. and SMITH, G. (1977) *Government Against Poverty? Liverpool Community Development Project, 1970–75* Oxford, Social Evaluation Unit, 40 Wellington Square

TOWNSEND, P. (ed.) (1970) *The Fifth Social Service* London, Fabian Society

TOWNSEND, P. (1974) 'Inequality and the Health Service' *The Lancet* 15 June, pp. 1179–90

TOWNSEND, P. and BOSANQUET, N. (eds) (1972) *Labour and Inequality* London, Fabian Society

VALENTINE, C. A. (1968) *Culture and Poverty* University of Chicago Press

WAITZKIN, H. and WATERMAN, B. (1974) *The Exploitation of Illness in Capitalist Society* New York, Bobbs-Merrill

WEBB, S. and B. (1963) *English Poor Law Policy* London, Frank Cass

WEBER, M. (1930) *The Protestant Ethic and the Spirit of Capitalism* London, Allen and Unwin

WEBER, M. (1949) *The Methodology of the Social Sciences* (edited by E. A. Shils and H. A. Finch) Glencoe, Illinois, Free Press

WEBER, M. (1964) *The Theory of Social and Economic Organisation* New York, Free Press

WEBER, M. (1968) *Economy and Society* New York, Bedminster Press

WEDDERBURN, D. (ed.) (1974) *Poverty, Inequality and Class Structure* Cambridge University Press

WESTERGAARD, J. and RESLER, H. (1976) *Class in a Capitalist Society: A Study of Contemporary Britain* Harmondsworth, Penguin

WILDING, P. (1976) 'Richard Titmuss and Social Welfare' *Social and Economic Administration* Vol. 10, No. 3, pp. 147–66

WILENSKY, H. (1975) *The Welfare State and Equality* University of California Press

WILLIAMS, F. (ed.) (1977) *Why the Poor Pay More* London, Macmillan

WINTER, J. M. (1974) *Socialism and the Challenge of War: Ideas and Politics in Britain, 1912–18* London, Routledge and Kegan Paul

WOLFF, R. P. (1968) *The Poverty of Liberalism* Boston, Beacon Press

WOOTTON, B. (1962) *The Social Foundations of Wages Policy* London, Allen and Unwin

YOUNG, M. F. D. (1971) *Knowledge and Control* London, Collier-Macmillan

EPIGRAPHS

COLLINGWOOD, R. G. (1961) *The Idea of History* London, Oxford University Press

LACAPRA, D. (1972) *Emile Durkheim: Sociologist and Philosopher* Ithaca, Cornell University Press

MACHIAVELLI, N. (1970) *The Discourses* Harmondsworth, Penguin

NIETZSCHE, F. (1969) *Thus Spoke Zarathustra* Harmondsworth, Penguin

TOLSTOY, L. N. (1966) *Resurrection* Harmondsworth, Penguin

Index